NOT MY CIRCUS

*Triumph Over Abuse, Trauma &
Family Secrets – A Journey
to Self-love, Pride & Remarkable Resilience*

BY
DELICIA NIAMI

Not My Circus–Book II in the ResilientAF Memoir Trilogy

Copyright © 2024 by Delicia Niami. All rights reserved.

No part of this publication in print or in electronic format may be reproduced, stored in a retrieval system, or transmitted in any form or by any means, electronic, mechanical, photocopying, recording, or otherwise without the prior written permission of the publisher.

Disclaimer

This memoir is based on true events. Some names, identifying details, and timelines have been altered to protect the privacy and confidentiality of individuals. The author has made every effort to ensure accuracy and authenticity to the best of their knowledge, but makes no warranties regarding the completeness or correctness of the information presented herein. The author assumes no liability for any errors, omissions, or damages arising from the use of this memoir.

Published by ResilientAF
https://www.delicianiami.com
Press Distribution by Bublish
Printed in the United States of America

eBook ISBN: 978-1-64704-804-4
Paperback ISBN: 978-1-64704-802-0
Hardcover ISBN: 978-1-64704-803-7

For my Mom

Trigger Warning:
This book contains references to drug abuse, sexual abuse, rape, pedophilia, and suicide.

SECTIONS

What Was I Thinking? 1
Unjustified 3
Stepping-Stones 11
Freedom 35
My Adventures in Europe 47
Shattered Illusions 91
Switzerland—My Forever Home? 107
Finding My Hippie Roots 117
Trustworthy Monster #2 125
Why Does My Body Hate Me? 131
Friend or Foe? 155
Uncharted Heartache 171
April 16, 2001 183
Introspection 207
Everlasting Love? 213
Unbreakable Bonds 227
Not My Circus 235

Not My Circus

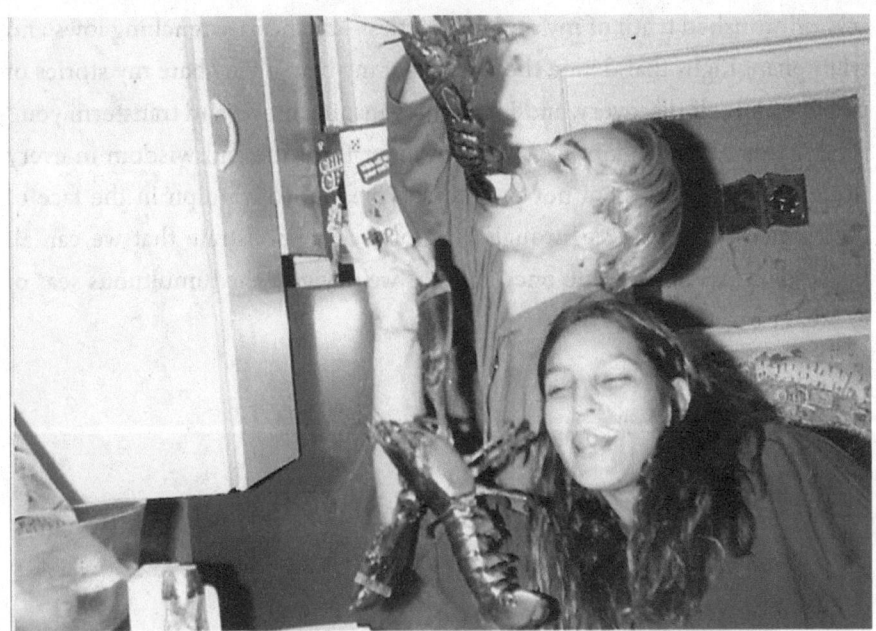

WHAT WAS I THINKING?

What if I told you that within the depths of our darkest experiences lies the potential for profound growth and resilience? Every trauma, scar, or wound we have endured holds with it the promise to not only heal, but to forge an unbreakable spirit.

In Kissing Asphalt, the first installment of my ResilientAF memoir series, I unmasked the transformative events of my childhood that helped shape me into the person I am today.

Not My Circus is the continuation of my journey into adulthood. Brace yourself for an unfiltered narrative that will ignite your spirit and challenge your preconceived notions. With every turn of the page, you'll witness the raw, unvarnished truth of my ongoing battles—the heart-wrenching lows and triumphant highs that define the essence of my being. I lay bare my stories of courage and self-discovery, and I hope they inspire, move, and transform you.

My aim is to kindle a flame of inner fortitude and wisdom in every reader, encouraging them not only to survive, but to triumph in the face of life's greatest adversities. Through my stories, I demonstrate that we can all be ResilientAF. So, join me once again as we navigate the tumultuous seas of existence together.

UNJUSTIFIED

Get off me, you motherfucker! The words I'd cried earlier that night still echoed in my head.

Under the moon's faint glow, I returned home in the wee hours, a customary weekend ritual. Mom was used to my late-night comings and goings. Ordinarily, I'd head straight to bed, but tonight was different. Instead of slipping into the comfort of my room, I stumbled upstairs, my mind still swirled with the events of the evening. Disgust overcame me. I searched the corners of my mind in a desperate attempt to figure out what had happened. My only desire was to cleanse myself of the abhorrence and filth.

I had become extremely inebriated at a local frat party earlier that evening. My best friend, Gertrude, had a new boyfriend, Brian, who was supposed to give me a ride home. En route to my house, we got a flat tire, and Brian entrusted another acquaintance to take me home.

Unfortunately, Brian's friend had other plans in mind.

In the pitch black of the evening, I emerged groggily from a drunken stupor. My consciousness sluggish while a relentless, suffocating weight pressed upon my inebriated self. The rough texture of the truck's vinyl seat rubbed against my skin, which amplified the searing pain that engulfed every inch of my existence. Slowly, I blinked to open my eyes. I found myself disoriented. Lost in a haze, it took me a few moments to collect my thoughts and clear my vision.

A large chest cast a shadow over me. The tender walls of my vagina were like a tomato scraping against a cheese grater. My legs dangled outside the passenger door, and the person responsible for my safety was now raping me.

Sobriety flooded my senses, and an unshakable power arose from within. With all my might, I shoved him away while I pulled up my underwear and pants. My voice erupted in a primal scream that echoed in my mind: "Get off me, you motherfucker!"

I ran as fast as possible away from the truck. I realized I had no idea where we were. Panic set in. I looked around and tried to get my bearings.

His words echoed in the distance, 'Come back!' In the eerie darkness, a figure raced toward me from the shadows, while another loomed ominously in the truck's bed. *There are two of them?*

"Come back. I'll take you home!" His voice sent shivers down my spine.

"Where the fuck are we, you asshole?" I shouted at him from the other side of the parking lot, attempting to get as much distance between us as possible. All I saw were a few streetlights, doors, and a vacant lot.

"Just come back. I promise I will take you home," he shouted.

Cautiously, I resigned myself to trust that he would indeed bring me home. The unsettling truth was that I didn't know how close or far I was from safety. I found my way back to the truck with a fire in my belly. Guardedly, I was powerless, yet an intense rage consumed me. The pent-up emotions from my past, including the violation I'd just suffered, converged into a seething inferno. Despite being vulnerable, my anger rendered me invincible.

The wheels of the truck rumbled beneath us and it became apparent that we had been less than a block from my home. To ensure he remained unaware of my exact place of residence, I requested he drop me off beyond my house. Without a glance back, I stepped out of the truck and slogged the remaining distance home.

How did this happen? I stepped into the shower and cranked the water to its hottest, hoping it would cleanse me of the filth and disappointment.

"Delicia?" I heard my mother call from the hallway.

"Yeah, Mom?"

"What in the world are you doing? It's almost 3:00 a.m."

"Showering."

"Why are you showering right now?"

"Can I talk to you when I'm done?"

Despite my best scrubbing efforts, it hadn't washed away any of the disgust nor the disappointment in myself.

I wrapped a towel around my hair like a turban, then reached for another to wrap around my body. Mom scowled as she stood at the door.

I brushed past her and huffed, "Mom, please come in my room."

While still intoxicated and suffering from a massive headache, I removed clothes from my dresser.

My mother looked at me like I'd lost my mind. "What has gotten into you?"

"Sit down, Mom," I replied somberly.

I put on comfortable sweats and a T-shirt as I sat on the bed next to her. While clutching her hand, I confessed, "Mom, I was just raped."

Her eyes turned bloodred, and I watched her anger soar. Consumed by a wave of rage, her hands clenched into fists that turned purple. Once Mom got us back from Baghdad, after our father kidnapped us, she remained fiercely protective of me.

"What happened?" she asked as she tried to contain her anger.

I attempted to explain, but she interrupted, "I don't care, we are going to the hospital and filing a police report."

"But, Mom, I don't know his name."

"Gertrude does, doesn't she?" Furious, she screamed, "call her . . . call her now!"

I had no desire to call Gertrude at 3 a.m. Reluctantly, I picked up the phone and dialed her number. It surprised me when she answered.

"Gertrude, oh good, you are still awake. What's the guy's name who gave me a ride?" I asked.

"I don't know, why?"

"Just tell me, what's his name?"

"I don't know. Let me ask Brian." I heard her talking to Brian in the background.

"Brian, what was the guy's name who gave Delicia a ride?"

"Why?"

"She wants to know."

"Carlos."

I responded, "Carlos what?"

"Why?" Gertrude inquired emphatically.

"Just tell me."

"What's his last name, Brian?"

"I don't know, Romanal, I think."

"Carlos Romanal?" I confirmed.

"Yes, why?" Gertrude repeated.

"Because he just raped me."

I heard her gasp as I hung up the phone. A mix of embarrassment and rage consumed me—the embarrassment came from being sexually assaulted. I experienced frustration with Brian for entrusting my care to someone who took advantage of me. In addition, I was furious because I had put myself in that situation.

Mom cried the entire way to the hospital.

A thick fog descended upon me that obscured my ability to comprehend the events of the evening. The weight of it all pressed on my shoulders. In addition, I took on my mother's heaviness, which only amplified the feeling of my being a burden. The mere thought of confronting her emotions, alongside my own, engulfed me to the point of shutting down. This had always been one of my coping mechanisms, a default response to any intense emotional upheaval that befell me.

In 1988, law enforcement rarely prosecuted rape cases. Particularly, ones that involved victims who were intoxicated. During this time, the police often struggled to acknowledge the significance of such cases. The lack of justice left many victims hopeless.

Despite my desire to escape, my mother stood resolute. She refused to let those responsible evade accountability. Though I wished to distance myself from the turmoil, her unwavering determination anchored me to the reality I had to face.

Mom and I arrived at the emergency room, and my mother conveyed the circumstances to the admitting nurse. She recognized the urgency and gestured for us to follow her.

The nurse led us to a room and informed us that the doctor would arrive shortly.

We waited in the triage room, and the medical staff requested urine and blood samples for testing.

When the doctor arrived, he asked my mother, "may I speak with you alone?"

"I would like to hear what you have to say," I interjected. I tried to remain calm and keep my snarky tone at bay. It baffled me that the doctor didn't address me directly, even though the heinous act was committed against my body, not my mother's.

He proceeded: "I'm sorry to tell you, young lady, we did indeed find signs of trauma in your vagina. It's clear someone violated you. In addition, there were pools of semen inside of you."

"Pools of semen?" I questioned with sincerity. How strange. I thought I'd woken up right when it began. "Are you sure?"

"I'm absolutely certain, young lady."

I tried desperately to piece together the events that had unfolded. In addition to the anguish that plagued me, I now found myself consumed with the fear and uncertainty of a potential pregnancy.

"After my findings, it was necessary to call the police," the doctor stated. "The sheriff will be here soon."

Waiting in the ER for the police to arrive was torturous. I flashed back to waking up on the vinyl seat, the pain pierced deep within my soul. The heaviness of a stranger on top of me thrusting something into my parched and raw vagina. I tried with all my might to recall anything that led to this moment, but only darkness came.

The officer from the Ventura County Sheriff's office arrived at the hospital hours later. After I explained that I had passed out from drinking, he jotted down a few things in his miniscule notepad. He looked at me with disdain and sarcastically stated, "I can't promise you anything, young lady, since you were inebriated, but we will be in touch."

Mom followed up with the sheriff constantly. My case went months without updates. In late May, right before my high school graduation, the vice principal and two deputies arrived at my English class.

The vice principal approached my teacher and whispered something in her ear.

"Delicia, please proceed to the office," Mrs. Bizzelle stated in a caring manner.

I was concerned something had happened to my mom.

Masky, one of the skateboarder kids who always mocked me for being a lesbian, shouted, "Oh, your girlfriend is in trouble. The dyke is getting arrested."

"Enough!" Mrs. Bizzelle snapped.

I arose from my desk and followed the vice principal along with the officers toward the administration building.

They took me into a corner office. A round table with small, dark blue plastic chairs were the only items in the room. The officers sat at one end of the table and motioned for me to have a seat at the other.

"What's going on?" I asked timidly.

"This is regarding the assault," one officer responded.

"Assault? Do you mean when I was raped?"

"Yes, ma'am. I'm afraid we will not continue pursuing your complaint any further."

"What? Why? You have his name and contact information. He raped me."

"Ma'am, the problem is his cousin was in the back of the truck with him, which gives him an eyewitness. You were drunk and by yourself. So it is their word against yours, and it just won't hold up in court. We're dropping the case."

"What? I'm so confused. Why? He raped me. Just because I passed out doesn't give him the right to violate me."

"Yes, ma'am. The problem is, he claims you said, 'Fuck me, fuck me, fuck me.'"

"What?" I shrieked! "I am a lesbian; I would never say that. Especially to a guy. How disgusting! There's no way I would say anything like that."

"I'm sorry, ma'am, but that is what was reported, and his cousin is backing him up on this claim. Try to be more mindful in the future."

Defeat enveloped me like a suffocating shroud. This entire debacle felt like a relentless onslaught that chipped away at justice and dignity. Because the alcohol rendered me unconscious, they dismissed my violation.

This bitter realization labeled me as the perpetrator, while those responsible for my suffering would go unpunished. In the eyes of the law, I wasn't a victim deserved of reparation. Rather, I was an inconvenience. The weight of injustice hung heavy in the air, which left me grappling with the harsh reality that my mother's quest for righteousness was futile.

Amidst the despair, anger burned within me—not just for myself, but for all women whose voices were silenced, whose rights were disregarded.

My lifelong dream was to become an attorney, but this incident sparked a newfound determination. I knew then, with certainty, that I wanted to become a criminal prosecuting attorney. I aimed to be a beacon of justice to restore dignity and rights for women in these types of situations. This wasn't just about seeking justice for myself anymore. I became increasingly focused on fighting for countless others who were silenced and sidelined by a failing system.

STEPPING STONES

Determined to put the painful incident behind me and move on with my life, I eagerly awaited my upcoming graduation from high school. I wanted to leave all the drama behind and embrace a fresh start.

Throughout my journey from kindergarten onward, I had repeatedly faced taunting and ridicule. Graduation day symbolized my long-held desire to say goodbye to the cruel school years once and for all.

This wasn't just an escape from the torment and nonsense that plagued me throughout my youth, it denoted my liberation. The prospect of moving out and gaining independence excited me to no end. No more having to be home by 6 p.m. for dinner or abiding by any more of my mother's rules. I was committed to moving out as fast as possible.

Since the age of fourteen, I had saved every penny that wasn't spent on weed—all with the dream of one day being able to move out on my own. Graduation marked the crucial last step before I set my plan into motion.

When commencement day finally came, I burst with excitement.

I headed downstairs, ready to embrace the day, and my mother greeted me with disapproval. "You can't wear that," Mom snapped.

"What's wrong with it, Mom? It's what I always wear, jeans and a T-shirt."

"That's the problem. It's your graduation day; you need to look nice. Go put on a dress or something."

"But, Mom, I hate dresses. And who cares what I'm wearing, you don't see it underneath my gown anyway."

"Go change, you'll look beautiful." She smiled and grabbed my cheeks as if I were five years old.

"Whatever," I exclaimed.

Her words dampened my spirit and I climbed the stairs once again, determined to find a solution that would make her happy. I selected a dress I thought would meet my mother's approval and made my way back downstairs.

"Much better!" she proclaimed.

"Can we go please, Mom?" I implored.

Off we went—my mother, her longtime boyfriend Ron, and me. Nile and Patrick, my older brothers, planned on meeting us there.

Upon arrival, I sought out the few friends in my grade. I had limited connections among the crowd because many of the people I hung out with had already moved on.

The teachers shuffled us in like ants marching to our queen; one by one we lined up in alphabetical order. Since my last name began with an N, I was near the back. This meant I had waited much longer for my glorious moment of freedom.

My turn approached, and the entire row stood up and made our way toward the stage. Excitement filled the air and the closer I got, the more my hands perspired with a nervous, clammy sweat. Then, I stood on the stair, and through the microphone, I heard it:

"Delicia Niami."

It seemed like a dream. I'd waited so long for that taste of imminent freedom. The school counselor handed me an empty diploma holder as I shook the principal's hand. At that moment, it felt as if someone had removed a ten-pound bag of sugar from my shoulders.

Once everyone had crossed the stage, the announcer declared: "will the graduating class of Newbury Park High School, 1988, please rise?"

An electrifying energy filled the air.

"Congratulations! You did it! You are officially outta here," the announcer proclaimed.

It didn't matter if we were friends or foes—we, the graduates, stood united in solidarity. We locked eyes, grabbed our caps, and launched them as far as possible into the sky, celebrating our collective achievements.

That day denoted the start of a new chapter for me. I looked at apartment listings in The Recycler months ahead to see what options were available. Virtually every person I contacted expressed reluctance in renting to a seventeen-year-old high school graduate.

Despite several months of searching, I had no luck securing a rental. Frustrated by my predicament, I confided in my brother Nile, hoping he might have a contact in Los Angeles who could assist me in finding a place. To my relief, Nile revealed someone he knew who owned a triplex in Toluca Lake. He rattled off the landlord's contact information and instructed me to reach out.

I was nervous but hopeful that he would rent to me. I dialed the number and someone answered.

"Hello, may I speak with Mr. Smith?"

"This is he."

"Hello, Mr. Smith, my name is Delicia. I'm not sure if my brother told you I would be calling or not."

"Oh, Nile, yes, he mentioned it. He said you might be interested in the apartment?"

"I am extremely interested. I just graduated and I have money saved up for the first few months, until I can find a job and get settled in college."

"Sounds good. Come down and take a look."

"Really?" I squealed like a six-year-old getting her very first bicycle.

He chuckled, "Yes, I'm familiar with your brother, no problem. Come check the place out, and if you like it, you can sign a month-to-month lease. Sound good?"

"Good? It's amazing! Thank you so much, Mr. Smith."

"My pleasure, young lady."

The following day, I embarked on the one-hour journey along the 101 freeway to Toluca Lake.

The apartment captivated me with its undeniable charm. Each unit boasted a petite front lawn, with concrete steps leading up to the entrance. Nestled in a neighborhood on Riverside and Pass, the location was remarkable, directly across from the renowned Warner Brothers Studios.

This place exceeded my expectations. It had a great layout with a spacious bedroom, large living room, integrated dining area and full kitchen, bathroom with a bathtub, and even a laundry room. What added to its charm was a small built-in wall compartment where the milkman would leave the milk in the olden days.

As I stood in the small laundry room, my thoughts drifted back to a time when milkmen were a regular sight. I envisioned the nostalgia and simplicity of life, with the driver making his rounds, delivering fresh bottles of milk right inside the miniscule door in the wall. I appreciated the apartment even more, as it held a tangible reminder of history.

This extraordinary find, all thanks to my brother's connection, had become mine. My heart swelled with gratitude because I realized how fortunate I was.

The following week, on August 8, 1988, I moved into my new apartment. Filled with excitement and a hint of nervousness, I embarked on this solo adventure by packing my belongings into a small U-Haul truck. With the generous help of friends like Jason, Marc, Cindi, LR, and a few others, I had the support I needed. Mom helped, too, and trailed behind the U-Haul to ensure my safety.

Upon arrival at my very first home away from home, I felt overwhelming joy. The long-awaited freedom I desired became a reality.

While I enjoyed living alone, I missed Gertrude and would often see her on the weekends. After one of our many visits, Gertrude's little brother, Bruce, came bounding toward my car. He cradled something in his arms.

My curiosity piqued. I rolled down the window and called out to him, "Whatcha got there, Bruce?"

His eyes lit up with excitement as he exclaimed, "It's a cat! I found it under the house."

I looked closer, and I saw the tiniest, most adorable black-and-white kitten nestled in his arms. The sight tugged at my heartstrings, and a surge of both concern and affection consumed me.

"Do you want it?" Bruce asked, his youthful voice filled with innocence and hope.

Caught off guard, I pondered his question. "What are you going to do with it?" I inquired, genuinely curious.

"I dunno," he said as he shrugged his shoulders, still clutching the kitten.

Without hesitation, he handed the little feline over to me.

I gazed at the defenseless creature in my hands and greeted its pure and gentle essence.

During our childhood, we were bound by a strict no-pet policy, because of my mother's severe allergy to animals. Our beloved Grey-cheeked Peruvian Parakeet, Rover, was the sole exception. In that moment, I held a choice in my hands, to rewrite the animal-companion chapter of my life.

I daydreamt about the joyful moments we would share, cuddling and playing together. The possibility of forming an unbreakable bond with this creature felt like an incredible privilege.

"Bruce, what am I supposed to do with her? She's so tiny. Did you see the mama cat?"

"Nope, I found her under a house, crying and alone."

The weight of responsibility settled upon me as I realized the kitten's fate rested in my hands. With no supplies, carrier, litter box, or food, I made a snap decision. "Okay, I'll take her. Thanks, Bruce."

The tiny kitten understood that the decision had been made. She crawled up my shoulder and nestled her adorable self behind my neck. The thought of her exploring in the car without a carrier made me a little nervous.

During the entire forty-five-minute journey, she stayed serenely perched on my shoulders, making herself comfortable, as if she'd discovered her sanctuary. The soft vibrations of her purring served as a calming soundtrack, soothing my worries.

Once we made it home, I introduced her to our bathroom, gave her a snuggle and a kiss, and locked her inside to make sure she was safe. I headed out as quickly as possible to the pet store. While I navigated the aisles, and browsed the varieties of cat food, toys, and accessories, a sense of purpose arose from within.

Having the ability to shape my life based on my own desires and inclinations gave me a taste of freedom. The constraints imposed by my mother were a thing of the past, supplanted by the limitless opportunities that awaited me in this new chapter.

I came to realize the joys of having a cat were indescribable. They weave their way into your heart, leaving a trail of love and whimsy in their wake. While we settled in and bonded, I figured out the perfect name for her: Cow. I named her cow because she reminded me of a Holstein cow. With her adorable markings, I couldn't think of a more fitting name.

From the moment this little ball of fluff came into my life, she emitted a unique lovability that was impossible to resist. In those early days, I observed Cow's graceful movements and playful antics, and I was captivated by her every action. With wild fervor, she would dart across the room, chasing invisible prey. Perched atop the tallest shelves, her wide eyes shined with a mischievous glimmer.

Every morning, as the sun's rays streamed through the window, Cow would awaken me with her gentle purring. Her warm presence by my side filled me with content. In her company, the world was brighter and more alive. In those moments, time stood still, and my worries melted away.

Cow had an uncanny ability to sense my moods. She offered comfort and support when I needed it most. In moments of sadness or stress, she would curl up beside me, her gentle presence a reminder that I was never alone.

As time went on, Cow became more than just a pet; she became a confidante, a companion and a source of unwavering love. In her eyes, I saw a reflection of my spirit, and in her purrs, I felt a connection that surpassed words. She reminded me daily of the importance of embracing life's simple pleasures.

Despite Cow's boundless affection that filled my life, I couldn't shake the lingering temptation to indulge in alcohol and drugs.

It was a troubling paradox. One would think that experiencing a traumatic rape while under the influence would be a wake-up call, prompting me to abandon the destructive path of drinking. Yet, against all reason, it exacerbated the problem, leading me further down a perilous path of self-destruction.

Intense shame consumed me after the rape; it demanded an escape and weed wasn't doing the trick any longer.

In my subconscious quest to bury those emotions, I turned to the alluring embrace of alcohol and heavier drugs. The numbing effect provided a passing sanctuary that enabled me to escape. Once I gained the freedom of living independently, it unleashed a floodgate, sparking an insatiable desire for excitement, diversion, and the nighttime thrill.

Every weekend, my friends and I would embark on outings to the club scene. We immersed ourselves in the intoxicating world of revelry, where the rhythm of pulsating music merged with the clinking of glasses. Marc, Jason, Cindi, and I formed the core of our close-knit posse, joined occasionally by LR, Tommy, Penny, and sometimes Michelle.

The evenings began with our ritualistic stop at Jack-in-the-Box, a popular fast food restaurant. I often pondered whether a car filled with people ordering only a single extra-large soda confused the drive-thru cashier.

After securing a secluded spot to park, we discarded the soda through the car window, making way for our concoction of vodka and orange juice. The forty-ounce soda cup filled with our homemade Screwdriver became the centerpiece of our rendezvous. With each sip, the potent elixir infused our conversations with a buzz that preceded our arrival at the nightclub.

Despite being only seventeen years old, I possessed a remarkable fake ID that provided me with access to the colorful world of gay town. I was privileged and lucky to venture beyond the constraints of my age.

My trusted friends and I became a united front, ready to conquer the night. The combination of youthful audacity and liquid courage propelled us forward. We embraced the electric energy of the nightlife and painted the town with our laughter and uninhibited spirits.

In those drunken nights, we danced with abandon and surrendered to the hypnotic beats that pulsated through our bodies. The disco lights and mind-altering atmosphere acted as a temporary salve, soothing the wounds that lingered beneath the surface. In that realm, we attempted to let go of our burdens and embrace a carefree existence.

The friendships we forged became the lifelines that kept us afloat. We were comrades in this battle against our own demons, finding comfort in each other's company.

West Hollywood's Santa Monica Boulevard was the backdrop for countless nocturnal adventures that my friends and I experienced. Among the myriad of bars peppering this iconic stretch, we had our select favorites. Rage, Mickey's, The Palms, and Mother Load to name a few. In these spaces, unforgettable memories became ingrained in our lives.

Just east of Laurel Canyon, at 7969 Santa Monica Boulevard, sat a legendary establishment—the home of Peanuts. What began as a lesbian bar metamorphosed into a thriving gay venue, complete with a dazzling drag show, that captivated audiences every weekend.

The vibrant energy spilled onto the sidewalk, drawing us into its magnetic embrace. Inside, a mid-size dance floor awaited, highlighted by a stage that commanded attention. It stood in front of a line of mirrored walls and acted as the canvas for our beloved drag celebrities to display their immense talents. Viva, Grace, Boy Tom, Lesbiana/Tangerine, and the enigmatic host Michelangelo—some females, some masterful impersonators—became the stars of our nights, captivating us with their remarkable performances.

The midnight show stood out as the highlight of the evening, a spectacle that evoked awe. The lights dimmed, and the curtains rose. Everyone sat enthralled, we witnessed a kaleidoscope of colors, music and transformative artistry that unfolded before our eyes.

The show ended and the dance floor regained its liveliness for the next few hours.

And then it happened—the timeless melody of Donna Summer's "Last Dance" permeated the air, signaling the imminent conclusion of the night. Jason, my best friend since I turned fifteen, and I would lock eyes. We'd grab each other's hands and take to the center of the dance floor. Our bodies swayed in perfect harmony, as if we were the sole inhabitants of this magical realm.

At the end of the evening, an unspoken ritual unfolded: "Last Dance" ended and bright lights flooded the dance floor. Jason and I would embrace as if parting ways forever. Yet, inevitably, we'd journey home together after a heartfelt hug.

In these transformative spaces, we found not only acceptance, but also a profound sensation of belonging. Our visits to Peanuts were more than mere outings; they became integral chapters in our ongoing narratives.

In the years that followed, our paths diverged: Marc headed off to San Diego State for college; Cindi was on her own East Coast adventures; LR and Linda moved up to Santa Cruz; while Jason, Penny, Michelle, and I remained in LA. The vibrancy of those nights would become cherished nostalgia. The echoes of laughter, resounding beats of music, and the shimmering presence of drag performers would forever dance in the corridors of my heart.

In retrospect, I discovered that my inclination for partying stemmed not only from the need for momentary oblivion; but also a desperate desire to regain control over my life. In those wild nights, I dictated my narrative, casting aside the victim label that haunted me for far too long. It was a fleeting illusion of power, a mirage that greeted me with open arms.

Deep down, I knew that genuine healing was unattainable at the bottom of a bottle, in a capsule of ecstasy, or a tab of LSD. The path toward healing required a different kind of courage—to face the pain head-on and to confront the demons that lurked within. Something I wasn't quite ready to explore.

During our days of glorifying West Hollywood, Jason stayed with me practically every weekend. Eventually, he was with me more days than not. After a few months of him being there, I suggested we make it official. I offered to charge him a hundred dollars per month to stay on my futon and share my place.

This arrangement was a win-win. It allowed Jason to leave his dad's house and take on additional responsibilities—a first for him. Also, my rent decreased to only three hundred dollars a month. This provided me some relief as I juggled multiple jobs, including having worked as a secretary for my brother Nile during some of his movie launches.

I attended community college in the evenings in addition to working full time, so I wasn't home much. Jason relied on his parents for financial support since he hadn't secured a job yet. Therefore, he enjoyed hanging around doing a whole lot of nothing during the day, but he was bored. Jason and I lived together for about two months when he invited his friend over one day to hang out with him. I came home late from school that day. Jason and his friend Danny were there to greet me with a home-cooked meal and smiles.

This was my first meeting with Danny, and he seemed sweet and good-natured.

Danny ended up staying with us for several days, so I finally asked what his deal was. I brought Jason to my room and closed the door.

"Jason, how long is he staying? I like him, but this place is tiny for three of us."

"Actually, I wanted to talk to you."

"Uh-oh ... what?" I asked with a wry look.

"Well, it's just ..."

"Just what, J?"

"He doesn't really have any place to go."

"What do you mean he doesn't have any place to go? Doesn't he have family?"

"He has family, yes, but ..."

"But what?"

"But his family kicked him out."

"What? Why?"

"They found out he is gay and they kicked him out on the street. He's been homeless for over a month."

"What? Crazy! How can a family do that to their own son?" I was shocked that anyone would do that to their child because they were gay. I realized things like this happened, but this was the first instance where I had a personal connection with someone who had been a victim of such blatant discrimination.

"It happens all the time," Jason replied.

"Wow. Well, what do you propose we do?"

"I was thinking we could share the futon. I'm sure he would be willing to pay you the same amount I pay," he responded.

"You would share the futon with him and you each pay one hundred dollars per month?"

"Yeah, if that keeps him off the street."

"Oh my gosh. Let's go talk to him," I stated.

"So, he can stay?"

"Of course! What the heck? I'm not going to let him be homeless."

We approached Danny.

"I know, you want me to go. Don't worry. You don't have to even ask," Danny blurted out.

"No, Danny, I don't want you to leave."

"You don't?" He tilted his head and smiled like a cute cocker spaniel.

"No, dork. I didn't realize you were homeless and your family was a bunch of fucking assholes who kicked you out on the street because you're gay."

"Yeah, that's pretty much what happened," Danny replied.

"How about you pay me one hundred dollars per month and you and Jason can share the futon. I keep the room, and we will all share the kitchen and bathroom."

"Really?" Danny responded, as if he'd just won the lottery.

"Yes, it helps me financially. It helps you by giving you a safe place to stay, shower, shit, and eat cheap. And it will help Jason with his boredom during the day," I said with a chuckle.

Danny jumped up, skipped over to me, gave me the biggest hug and what felt like a thousand kisses.

"Thank you, thank you, thank you. I can't believe it. You just met me, and you are giving me a place to live. You are the sweetest, greatest, most amazing lesbian on the planet."

"Oh, Danny, you are such a dork. If you are good in Jason's book, you are good in mine."

"I'm so excited. We are going to be friends forever," Danny said as he squeezed me even tighter.

After welcoming Danny into my life and reflecting on the painful circumstances of his family rejecting him solely because of his sexual orientation, my mind wandered into uncharted territory. It forced me to confront a haunting question: *What if my mother hadn't brought us back from Baghdad after we were kidnapped?*

I pondered the path my life might have taken had I grown up in Iraq, a place where being gay meant facing rejection, oppression, public humiliation, and even death. While I'd had my fair share of ridicule in the United States, it paled in comparison to what could have been. It's sobering to think that many LGBTQ+ individuals have suffered far greater hardships, including the ultimate price, even in my country. These thoughts weighed heavily on me and stirred up a tumultuous mix of emotions.

One evening, as Jason, Danny, and I gathered around the dinner table, enjoying our "framily" meal, the ring of the telephone pierced the air. I stood up and walked to the kitchen, where the phone had been affixed to the wall. A woman's voice greeted me.

"Hello...," she uttered hesitantly. "Is Delicia there?"

"This is she; may I ask who is calling?"

"Well, you don't know me, but my name is Barbara. I am married to someone who I believe is your cousin. His name is Wakim Al-Niami. Do you remember him?"

"I'm sorry, you have the wrong number. My last name is Niami, not Al-Niami."

"Oh, I'm sorry, let me explain. Is your father's name Hazim?"

"That was my father's name, yes, but I have no idea if he's even alive."

"Oh, he's alive."

"What? You know my father?"

"Yes, that is what I am trying to explain. Wakim, my husband, is your father's nephew."

"Okay. So?" I found it quite strange that someone from my father's side of the family had reached out to me.

"I found your name in the database here at Cedar's, and I didn't think it would actually be you. It was a shot in the dark, so I called."

This was unsettling. I didn't know what to say. I hadn't heard a word from my father since my mother took him to court to sue him for child support when I was twelve.

Memories of that day surged through my thoughts as this strange woman rambled on the other end of the telephone. I'd faced my father for the first time since our tumultuous kidnapping. At just five-years-old, he returned us to the States, and at twelve, I stood face to face with him in a courtroom. My mother urged me to ask him a simple question:

"Go ask him if he knows when your birthday is, go ahead, ask him."

Mom nudged me in his direction and I very reluctantly asked my so-called father, "Hazim, when's my birthday?"

He muttered, "um, March, um, March um 8th?"

I shook my head in disgust and said "no, it's March 6th."

In that moment, his answer hung in the air and my heart sank. It was a stark and painful revelation, one that left me knowing I was insignificant in his eyes.

It was disheartening to realize that my mom led me into such a painful circumstance, knowing full well that my father wouldn't know the answer. It felt like a cruel manipulation, a way to prove what I'd feared all along: I meant nothing to him.

The depth of disappointment and hurt ran deep. This echoed the profound realization that the father I yearned to connect with was, in reality, as distant as I'd feared, despite my fervent hopes for a different truth.

It shattered any illusions or longing I had for a relationship with him. This left me to confront the harsh reality that his absence from my life was not only physical but also emotional.

Prior to our court interaction, the previous time I'd encountered him was just before boarding a plane back home on my fifth birthday. Now I was getting a call from someone saying she was the wife of the nephew of my father?

I remained silent.

"Hello, Delicia? Is that really you? We have been looking for you for so long."

"You have?" I asked incredulously.

"Yes, years. Wakim is going to be so happy I found you. He said you used to play together in Baghdad when you were little kids."

"I'm sorry, but I don't remember Wakim, and I haven't heard from my father since I was five. I'm not interested in getting to know anyone from that side of the family."

"Really?" I heard the disappointment in her voice.

"Sorry but I have spent a good portion of my life trying to forget Hazim's side of my family."

"Oh, how heartbreaking. We are really good people. I know your father isn't the best communicator, but..."

"Isn't the best communicator?" I interrupted with disdain. "He hasn't tried to contact me since we left Baghdad on my fifth birthday. The last time I saw him was at court when I was twelve, and he didn't even remember my birthdate. Is this a joke? Am I on Candid Camera?"

She laughed. "No, we would really like to meet you. I understand if you aren't interested. But, please take down my number and call if you ever want to meet."

Hazim wasn't someone I desired to meet. I rarely thought about him—until the night when I received that mysterious phone call.

"Okay, but I'm not making any promises." I jotted down her number and kept it in a safe place.

I made my way back to the table. Both Danny and Jason were staring at me in astonishment, mouths agape.

"What was that?" Jason asked.

"Apparently a cousin on my father's side of the family wants to meet me."

"What? You should totally do it. What if he's, like, a rich sultan or something."

"Shut up, Jason. He's not a rich sultan, he's a nobody."

"You should totally meet them," Danny interjected.

"I don't want to talk about this anymore, guys. I will talk to my brother and see what he thinks."

When I brought up the topic with Nile, I noticed the indifference in his response. I never broached the subject with Patrick, as he had zero desire to know anything about Hazim's side of our family. After all, this was the man who backed my mother into a corner and demanded she give up her firstborn son for adoption.

Nile agreed to join me for a lunch meeting with them. A few weeks later, we found ourselves at a restaurant off Melrose. Both during and after our meeting, my cousin, and his wife appeared kind, so I continued to nurture the relationship.

Since 1977, Hazim had been back in California. He never attempted to contact us, which confused and hurt me deeply. His abandonment haunted me, making it even more challenging to comprehend his sudden desire to meet me after all these years. The scars of varied traumatic experiences were deeply ingrained, and I refused to entertain the idea of reconnecting with him.

My cousin and his wife's persistent reminders of my father's desire to meet us became a recurring source of discomfort. I found myself at a loss for words whenever they broached the subject. One key question consumed my thoughts: *Why*? I struggled with the puzzling notion of why, after all those years, my father developed a longing to re-establish a connection with me. *Was it true? Could I trust this? Was I willing to allow a small crack in the window of my heart he'd shattered into a million pieces? The pieces I'd worked so many years attempting to repair?*

Regardless of their persistent inquiries and my growing curiosity, I had to ensure my emotional safety. My response remained a steadfast "no, I'm not interested."

Over time, I pushed Hazim to the darkest corners of my mind and tried to forget the pain and disappointment he notoriously brought into my life. Given all the effort I put into keeping him at bay, I wasn't about to summon the ghosts of my past now, after fighting tirelessly to suppress them. Resolute in my choice not to reopen old wounds, I was proud of the stance I'd taken.

I embraced the path of independence and began charting my course—relying on my own capabilities.

Varied employment opportunities helped me to build a life detached from the shadows of my past. With each new job came a fresh array of challenges and valuable lessons. I confronted them directly, viewing each obstacle as a chance for growth and learning. Through these experiences, I developed greater self-reliance and a deeper understanding of my own worth.

My first step to venturing into the world of business was applying to temporary agencies. It wasn't long before I landed a position opening sweepstakes for The Advocate, The National Gay, and Lesbian News Magazine.

Although it was a lighthearted and mindless job, it began my foray into corporate America. The temporary job ended and I resumed my path of pursuing education and working as a server.

The people I worked for at The Advocate were determined to get me back. Every day, like clockwork, I received calls from the temporary agency requesting that I return to work for them. I wasn't interested in the position they were offering, yet their persistence knew no bounds.

"Hi, is this Delicia Niami? You just finished an assignment at The Advocate?" The temporary agency inquired for the fourth time.

"Yes, I did."

"Well, they loved the work you did, and they would like for you to come work for them on a part-time basis in their accounting department."

"I'm not interested in accounting, and I've never done it before. Why are they insisting on me?"

"I'm not sure. They are adamant and keep calling. They really want you to work for them."

"Fine by me, I need the money, so tell them yes, I would love to."

There was no interview required for the job; instead, I was to report to the manager of the accounting department first thing in the morning.

The Advocate was located on Hollywood and Orange, opposite the famous Grauman's Chinese Theater. The immersion into the glitz and glamour of Hollywood Boulevard resulted in an electrifying experience in its own right.

Armed with a solid grasp of the layout, I headed to my destination. My first stop was a quick check-in at the front desk. Security was tight in this openly LGBTQ+ workplace, which was reassuring. I entered the accounting department, and the team welcomed me with smiles and open arms.

"Hi, Delicia, welcome back!" said Susan, the vice president of finance. "We are so glad you took the position!"

"What position did I take exactly?" I replied with a crooked smile.

Susan laughed and said, "You will be doing accounts receivable with Christine."

During my time sorting sweepstakes, I worked alongside Christine as my supervisor. With a few years' seniority and a commanding presence, she left a lasting impression. We had an excellent rapport, and I was eager to work with her.

She greeted me with a warm smile. "I'm thrilled to have you back. Come with me, and I'll show you what we will be doing."

I followed her to a grey cubicle with metal framing. I settled in and noticed how much this resembled a simple school desk. However, this was different. It was an adult desk, and I was about to embark on real adult work.

My job was accounts receivable and I handled magazine subscriptions and managed incoming finances. I felt important. At the same time, I acquired valuable learning experiences.

Amidst the routine of my work, there was a remarkable experience that unfolded one special day. Drew Barrymore, the same actor I grew up watching on TV and in films, was imprinting her footprints at the iconic Grauman's Chinese Theater. As a child, her performances in movies like E.T. captivated me. I'd watched it ungodly numbers of times in the theater. Now, I witnessed her being celebrated as part of Hollywood's history and that filled me with joy.

I swelled with admiration and gratitude as I gazed down from the tenth floor. In that fleeting moment, I felt connected to Drew. As a survivor in her own right, her journey mirrored aspects of my own. Though she had no knowledge of me, it was as if we shared an unspoken camaraderie—an unbreakable bond forged through the challenges we overcame.

Through determination and hard work, I embarked on a steady ascent up the corporate ladder. Beginning in accounts receivable I gradually moved up to accounts payable. They acknowledged and rewarded my dedication and commitment. My boss sponsored part of my education to further my advances. After a short time, they offered me a promotion to the role of general ledger accountant.

My journey into the corporate world shed light on a sobering reality: the lack of support for teachers in our country. It struck me that after just a few years in the workforce, I was making more than my mother. She had dedicated over eighteen years of her life as a passionate and hardworking special education teacher. It was a glaring reminder of the undervaluation of educators and the challenges they faced in terms of financial recognition and support.

In moments like these, my mother filled me with admiration. I'd often wondered how she provided for us on her modest salary. Now, it dawned on me why Mom purchased The Stein Club, a bar she had owned that helped us financially but meant she was gone all the time. Her constant absence made us latchkey kids. Although I resented this as a child, I now grasped that, on a teacher's salary, raising two children alone wasn't feasible without an additional source of income.

In retrospect, I acknowledged my mother's absence during that time was driven by a deep-rooted love and determination to ensure our well-being, even if it meant making difficult choices. My anger transformed into empathy as I embraced a newfound understanding of the sacrifices she'd made for us.

During my time at The Advocate, my involvement in LGBTQ+ politics surged. In the summer of 1989, Orange County was hosting its first-ever Pride event, and this piqued my curiosity.

Eager for an atmosphere of empowerment in a county known for its conservative and non-liberal views, particularly concerning the LGBTQ+ community, I, along with my friends, decided to attend. We set out for Santa Ana, and our hearts overflowed with anticipation. When we arrived, we were confronted with the sight of protestors.

"Should we still go?" Penny inquired.

"Heck yeah. We can't let those people stop us; that's what this is all about. We have to fight for our rights!" Jason exclaimed.

"Yeah, I think he is right; we should go," I responded.

After we parked the car, the sounds of chanting led us toward the bustling crowd. An apprehensive atmosphere hung in the air. We navigated through the picketers who held signs spewing what they thought were hurtful words in our direction. Despite the tension, we shared a knowing chuckle amongst ourselves and walked past peacefully. We made a conscious effort not to provoke any unnecessary conflicts.

"You are all sinners, and you are going to hell," the demonstrators shouted.

We approached the park, and the gates were shut; which left us unsure as to what was happening. With the anti-gay rally taking place just outside the park, the city authorities decided not to take any chances and closed the event shortly after it began. This meant those already inside could not leave, while those on the outside were denied entry.

More people arrived as we gathered on the lawn. Regardless of the slanderous words being shouted in our direction, we remained calm, minding our own business. Jason, Danny, Penny, and I sat together and observed the scene for about thirty minutes. It was then that we noticed the police arriving, dressed in riot gear. They pushed the protestors back from the sidewalk.

.'0[The police formed a barrier, prepared and waiting for any potential outbreak of violence. They stood shoulder to shoulder, donning helmets and face shields and wielding batons. There were hundreds of officers whom awaited a confrontation between the LGBTQ+ community and the hate-filled demonstrators.

It was our responsibility to alter the world's perception of us. In a spontaneous moment, everyone began holding hands. We formed an incredible circle of love, and sang together in unison. It took forty-five minutes for the protestors to realize that their attempts to provoke violence were in vain. Slowly, they dispersed.

Once the protestors left, the riot police followed suit, and the gates to the park re-opened. This event became a poignant moment in LGBTQ+ history, and I take immense pride in having been a part of it.

My solo journey meant unrestrained freedom to party whenever the mood struck. Jason, Danny, and I indulged in an abundance of gatherings during our cohabitation. The fun led to our thirty-day notice to vacate the premises. After many complaints from the neighbors, it was time for us to move on.

Once we parted ways, Jason found his own place, while Danny and I shared a new home together in West Hollywood.

Nestled on Palm Avenue in the center of gay town, our little sanctuary was just a leisurely stroll away from the bars and the allure of it all. At the youthful age of nineteen, on the cusp of turning twenty, I found myself immersed in a gay paradise.

Among the multitude of condominiums and apartments that lined the street, our dwelling stood proudly as one of the few cherished houses. It was a captivating craftsman home that boasted original hardwood floors and a decor that harkened back to its 1930s origins.

Both bedrooms offered equal space, while a welcoming living room, a cozy dining room, a fully equipped kitchen, and a complete bathroom embraced our daily existence. And to top it off, a small backyard provided a tranquil retreat from the bustling city. Astonishingly, this incredible abode was ours for a mere eight hundred dollars a month—a deal by any measure. Oh, how we cherished those bygone days!

Just a stone's throw from our new home, Video West became Jason's workplace. Once again, the inseparable trio of musketeers reunited. Danny and I shared the house, but Jason's constant presence made it seem as though he, too, called our house home.

Danny and I embarked on our journey together along with our faithful feline companion, Cow. As someone who'd never owned a pet before, I must confess that I was ignorant about the responsibilities that came with taking care of a cat. Aware of the dangers that lurked on the busy street outside, I kept her indoors, despite her yearning to roam free.

Cow was always an indoor-outdoor cat, and she wasn't about to relinquish her wild spirit. She would seize any opportunity to escape, and one day, when she was in heat, she slipped through the door undetected. It was a defining moment of my inexperience, as I hadn't yet learned the importance of spaying or neutering pets. As a result, Cow became pregnant.

Months later, a bundle of adorable black-and-white kittens graced our home. I marveled at their minuscule size when I came home to find them nestled against their mother's belly, tucked safely within her carpeted cat tree. But our joy was short-lived.

That summer in Los Angeles, the worst flea infestation I'd ever witnessed plagued the city, and the tiny kittens became riddled with these relentless parasites. Try as I might, every effort I made to keep the fleas at bay was in vain. The kittens were too young for any conventional flea treatment or collars, according to the vet.

Desperate to save them, I pleaded with my boss at The Advocate to allow me to bring the kittens into the office. I didn't think about the possibility of fleas spreading in the building.

I approached Christine in my desperation to seek a solution to my kittens' flea problem.

"Christine, I know pets aren't allowed here, but this is killing me. I can't keep the fleas off my kittens," I explained, my voice filled with hopeful desperation.

She looked at me with a sympathetic expression and replied, "I understand your concern, but, unfortunately, we have strict policies against bringing pets into the office. It's a corporate space, and we need to maintain a professional environment."

Tears welled up in my eyes as I pleaded, "I'm not sure what else to do. The fleas are relentless, and I'm afraid of losing these kittens. Can you make an exception?"

Christine's gaze softened, her compassion apparent. She sighed, then said, "I wish I could help you, but I can't. Please understand that it's out of my hands."

Each morning and night, I would vacuum the cat tree, since Cow was determined to keep her babies there. I picked the fleas off each tiny kitten one by one with tweezers, but my actions only brought temporary relief.

In my quest to find a solution, I discovered that orange oil might help combat fleas. Regrettably, the acidity of the oil proved too harsh for their sensitive skin, and their soft, pitiful meows echoed in my ears with each swipe.

I witnessed their suffering which was an excruciating battle, one that tugged at the deepest depths of my heart. No matter what I tried, the agonizing truth remained—I could not provide the relief they so desperately needed.

Days passed and the horrific pests took their toll. Despite my best efforts, every few days, I'd come home to find a lifeless kitten's body drained by the merciless parasites. With each loss, my soul shattered. Never before had I bore witness to the miracle of birth, for it only to be followed by my first harsh reality of death and the suffocating weight grief bore on one's soul.

Thankfully, Cow survived the ordeal. But I bore the scars of the traumatic loss of her five tiny kittens. It taught me about responsibility, compassion and the delicate nature of life. This sparked a shift in my perspective. It prompted me to reevaluate my priorities and find the present moment, something with which I was unfamiliar.

Faced with this extreme loss, I began to understand that the trials and tribulations I endured had not been in vain. Rather, they provided me with the tools to navigate the obstacles I might face in life. Each loss became a lesson, shaping me into someone capable of weathering the fiercest of storms. I embraced the uncertain future with confidence, believing I would indeed find the strength to conquer whatever came my way.

FREEDOM

Consumed by grief, I found myself drawn to The Palms, the one and only local lesbian bar. Amidst the haze of cigarette smoke and the soft glow of neon signs, I sought refuge from my depression. Here, in this haven of acceptance, I discovered a fleeting reprieve from the ache, surrounded by familiar faces and kindred spirits.

The exterior of The Palms exuded an air of mystery; with its discrete light grey concrete and a blacked-out window that concealed the vivacious energy within. A carved metal palm tree adorned the entrance.

Inside was quite dark, even during the day. Small black pleather stools lined the bar, where you would normally find our friend Marie. Her presence added a familiar warmth to the atmosphere. The dance floor and DJ beckoned to me, which offered a space of freedom and self-expression.

Marie was adorable and always floated me free drinks. We shared a flirtatious relationship and engaged in playful banter and teasing. Our connection was something I didn't find with just anyone. I laughed and joked with Marie; I was lighthearted with her; she got me. It was all in good fun until Marie became involved with another woman, Deena. Deena's presence cast a shadow over our interactions and stifled the once-energetic exchanges between us.

Her arrival changed everything. Her imposing presence, towering at six-foot-two, dwarfed my five-foot-five frame. Marie's and my flirtatious interactions dwindled, constrained by Deena's watchful gaze. Our carefree banter and playful exchanges gave way to guarded smiles and distant conversations as we navigated the unspoken boundaries set by Marie's new girlfriend.

One fateful night, as my friends and I entered the bar, Deena's jealousy erupted like a volcano when she saw Marie and me. We were laughing and standing close to each other. She unleashed her fury with a series of accusations. In a drunken haze, she demanded that I speak to her at the bar, her voice saturated with anger.

Curiosity and defiance led me to comply.

"What are you doing here?" she bellowed as the foul stench of whisky surrounded me like a fiery dragon's breath and her spit drenched my face. It was clear thar her anger and aggression were fueled by the alcohol.

"Hey, listen, Deena, no big deal. I was just hanging out with your girlfriend, catching up," I said in a bit of a snarky tone.

"Hanging out? Is that what you call smacking lips?" she slurred.

"What? I wasn't 'smacking lips' with anyone." In a moment of courage, I puffed out my chest, hoping to project an illusion of might.

"Let's go outside, right now!" she huffed as she pointed her finger toward the door and sauntered off.

I looked at Marie with bewilderment. and ignored Deena's demands. I chose to remain within the confines of the bar, unaware of the storm that was about to unleash.

Suddenly, a forceful hand grabbed hold of my ear and pulled me outside against my will. In that instant, a distinct memory surged through my mind. I recalled a similar act of humiliation from my childhood.

Flashbacks of my mother dragging me out of a junior high dance, my ear painfully clutched in her grip, ignited a deep well of rage within me. As Deena dragged me, I wriggled and writhed and attempted to free myself from her grasp. Once we were outside, the fury in me reached its peak.

"How dare you touch me like that? Who the fuck do you think you are?" I seethed, my voice laced with rage and indignation.

Deena lunged toward me, seeking to assert her dominance. Consumed by anger, I swung at her face. Somehow, I'd imagined my strength was mightier than a furious six-foot-two amazon. Obviously, she was quicker, much larger, and stronger than me. She grabbed my neck and lifted me off the ground. My body, frail compared to hers, was helpless against her overpowering presence.

She carried me by my neck toward a nearby newspaper machine. Deena violently shoved me against it, her anger and dominance radiated through her actions. Her words echoed in my ears: "And don't you ever even think about looking at my girl again!"

When she released her grip, my body crumpled to the ground, my legs unable to support me. My friends, who witnessed the chaotic scene, rushed to my side. Among them was Danny, my trusted roommate. He recognized the severity of the injury and concern filled his voice.

"Honey, look at your leg! We need to get you to the hospital," he pleaded, his tone laced with worry. Blood trickled from my wound, that left a trail as we stumbled forward.

I brushed off his concern. "It's fine," I insisted, my voice shaky but determined. "I can't even feel it. Let's just go home."

Our house was a few blocks away, so we headed in that direction. Danny, always attended to my needs, thus, he took charge of my injury. He meticulously bandaged me up. The full extent of the damage became apparent—a deep, triangular gash on the back of my leg, an agonizing reminder of the altercation.

Deena's forceful push propelled me into the unforgiving metal of the newspaper machine, the sharp edges tore into my flesh. Stitches were necessary, but the mere thought of confronting that reality troubled me. I was exhausted and surrendered to the numbing embrace of sleep. The alcohol coursed through my veins and functioned as a temporary anesthetic, dulling both the physical and emotional pain.

Weeks later, Jason and I sat engaged in the sound of laughter and clinking glasses that reverberated through the gallows of The Palms. The early 1990s was a time when the specter of AIDS loomed over the gay community. When the world first heard of AIDS In the early 1980s, it was known as GRID, "Gay Related Immune Deficiency." The belief was that it only affected gay men.

During those times, a profound ignorance gripped society. Fear infiltrated every aspect of our lives and affected even the most basic displays of affection. We were afraid to hug our friends, to shake hands, to use the same public restroom for fear of transmission.

Looking back, it's easy to see how naïve we were, how misguided our fears may have been. But amidst the crisis, we grappled with the unknown, a disease that defied logic and reason. And in that uncertainty, the fear only grew, feeding off our ignorance and misunderstanding.

Jason and I sat together at The Palms surrounded by the laughter and camaraderie of our people, while the weight of society's paranoia bore down on us. We constantly faced the looming threat and I knew that the conversation we were about to have would be one of the most important of our lives.

The illness was both mysterious and ruthless, with a cloud of stigma that surrounded it. I vividly recall the constant angst it caused. Eventually, the Centers for Disease Control renamed it AIDS, "Acquired Immune Deficiency Syndrome."

It was impossible to avoid the topic.

Settled in a quiet corner, distanced from the crowd, Jason and I engaged in a deep conversation. We shared our fears and concerns with each other.

"You know, it's terrifying," I said, my voice thwarted with worry. "This disease is affecting so many people. It's becoming normalized and it's devastating. It's so scary. Do you know anyone who has gotten it yet?"

Jason nodded, his eyes reflected the shared worry.

"I can't help it, but there's a constant unease. It's like a cloud of panic that hangs over us. I worry for you, Marc, Danny and our other friends. It's so unfair!" I exclaimed.

Silence settled between us for a moment as we absorbed the significance of our conversation. The concern for Jason's well-being gnawed at me. I took a deep breath and mustered the courage to bring up something I'd been avoiding.

By this point, they were aware of the cause behind the virus, and testing was now available to determine if you had contracted it.

"Jason, please…you are my best friend on the planet, I need you to get tested," I pleaded, my voice trembled with desperation. "I can't bear the thought of you being infected and not knowing. We need to understand as much as we can so we can fight this together. They are starting to have medication. If you test positive, you can start the meds and keep your body fighting this beast."

Jason looked at me with defiant sadness. "I appreciate your concern, but what would I do if I tested positive?" his voice was heavy with resignation. "There's no cure, and the drugs they give you seem just as horrifying as the disease itself. I don't want to deal with that."

I became teary-eyed as I listened to him. The thought of losing him to this invisible enemy was unbearable. I reached out and placed my hand on his knee, my words trembled with emotion.

My voice cracked as I stated, "But, Jason, there's hope. There's research happening, advancements being made. We can't give up. Please, for your own sake, get tested. I can even come with you, if you want?"

The desperation in my voice was undeniable. I sank to my knees while I pleaded with him to understand the importance of the situation. The turmoil in his eyes revealed a battle between fear and love.

He reached down and lifted me to my feet with gratitude and sorrow. "I hear you, and I appreciate your concern," he said softly. "But right now, this is the only way I can protect myself, mentally at least. Don't worry about me. I'll be fine."

I knew I couldn't force him to do something he wasn't ready for, but the worry that lingered within me was gargantuan. We sat, lost in our thoughts, and I silently vowed to continue fighting for awareness, support, and a future free from the grip of AIDS.

Despite the lingering worry, I found solace in the comforting presence of my friend and trusted roommate, Danny. Our bond was strong, and even in moments of uncertainty, his understanding, and support never wavered. I was less worried about Danny because he was hyper-conscious about not only the prospect of getting AIDS but germs in general. His patience and humor brought lightness to my often-chaotic world. It empowered me to continue fighting for the causes closest to my heart, knowing that together, we might make a difference.

When one of our friends stumbled upon a magnificent house in East Hollywood, we couldn't resist. The sheer size of the place was mind-boggling, it spanned a whopping ten thousand square feet. It boasted eight bedrooms and even included a basement. We saw this as an opportunity to create a communal living experience and fill the rooms with ten of our friends, Jason amongst them.

We didn't comprehend the trade-offs we were making. The grandiose of this house blinded us to the potential downsides. Unbeknownst to us, the reality of living with so many people would soon reveal its challenges and limitations.

The constant noise, the lack of privacy, and the ever-present chaos was too much for me. I realized that communal living wasn't my jam. Within six months, the novelty wore off.

I left that bustling house behind and retreated to the quieter streets of North Hollywood. Parting ways with Danny and our friends was bittersweet. We created many memories together in that grand house, the laughter echoed through its vast halls. But I knew that in order to preserve my sanity and regain balance, I needed to find my solitude.

I settled into my new place in North Hollywood and reflected on the journey of Danny and me. It all began with the serendipitous encounter that led to us becoming roommates, and from there, our friendship weathered numerous storms as we embarked on countless adventures together.

I knew that Danny's support and understanding would be lifelong. He became more than just a friend; he was the person who brought order to my chaos. And even though we were no longer sharing the same physical space, our bond remained unbreakable.

I carried with me the lessons learned and my deep appreciation for the unique connection Danny, Jason, and I shared. Our intertwined journeys would forever be connected by the laughter, the adventures, and the enduring support we found in one another.

I realized once I moved out and began working at The Advocate that the actions you take as an individual can create a ripple effect. By embracing my identity, sharing my experiences, and standing up for my rights, I'd hoped to make a meaningful impact to a more inclusive and accepting society. Besides being part of the inaugural Orange County Pride, one of my most memorable moments in LGBTQ+ history was when Governor Wilson vetoed AB101. This proposed gay-rights bill was meant to stop job discrimination of LGBTQ+ people in the workplace. At the time, I was deep into politics, and my friends and co-workers followed this bill from start to finish. The day after Wilson vetoed it, the magic happened.

It started off like any other day: I went to work, then to school at Santa Monica City College. On my way home, I didn't listen to or follow the news because my spirit was broken. This bill was vetoed after such a long and arduous fight. Traffic came to a halt; The light changed, but nobody was moving. Time passed, and I became more irritated, as I still had a long drive and I wanted to get home and sulk.

Over the blaring music on my radio, I heard chanting. When I turned down the sound, the noise intensified. I rolled down my window, and tried to understand what was happening. Within minutes, people blocked the streets and the chanting became closer and closer. A sea of colors and empowering messages hovered in the air, supporting the LGBTQ+ community. The neon signs read: "Gay and Proud of It," "Being Gay Isn't a Choice," and "We work just as hard as our straight neighbors."

The crowds kept coming, with thousands of demonstrators marching down the streets of Los Angeles, fighting for our rights. Supporters got out of their cars and cheered them on as they marched past. All I could do was sit in my car and cry. I cried for the times I'd fought for my rights. I cried with gratitude that our mother rescued Nile and me from Baghdad. I cried for the times I was emotionally and verbally gay-bashed. I cried for all the LGBTQ+ people who had committed suicide. I cried for Danny and some of my co-workers, whose families had kicked them out on the street for being gay. I cried for every person who ever experienced discrimination, abuse, bullying, berating, or even death solely because of who they are. Lastly, I cried for the comradery and for my people banning together to fight for our freedom. I wanted to leave my car and march with them, instead I just cried and sat with a mountain of love, respect and gratitude.

I reflected on the injustices and pain felt by marginalized communities, and my mind drifted back to another dark chapter in history—the Rodney King riots. A series of widespread civil disturbances erupted throughout Los Angeles, in the aftermath of the acquittal of four LAPD officers involved in the beating of Rodney King. The riots lasted for six days, from April 29 to May 4,

1992. The events caused considerable damage to the city, loss of lives, injuries, and huge social and economic impacts.

The acquittal of the officers incensed many members of society. This deep frustration and anger served as the catalyst for the riots. The exonerations illustrated the systemic racism and injustices that plagued our criminal system, especially in Los Angeles.

Rioting erupted after the verdict was announced, with the epicenter in South Central Los Angeles, a predominantly low-income neighborhood. Frustration and rage spilled over into the streets, which led to acts of violence, looting, arson and vandalism. The unrest spread throughout the city and resulted in chaos and destruction.

I was in a unique position during the riots. The Advocate provided a front-row seat to the city that transformed into a frenzied battleground. Swarms of protesters flooded Hollywood Boulevard and more people gathered by the minute. Sirens, helicopters and the distant sound of crowds filled the air which created a tense and urgent atmosphere.

A decision had to be made whether we would close and send all employees home due to the danger. The city was in a state of emergency. Staying put or leaving were both dangerous. Ultimately, the company let us decide if we wanted to risk driving amongst the insanity.

I watched from my office window as people looted stores and fires spread across the horizon. The conditions were more frightening by the minute. Witnessing the riots from this vantage point offered a distinct perspective, where the chaos felt both immediate and removed. The panic in me grew. I experienced a combination of empathy, worry for my friends, public safety and apprehension for my personal welfare.

I observed the riots from above when a sense of exigence arose. I stepped away from the chaos momentarily, paced the floor and attempted to process the tornado of emotions that churned within. Once more, I gazed down upon the city streets and watched the billowing smoke rising from burning buildings. This cast an eerie glow against the dusky sky. The distant sounds of sirens, shouting, and shattering glass were getting closer.

I made the decision to brave it and get out of Dodge. Where I lived at the time was far enough from the riots to experience safety, provided there were no demonstrations happening in the Valley.

Groups of protesters and cops blocked the streets. A dense grey hue tinted the sky with a deep orange undertone. The smoke was so thick, it was necessary to cover your nose and mouth, while the acrid smell of burning buildings permeated the air.

The journey was both nerve-wracking and intense. My drive home took me on Hollywood Boulevard where people were looting and smashing store windows.

Throughout the drive, I experienced a mixture of concerns for my safety and the safety of my friends, whom I couldn't reach. The phone lines were down, and any form of communication was lost. I struggled with the deep empathy for the communities affected by the riots. I saw the devastation firsthand, and my resolve to continue standing on the side of justice with the voices of those impacted grew stronger.

Upon returning home, relief and gratitude enveloped me. The contrast between the chaos of the drive and the relative calm of the neighborhood was palpable. It was a clear reminder of the disparities and challenges encountered by different communities.

Rioters targeted and set ablaze a range of businesses, including grocery stores, gas stations, retail shops and liquor stores. The iconic images of burning buildings in flames, plumes of smoke rising into the air, and people fleeing through the streets became emblematic. The city's infrastructure suffered severe damage, with more than a thousand buildings destroyed.

Law enforcement struggled to contain the situation, and the National Guard was called in to assist. Authorities enacted curfews and declared a state of emergency. The violence and unrest subsided as community leaders, activists and residents worked to restore calm and began rebuilding.

In the days following the riots, life resumed as normal. Except it was anything but normal. While driving through the aftermath, my heart shattered. Burned-out buildings lined the streets; broken glass and graffiti was everywhere. Gas stations were burned to a crisp. The drive was unsettling, to say the least.

Los Angeles and the wider United States were both greatly impacted by the riots. The uprising highlighted social divisions and racial tensions, which sparked national conversations and calls for reform.

In the aftermath, there were efforts to improve police relations, invest in underserved neighborhoods, and to promote dialogue and understanding among different racial and ethnic groups. The events of the Rodney King riots continue to serve as another reminder of the need for ongoing efforts toward social justice. I was just starting to grasp these issues more deeply, and advocate for freedom. Not only for myself but for others as well.

Upon discovering the grievous injustices that exist in our world, I became resolute in my commitment to championing LGBTQ+ rights. This unwavering dedication has shaped my life in transformative and empowering ways. It began with the realization of my identity and a deep acceptance of myself as a gay individual from the early age of twelve. I came out in a very non-liberal high school and area at large, Newbury Park. As a young adult, coming to terms with my sexuality allowed me to embrace my true self and recognize the importance of fighting for equality and acceptance.

Being able to find a supportive community has been essential in my fight for gay rights. Attending Pride events and being involved in rallies and demonstrations has both connected and supported me. Belonging to these communities has given me the ability to enhance my voice and challenge discrimination.

Advocacy and activism are integral parts of my life, simply because I identify as LGBTQ+. Whether I'm participating in protests or marches, writing, or sharing my individual experiences, I have made a conscious effort to speak out against injustices and challenge harmful stereotypes. I believe each act, no matter how small, contributes to a collective movement toward equality.

Engaging in dialogue with people of varied opinions has been both challenging and rewarding. By connecting with those who have different opinions, I've been able to humanize the LGBTQ+ experience and foster understanding. By sharing my journey, dispelling misconceptions, and encouraging empathy, I have witnessed hearts and minds change, one conversation at a time.

I'm grateful for the allies who have stood by me in this fight. The support I've received from friends, family and organizations who champion LGBTQ+ rights has been priceless. Collaborating with these allies has allowed us to amplify our message and create a stronger, more united front.

The fight for our rights and the progress we have made, prove the incredible strength of the LGBTQ+ community. This fills me with pride. I celebrate every step forward, no matter how small, and remain committed to pushing for a world where every individual is treated with dignity, respect and equality.

MY ADVENTURES IN EUROPE

By 1992, I'd settled in Hollywood, once again. and was still working for The Advocate. My home was a tiny studio apartment tucked away behind the front main house. I had a ritual of parking my amazing little roadster, a Mazda RX-7, on the street outside.

One morning, I discovered my car was gone and anxiety took hold. *Was it towed?* Desperately, I checked the street signs for parking regulations and dialed the number listed.

"Hello, I'm calling about my car. It's an RX-7, and I parked it on Las Palmas and Melrose last night and it's not here."

"Do you have the license plate, ma'am?"

"No, I don't. Everything was in the glove box."

"What's the exact address it would have been towed from?"

"Around 714 North Las Palmas Drive."

"No, ma'am, I don't show any vehicles being towed from Las Palmas in the last forty-eight hours."

A sinking feeling swept over me and settled like a leaden lump in the pit of my stomach. I knew someone had stolen my car. The theft of my property left me stunned. It required me to navigate emotions I'd never faced before.

The feeling of being violated cut deep. It wasn't just the loss of my amazing little sports car; it was a reminder of the internal emptiness and loneliness that followed me. The despair I felt was hauntingly familiar. I froze, just as I did when I was molested at seven. A surge of panic and anger shortly followed. The financial and logistical worries deepened my sense of loss.

Then, I recalled the unfinished lesbian porno I'd been writing. Embarrassment enveloped me when I realized it was tucked inside the glove box. What terrified me was someone having stumbled upon it, which allowed them a glimpse into my clandestine realm. A realm that symbolized the elusive autonomy and liberation I had been deprived of since childhood. Writing was an escape, a refuge where I expressed myself without the fear of being threatened or muted. During those stolen moments, I uncovered a place where my voice felt heard, rather than stifled by my past.

As a child, I was silenced—rendered voiceless by those who held power over me. This made it difficult for me to assert myself or express my opinions. Everywhere I turned, the specter of my past abuse lurked, haunting even the most mundane interactions.

In this private realm of storytelling, I held the pen of authority, crafting narratives that celebrated passion, love and the unapologetic expression of desire. It was a complete contrast to the realities I'd faced outside of my writing sanctuary. In the world beyond my words, vulnerability seemed like a weakness, a dangerous invitation for exploitation and pain. But within the realms of my stories, it became a wellspring of empowerment, where I could surpass boundaries.

This shattered the illusion of invincibility that writing fabricated. Regardless, the flush of embarrassment faded, and I resolved to protect and nurture my voice.

After I received the insurance-claim money, I purchased a used Mazda B2000 truck. To protect my newfound possession, I invested in "The Club," a device touted to deter would-be thieves. Each night, I diligently secured it to my steering wheel.

About a month later, I stepped outside, and saw the empty space where my truck was parked. Panic set in. Tears streamed down my face. I checked the street signs, once again, searching for any wrongdoing on my part. Déjà vu enveloped me and I retreated to my humble abode to make the distressing call.

"What's the license plate, ma'am?" the man inquired.

I rattled off the number.

"No, ma'am. There's no record of that vehicle being towed," he responded.

Devastated, I sank onto my bed, surrounded by the disbelief that fate would be so unkind. *How was it possible that two cars could be stolen from the same person within such a short span of time?*

Naturally, my mother was always the first person I turned to in moments like these, and without thinking twice, I called her.

"Hi, Mama," I began, my voice weary.

"What's wrong, my baby?" she sensed the sorrow in my tone.

"I'm not sure how to tell you this, Mom…"

"What? What happened?" Her curiosity merged with concern.

"Well, someone stole my truck."

"What?" my mother shrieked. "How could this happen? Didn't your car just get stolen?"

"Yes, Mom. I need to move out of this neighborhood. This can't keep happening."

My friends' wealthy parents often sent them on luxurious trips to Europe. I would await their return so that I could live vicariously through their stories. I worked to support myself and finance my education, which left little room for travel.

My mom was aware of this and frequently expressed her desire to save money and send me on a trip to Europe. Despite my resistance, and regardless of her limited income, she was determined.

"You know what, Delicia? Enough of this. I'm tired of watching you work so hard only to have these things happen to you. I don't care if you like it or not; I'm going to save money for you."

"For what, Mom?"

"You've told me not to do this over and over again, but it's going to happen. I'm saving money so that you can go to Europe. End of discussion. You are my baby, and I've watched you go through so much in life, fighting hard for everything. Please let me do this for you, it's something I want and need to do."

"Really, Mom? I know you don't earn much…"

"Don't you worry about that. Stay where you are for now, take the bus to work, and when you come back, you'll have enough to rent a new place."

Silence settled between us, and I pondered her words.

"Mom, thank you so much. I really appreciate it. I'll take you up on that."

"You will?" Her excitement gushed forth like a bubbling fountain.

"Yes, Mama, I will. Thank you."

Over the next six months, my mom saved enough money for me to plan my European adventure. One night, she called me with an infectious enthusiasm in her voice.

"Guess what? I have money for you to go to Europe! With my tax return and some other funds, I have five thousand dollars for your trip, so start planning!"

In February 1993, I began the exciting task of organizing my trip. While I searched for plane tickets, I stumbled upon a fantastic deal: an open-ended round-trip ticket to London for just three hundred and fifty dollars. Without hesitation, I made the purchase and turned my attention to securing a rail pass and exploring hostel options.

I drew upon the wisdom and experiences shared by my well-traveled friends. After I read Rick Steve's *Europe Through the Back Door*, I crafted my itinerary. A long-awaited dream became a reality!

London would be the start to my grand adventures. This was followed by Amsterdam's coffee shops, Volendam's tulips, and then it was off to Paris. Bordeaux, Biarritz, Barcelona, Salamanca, and Switzerland's picturesque landscapes in Geneva and Zürich would follow. My interest in Austria beckoned me to Salzburg and Vienna. Finally, Greece called out as a main bucket list item, including Athens and the islands of Lesvos, Paros, Antiparos and Santorini.

With each passing day, the excitement within me surged as the trip inched closer by the minute.

When the time came, I handed over the care of my beloved cat, Cow, to Gertrude. Then I journeyed to LAX, my gateway to Europe.

The moment I boarded the plane, a whirlwind of emotions engulfed me - excitement, trepidation, wonder, and uncertainty.

Heathrow Airport reminded me of a lot of LAX. Maneuvering the airport was familiar and upon arrival in London, I peeked at my checklist of must-do experiences. I planned to spend three short days there:

1- Ride on a classic double-decker bus.
2- Savor the iconic dish of fish and chips.
3- Explore the West End theater district.

Each city I planned to visit had its own special set of must-see places.

Finding a double-decker bus was a breeze, but authentic fish and chips posed a challenge. Surprisingly, the scent of Indian street food filled the air, which overshadowed my expectation of traditional British cuisine. Undeterred, I persisted until I stumbled upon a hidden gem that satisfied my craving.

London spun me like a whirlwind, its energy animated in every bustling street and hurried passerby. It was as if the city itself never slept.

As a cannabis enthusiast, adjusting to the fast-paced atmosphere in London without access to marijuana was a challenge. The prospect of my drug of choice being decriminalized in my next destination, Amsterdam, filled me with excitement.

Once I arrived in Amsterdam, I found my way to the cozy pension, akin to a small family-run guesthouse or inn, where I would stay during my time here. The caring woman who ran the place welcomed me with open arms.

Eager to immerse myself in the atmosphere, I wasted no time and embarked on a stroll through the enchanting streets. Along the way, the cobblestone, coffee shops and charming stores called out to me. Cleanliness was not their strong suit. Heaps of trash floated lazily down the canal. Despite the lack of tidiness, Amsterdam exuded a unique and captivating vibe that entranced me.

I'd passed by several coffee shops until I found the one that looked the least intimidating. I took a seat at a booth and a server handed me a menu. It looked like an old-school photo album. Inside the small plastic sleeves, where a picture would normally go, little nuggets and small squares of hashish awaited my perusal. I'd never encountered names for pot before this; back home, it was either dirt weed or the good shit.

I inspected the menu, and was captivated. The buds, hashish, and enticing aromas they exuded brought a smile to my face. There were pages upon pages of different varieties, all at my fingertips.

The server approached and in perfect English with a heavy Dutch accent asked, "do you see something you like?"

"Do I see something I like?" I replied with delight. "I can't believe how many options you have! Do you have any idea how stoked I am? I'm sorry, this is just the coolest thing I've ever seen. Is there one you would recommend? I smoke regularly at home and I am over the moon about this. It's so awesome!"

"Wow," he responded. "I haven't had a customer this uber-excited in a while. It's refreshing."

"What do you recommend?" I asked again with a giant grin.

He flipped the page to the preferred bud of choice. "I'd try some of this kind."

"I'd like to try hash since I can buy weed at home."

"Yes, you can have both if you like," he responded politely. "In Europe, we mix the hashish with tobacco and smoke it this way."

"Can I mix it with weed? I don't like cigarettes."

"Sure, for you it might be very strong. But if you like it like this, of course."

"Awesome, thank you, that's what I'd like, please."

A few minutes passed and he brought both the weed and the hashish to my table, along with papers and a lighter.

"We have a pipe if you prefer or a water bong?"

"A bong would be amazing. I can roll a joint for later."

With anticipation and excitement, I mixed the hashish and weed together, and rolled the joint with care. The leftover mix was scooped into the bong. I ignited and inhaled the aromatic smoke, and reveled in the effects. It was a milestone I'd dreamt of for years, and now, I could check it off my bucket list.

That night, as if drawn by an invisible force, I navigated the intricate streets of the Red Light District. In that place, forbidden desires and hidden secrets merged, evoking an undeniable discomfort within me. The weight of my troubled childhood and the traumas I experienced shrouded my sense of self, particularly when it came to matters of intimacy.

It took a lot of courage to continue on this escapade. I walked through the dimly lit streets, and my past wounds resurfaced. This threatened to unravel the facade I'd built around my sexuality. The memories of molestations and the scars they'd left behind affected my ability to embrace my desires and experience comfort within my own skin.

The sight of women draped in seductive lingerie, sensually posed behind windows, only magnified my unease. Their enticing gazes and suggestive gestures triggered a whirlwind of conflicting emotions within me. On one hand, I found myself intrigued by the world of passion and desire they represented. On the other, the wounds of my past acted as a barrier, that prevented me from embracing and exploring my own sexual prowess.

While the women behind the glass pursued me with an intensity that made me feel desired, the dissonance within my soul intensified.

There was a part of me that relished the attention, no matter the source. In a passing instant, I perceived myself as attractive, noticed, and desired—a stark juxtaposition to the lack of confidence that plagued me regularly.

The Red Light District became a battleground for my inner conflicts. I wrestled with the desperation to be desired and the apprehension that lingered from my past abuse. It was as if the district's vivid colors and seductive ambiance mirrored the colorful yet tumultuous hues hidden within me.

I swiftly retreated, seeking safety in the sanctuary of my pension. Here, I allowed myself to navigate the intricate labyrinth of my own emotions, confronting the impact of my past on my sexual identity and liberation, or lack thereof. Healing would be a gradual process, one that required self-compassion and patience. I would need to unravel the complex layers that shaped my perceptions. I held on to the hope that one day I could embrace my sexuality without the burdens of my past.

The following day, I strolled along the picturesque canal, my mind fixated on finding a secluded spot where I could partake in the pleasure of smoking a joint. Anxiety gnawed at me. Fear of potential legal consequences loomed large in my thoughts. I couldn't afford to end up in jail, not when I'd just begun to see the world.

I spotted a quiet bench nestled in the corner and extracted the joint from its hiding place. I struck the match and ignited the tip. My anticipation intensified as the pungent aroma wafted through the air.

I took the first hit, and a police officer abruptly appeared on his bike. Terror overcame me, and I instinctively tucked the joint out of sight. At that moment, I braced myself for the inevitable confrontation.

To my astonishment, the officer rode past. My mind struggled to process this. It was in stark contrast to the reality I was accustomed to in the United States. An act like that would have, at a minimum, led to a citation or reprimand by law enforcement.

The contrasting attitudes toward weed left me bewildered. I found myself caught between the realms of what was permissible in this foreign land and the strict societal norms that were ingrained in me. The experience was strange and eye-opening, it offered a glimpse into a world where my chosen indulgence was accepted rather than condemned.

I exhaled, a billow of smoke poured above my head. Immediately, this released the tension that gripped my every muscle.

The following day, I was off to Volendam, a place that embodied the essence of the idyllic Holland I envisioned. The landscape of my mind was painted with a vivid scene of windmills that gracefully rotated amidst a backdrop of vibrant tulips.

The train rolled into the quaint town that unfolded before my eyes, as if plucked from the pages of a storybook. I discovered a workshop where skilled artisans crafted wooden shoes, a timeless tradition passed down through generations. I watched in awe as the cobblers masterfully molded antiquated footwear. Their hands danced across the material with precision and grace.

Volendam became a bridge between the past and the present, which allowed me to travel through the limitations of time. This realization ignited a hunger within me—a yearning to explore, to touch, to connect with the world around me.

With this newfound appreciation for the power of tactile encounters, I embarked on the rest of my journey, actively seeking opportunities to engage with history in a more intimate way.

I left behind the breathtaking landscapes of Holland and a stunning train journey to Paris greeted me. Rolling hills led the route adorned with an exquisite array of flowers.

My friend Marc, in his thoughtful generosity, had arranged for me to stay with his friends Aude and Laure.

Upon arrival, Aude and Laure greeted me with warm smiles and a comforting embrace, followed by the French customary kiss on each cheek. We embarked on the metro, while we navigated the intricate web of underground passages.

Aude spoke over the bustle of the crowd.

"It's unfortunate, but I have to attend school this week, so I won't be able to spend much time with you," she explained. "Laure will be here, and she's happy to show you around. She has a lot planned for you."

"Oh, that's amazing. Thank you, Laure. I'm looking forward to spending time with you and seeing Paris."

Laure just smiled and nodded.

"She doesn't speak much English, so I am sorry about that, but I am sure it will be fine," Aude proclaimed.

"I'm sure she speaks more English than I do French, but this should be fun," I said with a playful grin.

The prospect of having a local guide and a place to stay thrilled me. Despite the language barrier, Laure and I connected effortlessly, an unexpected bond formed between us. Such moments of instant connection were rare in my life, and I treasured them immensely.

Language became secondary to our shared experiences. Laure's infectious enthusiasm and genuine kindness bridged any communication gaps that arose.

With each passing day, our connection grew stronger, and Laure's presence enriched my travels. Her guidance added authenticity and local insight, which heightened my experiences of Paris.

Throughout the week, Laure took me to various hidden gems and off-the-beaten-path places that only locals knew about. In between our escapades, we drank the finest wines, smoked joints, savored delectable cuisine, and embraced the joie de vivre that Paris offered. The city became a backdrop for our cherished time together.

I approached the end of my time in Paris, and realized that the memories we'd made would last a lifetime. Parting ways with Laure was like leaving behind a kindred spirit, someone with whom I'd shared an extraordinary bond.

It is on rare occasions that I remember my dreams. During my time here, I had a dream that lingered. In it, I met a soulmate who was unlike any other person I'd encountered. She exuded a surfer girl's vibe; with short blonde hair, piercing blue eyes, and a tiny nose. In my dream, we'd experienced an intense connection and a depth of love that was surreal. I couldn't place this mystery woman—someone unfamiliar yet oddly familiar. Her enigmatic presence remained in my thoughts for weeks.

While in Paris, Laure introduced me to her boyfriend, Philippe. I informed Laure and Philippe about my trip to the South of France, and he proposed a thrilling ride on his Ducati. Despite the fact that my mother would be horrified, the idea enthralled me.

I slung my backpack over my shoulders, secured the helmet on my head, and hopped onto the back of Philippe's motorcycle. I clung tight to his waist the entire three-and-a-half-hour journey to Biarritz.

Despite Philippe's limited knowledge of English, he was familiar with the word sex. This was his one-word question upon arrival: "Sex?"

"No, thank you, Philippe, but I appreciate the ride."

With his head tilted to the side, he didn't appear to understand my response.

"No, Phillipe, I like women."

Again, he gave me a questioning look.

I fumbled through my French-English dictionary, and said, "J'aime les femmes" with a deplorable French accent, but he understood.

"Okay, see you," he said, kissing me on both of my cheeks before speeding off.

I found myself intrigued by the South of France. Lively cafés and boutiques lined the streets, which exuded a relaxed and laid back atmosphere that put me at ease. In the few days I'd spent here, I wandered along the golden sandy beaches, basking in the warm sun, and I immersed myself in the local culture.

Although I loved this destination, I remained steadfast in my commitment to my itinerary. The temptation to stay longer in one place was strong, but that meant I'd risk missing out on other wonders that potentially awaited me.

I left Biarritz behind and embarked on the next leg of my journey, Bordeaux. Here I indulged in two of life's greatest pleasures: wine and a bit of gambling.

I departed my final destination in France and reflected on the moments I'd spent in this incredible country. The bonds I'd made reminded me that life was meant to be savored.

The train ride to Spain was, once again, breathtaking. My first stop was Salamanca, one of *Europe Through the Back Door*'s must-see locations.

Known for its rich history and architectural wonders, Salamanca offered a unique blend of cultural heritage and magnificent landmarks.

After a few days in Salamanca, I was ready to hit the big city of Barcelona. Upon arrival, I immediately perceived an unwelcoming atmosphere. Perhaps it was my American background, but the people I'd met were unhelpful and, frankly, mean. They gave the impression that they weren't fond of me, and my high school Spanish didn't seem to be sufficient, despite my best efforts.

To prepare for my trip, I had read several books. Many discussed the necessity of being cautious in big cities, Barcelona was specifically mentioned. I remained vigilant, always on the lookout for potential thieves and their cunning tactics. Various guide books talked about the infamous "gypsies" who employed different methods to distract and rob unsuspecting tourists. I certainly didn't want to be part of that statistic.

One common technique involved squirting water into the air from a distance. When it landed on the target's head and the person looked up, accomplices would seize the opportunity to steal their belongings. Passports, money belts, fanny packs and cameras were all high on the list of desired items. Fortunately, due to my awareness, I avoided falling victim to such schemes.

As a solo traveler, I engaged in conversations with strangers more often than my otherwise-introverted self would have. In the hostel, I met Lupe, a friendly woman from Mexico City who spoke fluent Spanish and English. She seemed nice and I thought her language skills would be advantageous, so I asked if she'd show me around Barcelona. She agreed.

Together, we explored the city, visiting museums, landmarks and other tourist traps. During a relaxing break in the park, two strangers approached and sat next to us on the bench. It seemed awkward, but Lupe's friendly demeanor helped put me at ease.

In Spanish, the men began the conversation.

"Hola, ¿cómo estamos?" one of them asked with a smile.

"Estamos bien, gracias," Lupe answered. "¿Por qué estás tan cerca de nosotros?"

"Lo siento, pero ambas son muy hermosas y no podíamos pasar sin decir hola."

"What are they saying?" I asked Lupe, a bit annoyed by their proximity to us.

"He said he thought we were both so beautiful they couldn't walk past without saying hello."

"Wow, that was nice."

"Que muy linda," she said.

Lupe translated as Manuel and Frederico introduced themselves and invited us on an adventure.

"They want us to go somewhere with them," Lupe stated.

"Umm, where?" I asked with grand hesitation.

"¿A dónde vamos?" Lupe asked.

"A un restaurante, ¿tenemos hambre?" Federico responded.

"Sí, ¿pero a dónde?" Lupe insisted.

"Está un poco lejos de la ciudad, pero es muy lindo. Confía en nosotros, todo estará bien. Te prometo un gran día, ambos nunca lo olvidarán," Manuel said.

"He said it's far from the city but to trust them; it will be an experience we will never forget," Lupe translated.

"Well, that sounds straight out of a horror movie," I said with angst.

"I think these guys are trustworthy; it will be fine," she pleaded with her eyes for me to believe them.

"I'm very hesitant, but if you say so, I guess if we die, we die together."

Lupe turned to Manuel and said, "Valle, vamanos." And off we went.

A surge of terror coursed through my veins. Doubts gnawed at the edges of my mind. Despite my attempts to quell the rising tide of worry, unease settled deep within me.

With cautious steps, we followed the park path, my senses on high alert. Amidst the tranquil surroundings, my gaze fell upon a battered old Volkswagen Beetle. Manuel swung the door open, and revealed the torn seats in the back. I climbed in and my unease intensified with each passing moment. The engine roared to life, and the tiny car took off.

We ventured farther away from the city, and my anxiety tightened its grip. The thumping of my heart amplified with every kilometer we drove, urging me to listen to my internal voice of caution. Lupe clutched my hand in a silent display of solidarity.

"Don't worry. It will all be fine," she said in a calming voice.

"Okay, if you say so." My hands sweated, and I think she could tell I was putting all my faith in her.

We began driving up a windy two-lane mountain road, nothing but ocean on one side and mountain on the other. I imagine a look of panic crossed my face because Lupe squeezed my hand tighter.

"¿A dónde vamos?" Lupe asked.

"No te preocupes, ya casi llegamos," Manuel answered.

"He said we are almost there."

At the mountain's summit, one lonely building stood like a forgotten sentinel. We pulled into the parking lot and the air hung heavy with uncertainty. My hesitation grew as we came closer. The doors were closed and empty windows offered no clues as to what lay inside. It looked like an old, run-down abandoned building.

Upon closer examination, it became clear this was a restaurant that was closed.

"This place isn't open," I proclaimed as I gave Lupe a wry look.

"¿Este lugar está cerrado?" she asked the guys.

"No te preocupes," Manuel stated as he pulled out a set of keys from his pocket. "Este lugar está cerrado hoy, sí. Pero yo soy el dueño y hoy, aunque estamos cerrados, estamos abiertos solo para ustedes," he remarked with a smile.

"What did he say?" I asked with a bit of trepidation.

"He said he owns the place, and they are closed today. Except for us, they are open."

"What?" I inquired with a perplexed look.

"Pásale." With a slight nod, Manuel motioned for us to follow him and he swung open the door. The restaurant, devoid of any other patrons, echoed with silence as our footsteps reverberated against the polished floors.

"Porfa, ¿puedes ir a buscar la comida para que pueda cocinar?" Manuel asked Frederico as he ventured off to grab ingredients for our meal.

Manuel led us through the vacant dining area and the clattering sound of pots and pans being liberated from their hooks filled the air. He brought us to a table in the dining room near a bay window overlooking the sea cliffs of Barcelona.

"Siéntete como en casa. Siéntete libre de explorar. Deberías ir a ver la vista, es increíble." Manuel told Lupe.

"Come on, let's go explore. He said the view is amazing. They are going to cook for us."

"What? Wow, this is so cool. I'm glad we came," I said hesitantly as we ventured further into the empty restaurant.

"What an incredible view! Look, you can see all of Barcelona from up here." I continued.

There was a giant dance floor in the center of the dining area, and we took advantage of every square inch as mouthwatering smells wafted from the kitchen. Music filled the room, and Lupe danced with abandon, while I found myself unable to move with the same freedom.

"Casi listo, chicas." Manuel said as he popped his head out from the kitchen. "Por favor, tomen asiento."

The table was arranged by Frederico for our exclusive dining experience. The aroma of Spanish cuisine filled the air, tantalizing our taste buds and heightening our anticipation.

Course after course emerged from the kitchen. Gazpacho, a chilled tomato soup, refreshed our palates with its incredible flavors. The heavenly scent of Gambas al ajillo wafted through the air, while steak was seared before our eyes. Homemade tortillas completed the ensemble of gastronomic perfection.

We savored each bite, and the flavors harmonized with the breathtaking views of Barcelona. Laughter, bilingual conversation, and the clinking of glasses filled the air, creating an ambiance of pure joy and contentment. My fears seemed far behind me at this point.

The evening sun dipped below the horizon, casting a golden glow over the distant city below. Unease slowly crept back into my thoughts. Despite the incredible views from the deserted restaurant atop the mountain, it didn't quell the nagging doubts that plagued me. It appeared too good to be true, too perfect of an experience. I couldn't shake the doubt; I was certain there had to be a price to pay.

Questions swirled in my mind like a turbulent sea, each one more disconcerting than the last. *What did Manuel and Frederico expect for this extravagant gesture of hospitality? Would they suddenly reveal their true intentions, turning this idyllic evening into a nightmare?* The past taught me to be wary, to always expect the unexpected. It was difficult to savor the moment when the specter of uncertainty loomed over me. I was always on guard.

Despite my fears, the evening unfolded with no signs of hidden motives or ulterior expectations. Manuel and Frederico were impeccable hosts. Their genuine smiles and warm gestures contradicted the narrative of mistrust that was ingrained in me.

The night drew to a close. Manuel and Frederico drove us back to the hostel, then bid us farewell with a gentle kiss on each cheek, the traditional Spanish adieu. They expressed no desires beyond maintaining the connection we'd forged during those memorable hours. This evoked conflicting emotions in me of both relief and astonishment. They showed me a side of humanity I often doubted existed—a generosity untainted by hidden agendas.

We returned to our hostel and my thoughts swelled with conflicting emotions. I questioned my apprehensions and the walls I'd built to protect myself. *In my constant state of vigilance, had I unintentionally closed myself off from genuine experiences and authentic connections?* It was a subject that resonated deeply within me.

This served as a reminder, once more, for me to embrace the present and let go of the fear that constantly threatened to overshadow life's most incredible moments. I was already familiar with this concept, but it hadn't registered yet. I resolved to make a conscious effort to overcome this dread, and I had hoped this trip could serve as a catalyst.

This was a clear testament to the power of trust and the capacity for human kindness. It taught me that sometimes, just sometimes, it's okay to let go of my fears and allow myself to be embraced by the unexpected splendor life has to offer.

After I left Barcelona, my next scheduled destination was Geneva, Switzerland. I'd experienced hostility from nearly everyone in Barcelona, except for Manuel, Lupe and Frederico. My pension in Geneva provided a much needed relief. There, I was greeted by a warm and gracious Swiss lady.

"Welcome to Geneva; let me help you with your bag," she walked up the stairs to show me my room.

"Wow, you are so nice here," I replied.

"What do you mean?" she inquired.

"I just came from Barcelona and everyone was so mean to me there."

"Oh, honey, how terrible. I'm sorry that happened to you. We are mostly all nice in Switzerland," she said cheerily.

"What a relief! I'm happy to be here."

Geneva left me impressed by its immaculate cleanliness. The next locale on my itinerary was the tiny mountain town of Gimmelwald. I'd discovered the hidden treasure of Gimmelwald through my trusty guidebook, *Europe Through the Back Door*.

Even the locals were oblivious to its existence, emphasizing its insignificance. Whenever I mentioned Gimmelwald to a Swiss person, the conversation repeated itself.

"You mean Grindelwald."

"Nope, I mean Gimmelwald."

"There is no Gimmelwald in Switzerland."

At which point, I'd reach into my bag and retrieve my AAA map, eager to share the enchanting village of Gimmelwald with the locals. I'd unfold the map and present it to them. Their reactions were always similar.

"Huh, Gimmelwald?" they'd say with a confused look. "I didn't know it existed."

Nestled in a remote and untouched mountainside, Gimmelwald consisted of a few scattered houses and a youth hostel, which charged a nominal fee of five Swiss francs per night. Payment operated on an honor system. Upon checking out, guests would leave their dues in a cast-iron pot adorned with the word "Geld".

Just beyond the doorstep of my cozy log-cabin hostel, incredible hikes, and genuine Swiss experiences awaited. I'd planned to spend five days in Gimmelwald and indulge in nothing but hiking and relaxation. There were no stores anywhere nearby, so I brought all my food with me and anything else I needed during my stay. It was an opportunity to disconnect from the world and tap into the serenity of the mountains.

The sun rose on my first morning here, and I began my hike. The sheer magnificence of this country left me in awe. While living in Hawaii as a teenager, I'd encountered some remarkable places, but this was unlike anything I'd ever seen before.

I walked a few miles and was surrounded by the magnificence of the landscape. During my hike, I stumbled upon a colossal waterfall. Its sheer size and grandeur mesmerized me. A mystical ledge sculpted by nature offered a thrilling vantage point to sit and observe. For safety reasons, a sturdy railing sat alongside the cliff edge. This enabled visitors to experience the refreshing mist on their faces.

The spectacle was so extraordinary it left me utterly amazed. Despite not having hiked as far as I would have liked and it not being lunchtime yet, I savored my meal right there on the rock. That moment would forever be etched in my memory—a mind-blowing beginning to a journey whose full magnitude remained unknown.

The hostel was bustling with fellow travelers, many hailing from the United States and Canada. Evenings brought us together, sharing dinners and swapping stories of our discoveries.

As my departure date approached, conversations buzzed with excitement about our next adventures. Listening to the diverse plans and destinations was captivating.

"So, where are you headed next, Delicia?" Ryan, a guy from Canada, asked.

"I have Zurich next on my itinerary."

"Oh, wow, that is a huge change coming from here. Such a big city. Have you heard of Bern?"

"It's the capital of Switzerland, right?"

"Yeah, but it is a cool town. Some amazing people, too. You'd love it; you should check it out, eh."

"I'm not sure. I have a pretty tight schedule to stick to, but I can try. Instead of going to Zurich, maybe I could visit Bern for a few days."

"You totally should; it's so worth it," he replied.

"Okay, cool, I'll do it." Just like that, my itinerary changed.

My delightful stay in Gimmelwald came to a close, and the train meandered through Switzerland's incredible countryside. I marveled at the pristine scenery that unfolded before my eyes, curious about the adventures that lay ahead.

Once again, I was reminded that life's most miraculous moments often occur beyond the limitations of our deliberately constructed itineraries. Similar to my time in Barcelona, it was these unplanned encounters, spontaneous conversations with locals, and unforeseen detours that revealed the true essence of travel.

Upon arrival in Bern, I found my way to the youth hostel nestled along the tranquil banks of the Aare River. I was exhausted and I longed for a restful sleep. Tomorrow, the plan was to replenish my depleted food supply.

The hostel offered a welcoming atmosphere. I stepped through its doors and was greeted by fellow travelers from various corners of the globe. Their laughter and conversations filled the communal area.

After a smooth check-in process, I headed to my bunk bed in the dormitory. Nestled under a warm blanket, I found calm in the gentle lullaby of the flowing river. The sounds of the night comforted me into a restful slumber.

Morning light seeped through the curtains and roused me from my peaceful sleep. The prospect of Bern, a city that supposedly brimmed with culture and culinary delights, invigorated me. I donned my daypack, eager to embark on a new urban quest.

I trudged up the incline and noticed someone coming down the hill in the distance. When our paths intersected, I greeted her with a warm smile, hoping to strike up a conversation. She returned the gesture, her eyes twinkled with a spark of curiosity.

"Excuse me, do you speak English?" I hesitantly inquired.

"A little bit, yes," she answered.

"If I walk up this hill, can I find food?"

"Food?" she asked, bewildered. "Honey, it's Sunday."

"Yes, but I was hoping someplace was open and I might be able to find some food?"

"No, honey, it's Sunday. In Switzerland nothing is open on Sunday. It is a day of rest. Are you hungry?"

"Yes, very. I ate the last of my food while I was in Gimmelwald."

"You mean Grindelwald."

"No, it's this little mountain town, even the Swiss people don't seem to know of it."

She laughed. "I'll have to find it on a map. If you are hungry, you can come with me."

"Where are we going?" I asked.

"Follow me," she said, and continued down the hill.

We arrived at a modest house a few blocks away.

"Come on," she stated as she walked in the hallway. "Shoes off, please."

As a native of Los Angeles, I hesitated to enter strangers' homes after just meeting them on the street. However, considering my previous experience in Barcelona and the fact that she appeared to be in her eighties, I pushed past my comfort zone and embraced the unexpected.

"What would you like to eat?" she asked with a smile.

"Really, you're going to feed me? How kind of you," I replied with gratitude.

"Of course. You are hungry, there is no food, and I will feed you; it's the Swiss way."

"Wow, that's very different coming from LA. Thank you."

I enjoyed the many varieties of jams and breads she brought to the table along with other leftovers.

"How do you like Switzerland?" she asked.

"So far, I love it. The people have been so nice and welcoming, and it's one of the most spectacular countries I've ever seen."

"Oh good, so glad you are finding you like it here."

"I'm staying at youth hostels because of my budget while traveling. The people I am meeting are mainly Americans, Australians, Canadians and travelers from other European countries. I'm excited to immerse myself in the culture of where I am visiting, you know? My goal is to meet Swiss people while I'm here, not other Americans or Canadians."

"I will be right back!" she exclaimed, as she skipped to the kitchen.

Excitedly, she came back to the table and proclaimed, "My granddaughter is going to come get you, and you get to have dinner with a real Swiss family! Her husband is American; you will love them. Oh, but you just ate. It's okay; you can eat again."

I was flabbergasted. We'd only crossed paths minutes before on the street. Now, this kindhearted woman was not only providing me with a meal but also arranging for her granddaughter to do the same. I'd stepped into a different world—one where strangers were not to be feared but embraced.

To my surprise, the elderly woman's grasp of English was far more than just a "little bit." While we waited, we engaged in meaningful conversations on diverse topics. The connection we forged in such a brief time was remarkable.

When her granddaughter arrived, I bid farewell to my newfound heroine, grateful for the chance encounter. I embarked on yet another venture, delving deeper into the generosity and warmth of the Swiss people. Her granddaughter introduced me to the rest of their family, and we all shared a delicious meal together.

"What have you seen since you have been in Bern?" her husband asked.

"Not much, really. I came from Gimmewald and spent the night in the hostel, and then I met your grandma."

"Do you mean Grindelwald?"

"No, Gimmewald. It's a tiny mountain town."

"Oh, well you should definitely check out the Grosse Schanze while you're here. It is a huge lawn area in front of the college where people hang out. Also, the Kleine Schanze—it's a fantastic park where you can play life-size chess. If politics interests you, visit the Bundeshaus."

"Wow, that sounds fantastic."

When she dropped me off at the youth hostel, profound gratitude enveloped me. The events of the day replayed in my mind, and I found myself lost in reflection. The extraordinary people I had encountered and the places I'd seen were like puzzle pieces fitting together to form a structure of warmth and hospitality.

Nowhere else had I experienced such a profound sensation of being welcomed and embraced. The barriers I once held on to were shattered by the genuine connections I made with strangers, acts of kindness I received, and the openheartedness of the Swiss people.

I closed my eyes and cherished the memories of the day.

Despite our differences, there exists an underlying human connection that transcends borders and can bring us closer, if we approach life with open and receptive hearts.

The following day, I set out for the Kleine Schanze. I was captivated by the breathtaking landscape and tranquil atmosphere.

Two guys rode past on bikes and said, "hello."

"Hi," I shot back at them.

They parked their bikes and took a seat on the bench next to me.

"How's your afternoon going?" one of the guys asked in an accent I hadn't heard before.

"Great, how about you?" I responded with hesitation. Although I had experienced several delightful moments with people thus far on my European adventure, I was not prepared to let my walls down. I knew solo travel made me a target.

"Excellent now that you said hello to us," he replied with a smile.

I was perplexed. They said hello to me; why wouldn't I say it back?

"Where are you from?" I asked. "Your accent is unique. I have never heard it before."

"We are from Ghana, and you?"

"Where is Ghana? They stopped teaching us geography in fifth grade in the states."

"It's a country in Africa."

After introducing ourselves, we chatted for a bit, and then Philip, one of the guys, asked, "Have you ever tried African fufu?"

"African what?"

"African fufu. It's a staple dish in Ghana. We were just going back to our place to make some. Would you like to join us?"

"Sure, why not?" the words shot out of my mouth before I realized what I'd said.

"Okay, let's go then."

Philip and his friend, Jay, walked their bikes as I strode next to them along the cobblestone streets. Within fifteen minutes, the neighborhood underwent a stark transformation. We literally crossed the street from affluence to poverty. Their apartment was so cramped that it was difficult to move. With just one bedroom, it accommodated eight people, pushing the limits of space and comfort.

Philip and Jay left me with the rest of their crew while they went to cook. I was unfamiliar with everyone and it was challenging to comprehend their accent. After about forty-five minutes, Jay and Philip emerged with a bowl filled with what look like chicken wings in red sauce with little pools of oil floating on the top. A large tortilla-like object filled another bowl.

Philip demonstrated how to eat fufu. He tore off a piece of the gargantuan flatbread, scooped up some chicken with the tortilla, dipped it in the oily sauce, and devoured it. He sucked and slurped the juices from his fingers, and my stomach churned a bit. But my internal thoughts cried out, when in Rome, and I followed suit. I grabbed a piece of bread and went for it, I even slurped my fingers. The flavors were unique and full of spices. The manner in which it was eaten went against everything I'd been taught in "Manners101" and would have appalled my mother. Nonetheless, I thoroughly enjoyed the experience.

I hadn't smoked hashish or weed since I parted ways with Laure and was longing for it. The people here made me think I might get lucky in the drug department, if I could muster up enough courage to ask. Amidst shoving oily chicken wrapped in bread in my mouth, I blurted out:

"Does anyone here know where to get hash?"

Their surprised reactions echoed through the room. "You smoke?" they asked.

"Absolutely," I replied.

"We can definitely help you out. After we eat, let's head back to the Kleine Schanze and look for Bucher."

I didn't grasp the meaning behind their words, but I was thrilled at the prospect. Once lunch was over, we returned to the park and waited on a bench. Soon enough, a young blonde woman with long hair and a guy in a leather jacket approached.

"Wie geht's Bucher?" he asked.

"Wie geht's Philip?" he responded.

With their brief exchange, Philip turned to me and said, "come on, let's go."

Similar to a drug deal in America, we walked along the river's edge until we came to an alleyway. Behind a large trash bin, I watched as Philip and Bucher made the exchange. In less than thirty seconds, he was on his way back, hash in hand.

"Let's go," Philip said.

We followed Bucher and his girlfriend through the passageway of the train station to an elevator. We took it to the top floor, where a cafeteria awaited, just in front of the University of Bern.

A breathtaking view unfolded before us: There was a vast expanse of green grass, spanning an area equivalent to several football fields, with rows of trees standing in perfect alignment. On the opposite side, a walkway adorned with a protective wall offered a panoramic view of the magnificent city of Bern. There was no doubt in my mind this was the Grosse Schanze, a sight to behold.

"Is this the Grosse Schanze?" I asked.

"Yes, we can smoke freely here," Philip replied.

"Really, wow. The cops don't care? Is it like Amsterdam?"

"Kind of. You can get in trouble here, but the police don't come up here often."

Bucher rolled a joint and introduced himself to me along with his girlfriend, Michelle. We sat atop the three-foot wall overlooking the city and smoked a joint made from hashish and tobacco. Despite my aversion to cigarettes, that was the way they did it here, so I couldn't be choosy if I wanted to smoke.

There were many other Swiss people lounging on the grass; playing instruments, reading books, and smoking joints. We were enjoying our smoke when Bucher's friend approached us. After exchanging some words in Swiss German, she introduced herself in her best broken English.

"Hi, I'm Sandy. Are you from the states?"

"Hi, I'm Delicia. Yes, I'm from California."

"Oh, wow, it never rains in California," she said in a singsong tone.

After spending the afternoon hanging out and attempting to communicate despite the language barrier, we got along quite well.

"Where are you staying tonight?" Sandy asked.

"The youth hostel," I replied.

"What?" She reared back her head as if she'd never heard of such a thing.

"You know, the youth hostel, by the river."

Again, she looked baffled. I searched through my pocket translator for the word hostel in German.

"Die Jugendherberge," I said in my best broken German.

"Ah, die Jugendherberge. No, no, you come home with me," she insisted.

"Really? Awesome, thank you," I accepted with a smile, knowing this would give me more insight into a real Swiss family's life.

That night, Sandy and her parents warmly welcomed me, fed me delicious food, and provided a comfortable bed. The experience left a profound impact on me. I was grateful for the opportunity to forge a new friendship. Switzerland, notably Bern, was growing on me in ways I hadn't expected.

The following day, Sandy and I returned to the Grosse Schanze. While I listened to the melodic conversations in Swiss German that surrounded me, one of the most stunning individuals I'd ever seen immediately captivated my attention. She approached us, accepting the standard Swiss three-kiss greeting from everyone in our group with grace. An extraordinary flutter of butterflies danced in my stomach, this surpassed the feeling I had experienced when sharing my first real kiss with Cindi at fifteen.

Sandy introduced us.

"This is Nadine. Nadine, this is Delicia. She's from California."

Familiarity tugged at my memory, but I couldn't figure out why. I extended my hand toward her. She grabbed me and placed three gentle kisses on my cheeks, one after the other, left, right, then left again. The touch of her lips against my skin gave me goosebumps, and an electrifying intensity lingered.

Nadine beamed the most miraculous smile in my direction and said in her best broken English, "it is so nice to meet you. You have a very beautiful smile."

Tongue-tied and captivated by her presence, I struggled to find my words but stammered out, "It's...uh...really nice to meet you. You have... um...incredible eyes." I locked my gaze with hers, and her eyes sparkled like crystallized pearls from a tropical paradise. They left me mesmerized.

Nadine and I connected instantly, forging a bond that surpassed language barriers. Despite her limited English and my complete lack of German, other than the time I sang "Silent Night" in my elementary school play, we communicated effectively. Our conversations were a mix of broken phrases, gestures, and shared laughter. It soon became clear to both of us that our connection ran deep. In just a few days, we became inseparable. We navigated the city of Bern together and created memories that would remain with me for a lifetime.

Two days after meeting Nadine, we sat in the cozy coffee shop waiting for the rain to subside. Suddenly, a realization struck me like a bolt of lightning. This was the girl from my dream—the one I saw while I was in Paris with Laure! The revelation left me in a state of disbelief, prompting me to question my sanity. That night, I delved deep into the catacombs of my mind, determined to retrieve every detail of that dream. The fragments slowly pieced together, and the undeniable truth emerged: I had indeed dreamt of this woman weeks before our encounter.

The sheer revelation of my dream that foreshadowed meeting Nadine left me in awe and wonder. It appeared as if the universe was attempting to unite us, intertwining our destinies in a way far beyond my comprehension. Considering Bern was never on my itinerary, this had to be kismet.

I pondered what this meant. *Did I just meet the love of my life?* I believed the universe was always writing me the greatest love story, but was this it?

Shortly thereafter, Nadine introduced me to her boyfriend, Roger. Despite knowing Nadine was straight, our cosmic bond and connection remained undeniable, and I cherished it dearly. Roger and I grew close as well, expanding my circle of friends.

Never in my life had I been as liked and socially accepted as I was in Switzerland. The connections I forged there were genuine and incredible. Although language was a barrier almost everyone understood enough English to bridge the communication gap.

A few days later, I ventured out to the Grosse Schanze by myself, hoping to meet up with Bucher, Nadine, Sandy and the gang. I wandered over to the life-size chessboard, which was closer to the entrance of the school, and observed someone with a giant Afro smoking a joint. As I neared, I became even more curious.

Without hesitation, I marched up to him and proudly said, "Hello, wie geht's," in my best German.

He gazed at me, with a single eyebrow raised, and uttered in impeccable English: "We are doing well, and how are you today, young lady? Would you like to share our joint? I'm Danu, and this is Oli."

"You speak great English, Danu."

"I was married to an English lady," Danu said as he puffed on the long joint.

He stood about five-feet-five-inches tall and his Afro made him at least a foot taller. He was pretty fly for a white guy, especially in 1993. Oli was tall and spoke perfect English as well. I was hopeful they would help translate for me during challenging conversations with others who did not speak as much English as they did. Danu, Oli, and I became exceptionally close and spent time together daily after our initial meeting.

By this time, my itinerary had me in Greece, far beyond where my physical presence lay. The idea of remaining steadfast to my itinerary went by the wayside. I'd met so many amazing folks along the way, that I kept extending my trip by the day. People liked me and were genuinely interested in getting to know me, a sensation I'd only experienced from a select few up to that point in my life.

Daily, random conversations led to the question of where I was staying each evening. My answer was always the youth hostel. Every person was adamant I come home with them and have dinner with their family, which provided me an internal glimpse into the Swiss culture and family life. The loving, open, and welcoming nature of the Swiss people shocked me.

I fell in love with Bern, and everything about it. Something about this place resonated deep within my core. I had to be either part-Swiss or Swiss in a past life. There was no other explanation for the intense connection I held for this tiny country. Switzerland was no larger than a pinhead on the map, but it held an enormous piece, bigger than words could express, of my heart.

Within the first few weeks of meeting, Oli, Danu, and I were spending most of our time together. Danu allowed me to stay on his couch; in exchange, I would cook him meals, something he longed for after being single for so long.

Oli moonlighted at the city's most notorious coffee and tearoom, the Reitschule. I was still quite naïve at this stage of my life, and I remained oblivious to the anarchy surrounding us. Until then, my understanding of anarchy primarily came from the Sex Pistols' music and the scanty bits taught to us in school. I knew it involved people rising up against the system, but its true essence eluded me.

Each evening, we would visit the restaurant before heading to the teahouse. A perfectly balanced meal awaited our tastebuds for a mere five Swiss francs! It was here, at the Reitschule that I experienced raclette for the first time. A cart emerged, gliding across the floor, bearing an enormous wheel of cheese—undeniably the largest I'd ever laid eyes upon. An element on the cart skillfully heated it, resulting in a tantalizing golden-brown crust on its surface. The mere sight of this provoked an insatiable craving, causing my mouth to water uncontrollably.

"Oli, what is that?" I asked with enthusiasm.

"Raclette, you have never tried it?"

"No, I've had fondue but I've never heard of raclette."

"It's a specialty Swiss dish; you have to try it."

As an ardent cheese enthusiast, there was no way I wasn't going to try this delicacy. They approached our table and the servers retrieved chilled plates from beneath the metal roller cart. Cold potatoes, pickled onions, and miniature gherkin pickles were placed in front of us. The raclette emitted a powerful aroma that permeated the entire restaurant. I didn't understand the purpose of the assortment of cold vegetables before me, but all would soon become clear.

Oli must have noticed my confusion. He reassured me, "Just wait. You'll see."

The peculiar apparatus with the mammoth wheel of cheese arrived at our table. The waitstaff repositioned it, transforming the orientation from horizontal to vertical over my plate. Then, the cheese was scraped off, allowing it to cascade onto the bed of vegetables before me. Eager to indulge, I took my first bite of Raclette and it was everything I'd made it out to be, delicious! To this day, Raclette remains my favorite Swiss meal.

In 1993, cell phones were rare, and genuine conversations thrived. People engaged with one another. Since this establishment embraced anarchy, they granted the freedom to enjoy joints inside of the tea shop. Smoking joints, drinking tea, playing games, and having unforgettable conversations made for some of my most memorable nights.

Oli instigated my decision to learn Swiss German. We gathered to enjoy our customary dinner at the restaurant, and I'd realized that Oli mentioned my name several times within the midst of his conversation.

"Was, Oli?" I asked in German, and then I switched to English: "What? Why do you keep saying my name."

"Neut," Oli said with a coy smile. Neut was the Swiss German way to say "nothing."

From that moment onward, I made a commitment to learn Swiss German. My approach was to analyze people as they conversed, tune into

German television, and delve into books written in German, which initially appeared as indecipherable gibberish to me.

It all began with two words: oofa and uppa. I carefully observed a girl who spoke using expressive hand gestures that moved upward when she said "oofa," which meant up, and downward when she said "uppa." This began the inception of my Swiss German linguistic venture.

Oli and the others were flabbergasted at the strides I'd made in mastering Swiss German. I believed that my ability to absorb various languages was influenced by the experience of being taken to Baghdad at four. There, I was thrust into a position that demanded my immediate acquisition of Arabic.

Within a few weeks of my dedicated efforts, I began to grasp and express myself in broken Swiss German. I remained in Bern for an additional three months, and by the time I departed, I could engage in light conversations with the locals. The knowledge of Arabic proved invaluable in speaking Swiss German and German, as both languages feature guttural sounds many Americans struggle with. For me, those sounds came naturally.

The time came to move on. I desired to stay in Switzerland, but I recognized it was necessary to finish my trip and head back home at some point. Plus, by this point I'd been gone for over four months, and I was really missing Cow. Also, money was running out, and I knew I had just enough to get me through the end of my trip. Therefore, leaving Switzerland at that moment felt opportune.

A few days prior to my leaving, Nadine approached me and said, "I have lived here my entire life, and you know so many more people than I do."

"Really? It seems like you are friends with a lot of people."

"Yes, but I know these people," she stressed. "You know these people, those people, those people and those people." She pointed around to the groups huddled in various places.

"Huh, I guess you're right," I replied. I glanced around and felt a wellspring of pride. She was right. I was the popular kid for the first time in my life. I was the one everyone wanted to know, the one people were intimidated to approach because I was the "cool California girl." My mind basked in the glow!

Until now, I had never experienced being the person others were excited to see. Even though it was happening right before my eyes, it was difficult to believe. It stood as an absolute contrast to the memories of being picked on, teased, having my hair pulled, being talked down to and silenced by others. I was the kid who they made stand in the corner wearing the dunce cap. It was hard to comprehend being the center of such warmth and acceptance.

But now, here in Bern, Switzerland, everything was different. People loved and embraced me wholeheartedly, and though I couldn't quite grasp the reason, I savored every moment. This newfound sense of belonging left me both exhilarated and perplexed. I contemplated moving on from this place, but I wondered, *am I crazy for wanting to leave?*

Oli, Danu, Padu, Nadine, Sandy, Bucher, Philip and the entire gang all came to say their goodbyes. Their presence, as I boarded, stirred up a plethora of emotions. I reminisced about the countless moments we'd shared and the many incredible individuals I crossed paths with during my time in Bern. The train set in motion, and I pondered when I would have the chance to reunite with my new friends once more.

There was a tinge of sadness as I passed through Zurich, the city I'd originally planned to visit. I assured myself I would come back to see it, along with my newfound friends in Bern. My journey carried on with a longing for the connections I'd left behind.

Austria unfolded before my eyes as I explored Salzburg, Innsbruck and Vienna. The country had its own appeal, and I treasured the moments I'd spent there. Sadly, Austria found itself in an unfavorable position after my departure from Switzerland. I longed for the place I had grown so attached to, Bern.

I resisted the urge to look back and attempted to focus on my upcoming travel. While I re-planned my itinerary, I neglected to think about the civil unrest or political upheaval that surrounded me. Little did I know that destiny led me to select a train route that would carry me through the center of a war-torn former Yugoslavia. During this tumultuous time, I wasn't aware of how dangerous it was to travel from Austria to Greece.

The train conductor was from Hungary and took a liking to me. In an effort to be friendly, he sat next to me.

"Hello, my name is Ishkav," he said and reached his hand out to greet me, American-style.

"Hello, Ishkav. I am Delicia," I responded.

"Ticket, please," he asked.

I handed him my ticket, he punched a hole in it and said, "I am a hungry boy."

With a serious expression, I questioned, "Why aren't you getting any food?"

He looked at me and laughed.

"What's so funny?"

"I am a hungry boy," he repeated.

"Yes, they have food on the train," I stated.

"No, you don't understand. I am a hungry boy, from Hungary, the country," he emphasized.

"Oh!" I exclaimed as the light bulb went on above my head. "How silly of me. I am from America."

We both laughed, and he went on his way.

Upon reaching former Yugoslavia, police officers boarded the train and began requesting passports from select passengers. "Passaporte," an officer demanded.

Startled by the sudden order, I handed over my passport, assuming he would inspect it, stamp it, and move on to the next person. Instead, the officer whirled around, mumbled something in a language I didn't understand, then walked away with my passport. The gravity of the situation sank in. At my youthful age, the last thing I wanted was to be stranded alone in Europe or, even worse, caught amidst a war zone without proper identification. Desperate for assistance, I rushed to find the friendly Hungarian conductor for help.

"Excuse me, where is he going with my passport?" I pleaded.

"Office," he stated, and he pointed to a tiny brick building next to the train. A line of several English-speaking people greeted me upon exiting.

"What is going on here?" I asked a backpacker who displayed a Canada sticker on his pack.

"We forgot to get our visas, so we have to get one here."

"Oh, thank goodness." The fear in me subsided.

An officer who, thankfully, spoke a bit of broken English greeted me. After responding to a few simple questions, he stamped my passport, and I was back on the train.

I looked forward to learning about history in life-size proportions in Athens. Upon disembarking from the train, I found my bearings and headed for the subway. This was the dirtiest, most disgusting thing I'd seen thus far. Everyone crammed in like sardines and gripped the bars above for balance. The fragrance was sickening; it resembled the body odor of a thousand hikers who'd been on a trail for months. I was exhausted and disgusted. All I wanted was rest.

When I located my hostel, it too, proved to be the most repulsive and revolting place I'd ever come across in my entire existence. "Roach motel" would be too nice of a description for this wretched abode. It was well past midnight, and weariness consumed me. I craved sleep, and the option of finding an alternative accommodation seemed futile. I found myself trapped in this horrid place, with no choice but to tolerate its nightmarish conditions.

The room had a twin-size bed frame, topped with a single sheet and a thin piece of egg-crate foam that attempted to give it some sort of semblance of comfort. The bathroom, which was outside of the tiny room, was miniscule at best. I flicked the light switch, and a repugnant sight met my eyes: someone had smeared feces on the wall next to the toilet, which created an unsettling streak of brown.

The absence of any toilet paper only added to the grim realization this was likely the reason for such a vile scene. The sink barely emitted a trickle of water which added to the dismal conditions. The sheer state of degradation left me in disbelief, unable to comprehend the depths of its repulsiveness.

I was beyond exhausted, so I decided to tough it out for the night. Every moment I spent in bed, I remained on high alert. I anticipated the unwelcome presence of roaches scampering across my face. Sleep evaded me. The moment the sun rose the next morning, I grabbed my belongings and checked out of the hostel.

Undeterred by my disturbing experience, I forged ahead with my plans in Athens. The Parthenon, with its magnificent structure, and Olympia, the historic stadium of the ancient games, were two sights I couldn't miss.

Eager to continue my journey, I wasted no time and boarded the earliest available boat to Lesvos. I gladly left the city of Athens behind and set sail toward the picturesque island, ready to explore.

By this time, I'd embraced my identity as a lesbian for several years. Lesvos, often hailed as "the place to go for lesbians," captivated my imagination with its promises of a ladies utopia. I envisioned colorful gatherings of empowered women, dancing, laughing, and reveling in the freedom to be their authentic selves. Excitement surged through me as we set out to sea on this journey to experience this haven I'd heard so much about.

I stepped onto the island, and was greeted by an eerie stillness. It gave the impression of being completely deserted, with a noticeable absence of women. I learned that it was a time when locals dominated Lesvos, and the vivacious lesbians I'd envisioned were nowhere to be found.

Determined to make the most of my time, I settled into the hostel and allowed myself some much needed rest. A few hours later, fueled by curiosity, I ventured out in search of the elusive gathering of women. I approached the local innkeeper, who guided me in the right direction.

I stepped into the bar with anticipation, only to find it empty. Just a few elderly male patrons were in attendance.

It showed me that even the most hyped destinations can fail to meet our expectations. I made the conscious decision to not let this define my experience on Lesvos. I would forge my path and embrace the island in the limited time I had to spend here.

"Hey, lady, can I buy you a drink?" a young fellow in the bar said as he approached.

"No, I'm good, thank you," I responded.

"Come on, you're in a bar. You gotta drink. What do you want?" he insisted.

"I'll have a Sex on the Beach," I replied.

One eyebrow shot up and he exclaimed, "Well, okay, let's go." A warmhearted chuckle followed.

"Never mind, I'm okay, I don't want anything," I replied.

"I'm just kidding with you, lady. Let me buy you a drink," he pleaded.

"Okay, but just a drink, nothing else," I stated firmly.

"Of course, and some polite conversation," he shot back.

This made me smile. "Oh, I got a smile out of you," he joked.

"Look, man, I really appreciate the drink, but you are barking up the wrong tree."

"What does that mean?" he inquired, thinking for a minute. "Oh…are you a lesbian?"

"Yep, I'm a lesbian. Where in the heck are all the women?" I asked with enthusiasm.

"No, it can't be true. You are too beautiful to be a lesbian."

"What is that supposed to mean?" I questioned with a bit of disdain in my voice.

"Most of them don't look like you. Anyway, I'm sorry to tell you, but you just missed them. You should have been here a month ago; this place was swarming with 'em. Women everywhere," he responded.

I tried to enjoy a few days on the island; however, amidst the scenic landscapes and relaxed atmosphere, my thoughts wandered back to Switzerland. I found myself consumed by a longing for the friends I'd left behind.

The next stops in Greece included Paros, Antiparos and Santorini. Paros didn't leave a lasting impression, but Antiparos was a captivating place.

One particular day, I strolled around the island and an unexpected confrontation with a family of turkeys occurred. From a distance, they appeared enormous, and for a moment, I mistook them for ostriches. My imagination drew parallels with characters like Doctor Dolittle or Snow White, as I had an innate desire to pet them. Unbeknownst to me, turkeys could be quite territorial and aggressive, especially when protecting their young.

With a naïve and innocent intention, I walked up to the turkeys and extended my hand toward them. I whispered, "Here, turkey, turkey." The scene took an unforeseen turn when one of them hissed at me, signaling its discontent. I recognized the potential danger, and I inched backwards, keeping a watchful eye on the gargantuan birds. A surge of adrenaline coursed through me as I attempted to stay collected. I understood now that their protective instincts heightened in an instant.

Without warning, the giant turkey chased me. Fear propelled me to turn around and sprint down the dirt road as fast as my legs could carry me. To my surprise, I learned that turkeys are lightning-fast runners. I ran, while onlookers found amusement in this comical scene. Desperation pushed me to seek refuge in a nearby store, where the employee shooed away the persistent beast. Breathless and grateful, I thanked the kind lady and requested to stay for a while to ensure my safety.

After the exhilarating chase, my appetite was voracious. I stopped at a small restaurant along a dusty road. There, an elderly gentleman with a distinguished head of salt-and-pepper hair and a meticulously groomed handlebar mustache greeted me.

"What can I get for you this evening, young lady?" he inquired.

"I will have the grilled octopus."

"Excellent choice," he said as he sauntered back toward the kitchen.

I stared at the purple, yellow, blue and orange in the sky, and I thought about how frightening the turkey experience was. In the next moment, my thoughts drifted back to Switzerland and the amazing friends I'd made there.

He brought out my octopus and set the plate before me, it looked amazing. The first bite tasted like a tiny piece of heaven fell from the sky onto my plate. It was incredible, and I gobbled down the entire plate within minutes.

When he emerged again from the restaurant, he wore a look of astonishment as he glanced at my empty plate. His eyes widened in surprise, unable to conceal his perplexity at my insatiable appetite.

"Wow, you were hungry," he stated.

"That was the most incredible octopus I've ever eaten."

"You liked it that much? I'm Nick, I own the place. I caught it this morning."

"For real?" I asked with excitement.

"Yes. What are you doing tomorrow?" he inquired.

"I don't have any definitive plans."

"Would you like to come fishing for octopus with me?" he questioned.

"Sure, sounds awesome," I responded, surprised at my lack of apprehension.

The following morning, I met with Nick at the restaurant, and together we made our way to the dock. The previous night in order to avoid mosquitoes, I'd covered the bed with a net and used sheets to protect my body, leaving only my face exposed. Regrettably, this proved to be a grave mistake. When morning arrived, I discovered a staggering twenty-three mosquito bites on my face, neck, and even scalp. Despite my intentions to learn the art of catching octopus, the incessant itching and discomfort stole my attention.

Nick's fishing prowess led to the successful capture of several octopi during our quest at sea. Back at his restaurant, he skillfully grilled them for us to enjoy. We sat on the patio, savoring the delightful meal and each other's company.

What struck me the most, however, was the genuine respect and consideration Nick displayed throughout our time together. Despite being unfamiliar with each other, he never uttered a word or made any gesture that was inappropriate. It was a breath of fresh air, a rare and welcome experience in a world where such interactions were far from guaranteed.

These encounters with Nick and other men during my journey challenged the perceptions I had developed of men in particular as a result of the abuse I'd endured. Their respectful and appropriate behavior began to chip away at the walls of apprehension and discomfort that I'd built. It was a glimmer of hope, a fleeting moment where I felt the tiniest bit more comfortable around men. Although this was a small step in my healing process, it was a reminder that not all interactions needed to be tainted by fear and mistrust. This lesson had eluded me for far too long.

My final destination in Greece was Santorini. I anticipated the opportunity to experience its captivating cinematic charm and quintessential Greek allure. The white edifices perched upon the cliffs, the spellbinding sunsets, and the immaculate beaches composed a mesmerizing scene that appeared almost surreal in its perfection. My plan was to spend a full two weeks in Santorini.

Starting fresh in the morning, I was eager to explore the main town. I walked along the road that hugged the steep cliff side. A moped zipped past me, which interrupted the tranquil ambiance. Suddenly, the moped decelerated and executed a U-turn, coming to a diagonal halt just ahead of me.

The rider revealed a disconcerted smirk that sent a shiver down my spine. In a moment, my worst fears materialized. I realized I was in a dangerous position, and my instincts screamed at me to escape.

Disheartened, I thought, *here we go again*. Just as I regained a miniscule amount of faith in men, the universe seemed to conspire against me. This interaction provided me with a counterbalance that perpetuated my doubts and reinforced my reasons for mistrust.

I ignored him and walked around his moped. He moved his bike to block me again.

"What?" I asked, wondering what he wanted with me.

He acted like he couldn't speak English and gestured for me to hop on the bike.

I politely declined, "No, thank you," and walked on.

"Ney," he crooned, as he nodded his head and pointed to the back of his seat.

"No, thank you," I said again, a bit more pronounced.

"Ney," he continued with a depraved smile.

I remembered a conversation I'd had with Marc. He warned me that "ney" meant yes in Greek and that it confused him when he visited.

"No, as in the American no," I shouted, getting more aggressive with my tone.

"Ney," he said as he reached out and grabbed my shirt, pulling me toward him.

"No," I roared, with fear and anger in my voice.

With a tight grip on my shoulders, he attempted to place me on his moped. In a split second, I yanked my arm back and delivered a powerful punch to his stomach. The impact doubled him over in pain, which granted me the opportunity to break free.

I ran across the street to the houses on the hillside. I'd hoped I would escape whatever he planned to do with me. The sound of his enraged pursuit echoed behind me, and his furious voice bellowed, "I catch you, I kill you."

The fear in me grew. I spotted an empty garbage can and slid inside, in an attempt to hide. His voice sounded closer and closer. I held my breath while I prayed he wouldn't find me. My only defense was to hunker down and embrace the stillness. I hoped for a divine intervention to keep me safe from harm.

Gradually, his cries dissipated into the distance. Slowly, I raised my head and scanned my surroundings. Time was of the essence, so I acted quickly.

With all the speed my trembling legs could muster, I leapt out of the trash can and sprinted toward the road. With desperation, I waved down the first passing car while I stood in the center of the cliff-top highway.

The occupants of the vehicle struggled with my English, but witnessed my distress. They appeared to understand the urgency and opened their doors, which allowed me to seek refuge. With a swift getaway, we sped off and left the moped man oblivious to my whereabouts.

Among the captivating destinations that I wanted to explore, Greece held a special attraction. This was the place I'd longed to visit the most. It was where I envisioned myself able to experience the wonders of its ancient history and movielike landscapes. I refused to let this single experience soil my memories of Greece.

From the moment I'd left Switzerland, I knew that I had to return to the land of the Swiss. And so, on a spontaneous impulse, I decided to cut my time short and alter my flight's course, steering away from London and I charted a flight directly to Zurich.

Despite my intense longing for my cat, there wasn't a desire to go back home pulling at my heartstrings. Instead, my urge to revisit Bern was constant. Therefore, I returned to the location that had such a profound impact on me.

After flying from Santorini to Athens, then to Zurich, and a train back to Bern, I surprised my friends with a visit to the Grosse Schanze. The atmosphere was filled with joy as people hurried toward me, treating me as if I had just returned home from a long journey. Danu demonstrated his unwavering hospitality and offered me a place at his house for as long as I wanted.

My stay in Bern extended my trip for an additional two months until my financial resources ran dry. Determined to find a way back to London, I used my last remaining francs to purchase materials from a local art store. This enabled me to create necklaces. No one taught me this craft, I learned on the fly.

With a handful of self-made necklaces, I ventured toward the university and proclaimed, "I'm selling necklaces" in Swiss German. To my astonishment, within minutes, all the necklaces found buyers. The demand grew, which prompted people to ask for more. Day after day, I crafted and sold necklaces until I amassed enough funds to secure my ticket back to London.

On the long train ride back, I reflected on my time in Europe. My adventures exceeded my expectations. This journey taught me, once again, to embrace the present moment. I learned that freeing myself from the constraints of sticking to an itinerary opened up possibilities beyond my imagination. By savoring each experience as it unfolded, I discovered surprises around every corner and the joy of living in the present.

It also taught me that tearing down the walls I'd built up over a lifetime proved crucial for shaping my future self.

Among the countless blessings of this expedition were the incredible individuals I encountered along the way. These remarkable souls shattered preconceived notions and shifted my perceptions of the world. I was no longer burdened by the belief that all men were threatening or abusive. Throughout my travels, I met several extraordinary men who defied these stereotypes and inspired me with their kindness, respect and genuine care. Their mere presence illuminated the path to healing and began to restore my faith in humanity.

However, it was in Switzerland where I experienced a love and acceptance that surpassed anything I'd ever known. The warmth and affection extended to me in this incredible country was unbelievable, leaving an eternal tattoo on my soul.

SHATTERED ILLUSIONS

On a warm August day in 1963, a significant event unfolded that would shape the course of my family's history: the birth of Patrick. He would have been my eldest sibling if my mother had been granted the opportunity to embrace her firstborn child. Instead, Hazim gave Patrick up for adoption. My mother didn't have a chance to even glimpse at him.

Hazim, who would later become my father, was the main financial provider in my parents' relationship. Once he found out Mom was pregnant, he presented her with a difficult ultimatum: "it's him or me."

Hazim insisted she place her son up for adoption or else he would leave, taking the financial support my mom so desperately needed with him.

He was hesitant to marry her because he was unsure whether she wanted to be with him because of the child or because she loved him. In Hazim's perspective, if she gave up her son, it would prove her love for him was real.

Forced to confront the harsh reality of his circumstances, my mother's eldest child became a troubled individual from an early age. Patrick found himself in a family with two older sisters who were the biological children of his adoptive parents. One fateful night, something transpired that caused his parents to reach a painful decision, leading them to pack Patrick's belongings and cast him out onto the streets. The reasons for this bewildering turn of events would unravel in time. Meanwhile, Patrick delved into the grim underworld and engaged in the perilous act of prostituting himself to survive.

I knew nothing of Patrick until I was thirteen years old. We were living in Sun Valley, at the northernmost end of North Hollywood, and my mother told me the story of my eldest brother. My mom said she became pregnant before marrying my father. On Patrick's twenty-first birthday, Mom began her investigation to find him. After a year of searching, she received a message from a private detective informing her my long-lost brother wanted to reunite with our family.

The much-anticipated meeting arrived on Mother's Day in 1986.

A tall figure caught our attention, and a surge of recognition ran through me. My mother called out his name, and Patrick turned around. When he saw her, his face broke into a grin. They embraced as if they'd shared a lifetime together and they both cherished the long-awaited meeting. Though he appeared uneasy, his jubilation overshadowed any apprehension. The resemblance between us was striking. We introduced ourselves, and Patrick expressed his excitement.

We headed inside the restaurant, eager to celebrate and share a meal together.

From the moment Patrick and I met, a remarkable bond unfolded, as if we were kindred spirits. Throughout the day, our conversations flowed endlessly and we never lacked topics to explore. We realized our senses of humor matched seamlessly, and our shared interests established a sincere connection between us. Patrick's desire to know me filled me with longing and excitement to establish a deeper connection with him.

Nile was already eighteen, out on his own, and appeared disinterested in forging a connection with me in adulthood. Our interactions remained limited to obligatory gatherings during family occasions and holidays. Nile's lack of interest left me feeling overlooked and dismissed.

Over the next several months, Patrick and I embarked on the journey of getting acquainted. We delved into shared experiences, went out to dinner, attended concerts, and immersed ourselves in each other's company. My admiration for him grew. I discovered a genuine camaraderie and appreciation for who he appeared to be.

Patrick and I nurtured our relationship throughout my late teens and early twenties. During this time, the knowledge of Patrick's recurrent trips to Thailand lingered in the periphery of my awareness. Only as time passed and I matured, did I begin to understand the weight and significance of his journeys.

Emblazoned on the license plate cover of his sleek black Corvette was a phrase in Thai, which always piqued my curiosity. Although I never found the nerve to inquire about its meaning, I assumed Patrick held a strong fondness for Thailand.

Through our shared experiences, a deeper connection with Patrick took root. It was during these transformative moments that curiosity filled me, gradually eroding my hesitation.

"Patrick what does your license plate cover say?" I finally asked him.

"I'll tell you someday," he responded, his words veiled in an air of secrecy that only intensified my curiosity.

Instead of pursuing it further, I left it. Realizing this was not the right time.

Similar to Nile, Patrick possessed a remarkable entrepreneurial spirit and a keen business acumen. However, while Nile channeled his talents toward noble endeavors, Patrick ventured into a realm society deemed controversial and morally questionable. Patrick established his own pornography company, PR Simon Productions. His company focused on a highly specialized market, pushing the boundaries of conventional sensibilities.

It centered on a particular niche within the LGBTQ+ community known as "bears"—overweight, hairy, big, and tall gay men. Patrick's business thrived and captured the attention and desires of individuals worldwide. Customers from diverse backgrounds and all corners of the globe, including Japan, Germany and Africa, would send him substantial sums of cash through the postal service. With eager anticipation, they awaited the arrival of their coveted chubby-bear VHS tape in the mail. PR Simon Productions was a one-man show that thrived due to his creative vision and dedication.

Curiously enough, both my brothers found themselves immersed in the world of production, albeit in vastly different spheres. While one delved into the realm of adult entertainment, the other pursued a different, more conventional path. In hindsight, I realized I might have overlooked a crucial clue pointing me toward my own destined role as a producer.

After arriving from Switzerland, a burning desire to return and live there forever consumed my thoughts daily. In order to save money, I approached Patrick for support and a possible place to stay in San Francisco. If he was willing to assist me, I'd be able to make my way back sooner rather than later. To my relief, Patrick agreed.

During my stay, I slept on the couch in his two-bedroom apartment. Patrick used one room as his bedroom, while he dedicated the other room to the process of video reproduction and fulfillment.

Baker's racks adorned the office walls, which created a display that covered every inch of available space. At the main command station, I handled tasks such as processing orders, duplicating videos, packaging, and stamping items for delivery. This bustling hub buzzed with activity and brought Patrick's productions to life behind the scenes.

Our agreement was, that in exchange for rent, I would work for him by processing and filling orders as well as reproducing VHS tapes. Besides working for Patrick, I took on two server jobs during the evenings, diligently saving every tip I earned to further accelerate my goal of returning to Switzerland.

San Francisco proved to be advantageous, as the city attracted a considerable number of German tourists. This allowed me the opportunity to practice High German and embrace a small taste of familiarity amidst the streets of San Francisco.

While coexisting with Patrick, the haunting memories of my past returned with a vengeance. The unsettling environment triggered me. I wanted to escape. My brother unknowingly became the catalyst for a storm of emotions, dredging up the deep-seated wounds of severe sexual abuse and trauma I had long suppressed.

The demand for his bear videos surged, and Patrick's creative endeavors expanded to encompass a broader spectrum of audiences. Branching out from his niche, he ventured into producing "Daddy" videos tailored for gay men, as well as "Mom" videos that catered to an alternative audience.

I learned Patrick's involvement in the adult-film industry extended far beyond entrepreneurship. He became the charismatic star of his own original productions, donning many hats as the writer, director, casting director, producer, and star. "Slick Rick" became his porn-star name.

The revelation was as unsettling as it was unexpected. It shattered the illusion I held of my brother. To discover his role of directing and producing adult films was shocking enough, but the news of him also starring in them left me in disbelief.

A philosophical conflict consumed me; I grappled with the disparity between the Patrick I'd grown fond of and "Slick Rick."

Regardless of the choices Patrick made, I remained steadfast on my path. His life decisions, however disgusting I found them, would not deter me from my goal—returning to Switzerland, where my future awaited.

During our time living together, Patrick and I shared some unforgettable moments. One year, we let loose and embraced our playful sides by dressing up as Beavis and Butt-Head for the Exotic Erotic Halloween Ball. This was no ordinary event; it was an extravagant and avant-garde celebration of sexuality, freedom and self-expression. This event drew in crowds from all over the world.

Given my history and personal boundaries, the idea of donning anything exotic or erotic, especially with my brother, made me squirm. But being the supportive sibling he was, Patrick and I struck a deal. I reluctantly agreed to attend his sex party, provided that he agreed to wear a non-threatening, non-sexual costume—Butt-Head.

As nervous as I was, I stepped into that wild and eccentric world and something magical happened. Amidst the laughter and the sheer absurdity, a bond formed between us that surpassed anything I'd experienced with Nile.

Beyond the lightheartedness, our living together also fostered meaningful conversations, many of which left a deep impact on me. One particular discussion shook me to my core, it evoked powerful emotions and provoked intense introspection.

"Hey, Delicia. You know how you were born gay?" Patrick asked earnestly.

"Umm, I'm not too sure about that. I think if certain things hadn't happened to me, I might not be gay. I could be bi?" I replied.

"Well, you know how people say they are born gay?" he asked again.

"Yeah, I've heard some people say that."

"This is why I am the way I am," he confided.

"What do you mean?"

"Well, you know that I was kicked out of my house at fourteen, right?"

"Yeah."

"Do you know why?" he asked.

"No, why? I've always been afraid to ask you," I responded.

"It's because I would sneak into my sisters' room at night and do things to them. They didn't think it was right, but they weren't my real sisters, so I figured it was fine. My dad didn't think so, and he kicked me out. Since I was a little boy, I've liked little girls."

"I thought your sisters were older than you. And what are you talking about, you like little girls? And what the fuck, Patrick, you're comparing being gay to being a pedophile?"

"No, I was just trying to get you to understand that I've been this way since I was born. Ever since I was little, all I can remember is liking girls much, much younger than me."

The pieces of the puzzle began to fit together in my mind, and a fierce anger simmered within me, like scorching embers that seared my soul.

"Umm, what are you saying, Patrick?" I tried to remain calm.

"I like little girls," he replied, as if it were normal.

"Like, little, little girls?" I questioned with a furrowed brow.

"Well, I like them virgins. Nine or ten is my preference" he said nonchalantly.

My eyes widened in disbelief, leaving me utterly bewildered and speechless.

"Is that why you are always going to Thailand?" I asked angrily.

"Yes, I buy little girls there. But don't worry, I treat them kindly. I make their first time special, and I never hurt them. If I didn't buy them, someone else would, and most of these guys are assholes and treat these girls like shit."

My jaw dropped to the floor, and I grappled with how to handle the shock and disgust I felt. I lived with this repulsive pervert! The loathing stirred a storm of emotions within me.

"Now do you want to tell me what your license plate cover says?" I demanded.

"It says, 'I love little girls,' in Thai. Please, understand, this is not my choice," he confessed, "I have battled with this internal struggle for a long time, I tried desperately to find my place in this world while I dealt with my internal demons. I never wanted to harm anyone." His voice quivered with vulnerability.

My mind spun out, while I tried to comprehend the unimaginable. It felt like the ground crumbled beneath me, leaving me suspended in a void of disbelief and anguish. How would I reconcile that my older brother, the one I'd admired and longed for, the one who understood me, was nothing more than a degenerate?

The weight of this revelation crashed down on me. The memories of my childhood came flooding back. Repeatedly, I'd faced the unthinkable; my psyche, sexual soul and emotional well-being had been broken on so many levels.

His intentions may not have been to hurt the girls during his frequent trips to Thailand, but the undeniable reality was that he was inflicting deep wounds upon them. I knew this firsthand, since, daily, I experienced the devastating aftermath of my abuse.

My mind reeled. I attempted to calculate the number of innocent lives he'd tainted. Four trips a year, year after year… I computed the numbers in my head and became more nauseated with each passing second. The sheer magnitude of his depravity devastated me. It threatened to devour me entirely. Consumed by the urge to scream, I hungered to let go of the pain and anger that flowed through my veins. The sickening knowledge festering within me needed to be purged.

It was impossible for me to stay silent. His victims deserved justice, and it was my responsibility to speak out. Confronting the truth and finding the courage to protect others from the anguish that plagued me was important.

"Patrick, it's obvious your mind is misfiring," I said. "You really don't think you are hurting these girls? Someone molested me when I was a child; do you have any inkling how much pain, suffering and trauma that has caused me? Of course you're hurting them! And in a big way. You don't see it, but you definitely are! And it's not okay!"

"I never wanted to hurt anyone. It isn't right but I can't help myself. I treat them nice, it's better me than someone else who won't treat them well. These girls get sold either way."

"But, Patrick, if you didn't buy them and other guys didn't buy them, there'd be nobody to sell these girls to, so this would be a moot point. Sadly, its people like you who perpetuate the problem, especially by justifying it, saying you were 'born this way.' I mean, come on!"

"Look, I understand what you're saying, but it's not that simple. I can't control the actions of other people, and there will always be someone out there willing to buy these girls. I thought I provided some sort of protection for them. Despite this not being a perfect solution, I convinced myself it was preferable to leaving them in the hands of someone who wouldn't treat them as nice.

"Patrick, come on! You might think that you're providing some level of love or whatever, you're not! When you think about it you are not showing them love, instead what you are doing is robbing them of their freedom and innocence. You're also violating them, do you really think they would choose to be with you if they weren't being sold to you? Come on! Give me a fucking break Patrick!

"Instead of justifying your actions, consider focusing on ways to actively combat the problem. There are so many ways you could actually show them love, by doing your part to stop the madness! What about supporting organizations that work to rescue and rehabilitate these girls? What you are doing is just perpetuating the problem not 'showing them love'. What the fuck Patrick, going to Thailand to buy little girls that is so disgusting and you are not 'showing them love,' I beg to differ!"

"I don't think I can stop the desires I have, and don't you think it's better if I do it someplace where it's accepted? In this country, it is so taboo that even if I wanted to get help, I can't. They would arrest me before I finished talking. It's not something I have an outlet for, and I am doing it in the best and safest way I can think of."

"Please come on, Patrick; imagine if I were one of those little girls. That's how young I was when I was first molested. I was seven! It has taken such a huge toll on my psyche and my emotions; it's robbed me of my sexual freedom. The abuse has stolen my joy on so many occasions. The suffering stripped me of my childhood. Please try and think about me the next time you are planning a trip to Thailand," I pleaded, knowing this strategy probably wouldn't change anything.

The weight of our conversation hung in the air, and tension filled the room. Frustration arose within me, and I recognized the need to step away to regain my composure. I sought time alone, hopeful this would allow Patrick an opportunity to understand the seriousness of his actions. With the aim of deterring a recurrence of this madness, I'd sincerely hoped that a poignant image of his abused baby sister would fill his thoughts.

The revelation of having a pedophile brother was a devastating blow. Additionally, it threatened the fragile perception of security I'd just started to rebuild for myself.

I grappled with the profound question of forgiveness despite such a betrayal. I'm haunted by the scars of my past. To reconcile my pain with the reality of my brother's actions, and the wounds of my childhood only intensified the turmoil.

Instead of choosing bitterness and permanently ending my relationship with my brother, I realized that forgiveness wasn't about making excuses or endorsing his behavior. Instead, it was about reclaiming my agency and refusing to be consumed by hatred.

After I contemplated this matter for several weeks, I embraced the concept of radical acceptance, a mindset I instinctively cultivated from an early age. Despite my deep-seated despise of my brother on multiple levels now, I recognized the significance of having a sibling who loved and cared for me. I wrestled with the decision of either severing ties with him over his inevitable actions or embracing complete acceptance. Ultimately, I chose the latter, acknowledging the reality of who he was while choosing to maintain a relationship with him.

Forgiveness became a gift I gave myself—a way to break free from the shackles of the past and embrace a future filled with hope and healing.

This was a difficult choice. Unfortunately, throughout my childhood and young adulthood, I'd encountered several people who had engaged in inappropriate behaviors toward me regularly. Through candid conversations with some of these individuals, I came to believe pedophilia is a serious mental illness. These people genuinely think their actions are driven by an expression of love. Our society should no longer treat this as a taboo subject.

I often contemplated the potential ripple effects on our world if individuals who had pedophilic tendencies could discuss their mental health challenges with trained professionals. Creating a safe space could potentially lead to profound positive changes. From my personal perspective, it seems evident that addressing pedophilia as a mental health concern warrants significant attention. The combination of research, medication, therapy and other methods may become viable treatment options in the future. Perhaps, by approaching this with empathy rather than hate and abhorrence, we may pave the way for more effective strategies in healing this horrific behavior.

I've experienced the profound effects of pedophilia since I was seven years old. The scars run deep. They have shaped my perception of the world and have left a permanent mark on my psyche. In the midst of darkness, I clung to the idea that addressing this forbidden subject could spark grassroots transformations.

My experiences have taught me that silence only perpetuates the cycle of abuse. By breaking the silence and fostering open discussions, we empower survivors to reclaim their narratives and confront the societal structures that enable such atrocities. By addressing this issue directly, we can create a safer world for future generations, where children are shielded from the horrors that haunted my childhood.

A few weeks later, Patrick revealed he had an interview for a 'Mom' video. A vortex of emotions churned within me. I was unsure what this meant for me and my workday, and I was concerned, to say the least.

"Okay, do you want me to leave? What time is the interview?"

"It's at three, but you don't have to leave; just stay in the room and don't come out. You can make copies of videos. It shouldn't take more than twenty minutes," Patrick replied.

"Okay, sounds good," I responded with apprehension.

The impending interview loomed before me like a crossroads, a pivotal moment with the power to reshape not only Patrick's path but also the contours of our relationship as siblings, once again. I needed to approach this chapter in Patrick's life with as much of an open mind as possible.

I busied myself by duplicating VHS tapes and managing incoming orders, when a faint but distinct voice echoed from the other room:

"Hi, welcome."

Instantly, I recognized it as the cue, the unspoken signal that urged me to remain silent and within the confines of the office.

I waited, while I worked quietly. I concealed my presence and tried to ignore what was happening outside those walls. Fortunately, my reliable sidekick, Cow, was an anchor for me. I embraced and stroked her fur, and she somehow reassured me that no matter what challenges lay ahead, I could find stability in my dependable feline friend.

Their conversation filled the air, flowing into the room until it faded into silence. I was in dire need of using the restroom, but I couldn't risk being seen while she was present.

I waited, listening attentively for any sign signaling it was safe to come out. Time dragged on, each passing second heightened my urgent need to pee.

This necessary human function clashed with the requirement to remain hidden and created discomfort and anxiety in me.

I cracked the door and peered through the narrow opening to ensure the woman was no longer present. What awaited me on the other side was an unexpected sight—a glimpse of my brother's nakedness and a remarkably flat ass. I shut the door, my mind constantly replayed images of what unfolded outside of the office.

An intense repulsion overwhelmed me. Even the grounding energy of my beloved Cow didn't help me escape. I scanned the room and frantically searched for anything that would shield my ears from the sounds I knew would soon reverberate from the living room. I looked around desperately for a pillow, headphones, earmuffs; anything to help me create a barrier.

But my efforts proved futile. There was no object within my grasp that provided the silence I desired. The impending sounds penetrated into the room and amplified with each second that passed. There was no escape or shielding myself from the uncomfortable reality.

I spun in the office chair while memories of my childhood abuse surged to the surface and intertwined with the present moment. A familiar knot of anguish tightened in my stomach as sexual moaning sounds surrounded me. I pressed both index fingers into my ears in an attempt to create a physical barrier against the impending auditory assault.

I softly hummed and spun the chair in circles. I desperately sought stillness within the depths of my being. The sounds of my voice echoed from within in an effort to silence the hauntings of my past.

The office chair became a refuge, a cocoon of self-preservation amidst the chaos. Tears streamed down my face and I switched off between clutching my cat like she was a security blanket and plunging my fingers as deep into my ears as possible. I willed myself to withstand the onslaught, to bear the intrusive sounds that shook me to my core.

When Patrick entered the room, he found me spinning in the chair, my fingers still plunged in my ears, lost in a whirlwind of motion.

Startled by my behavior, he shook my shoulder to get my attention. He'd inquired with a hint of jest, "what are you doing? She's gone now, you can come out."

His words cut through the air and jolted me back to reality. I released my grip and ceased my frenzied spinning. Though his tone may have been lighthearted, the residual unease lingered within me.

I took a deep breath and mustered the strength to form a slight smile and said, "I just needed to use the restroom." What transpired had a significant impact that couldn't be easily dismissed, and I'd sincerely hoped Patrick had perceived the gravity of my unspoken turmoil.

"Okay, cool. " I said as I brushed past him.

Consumed with revulsion and disgust, I desperately needed to get out of the apartment. Every fiber of my being craved escape and fresh air. Thoughts of Switzerland consumed my mind. I fixated on the question of how swiftly I could return.

I didn't have the support of my mother or many of my friends since they weren't keen on me moving to a country almost six thousand miles away. Nonetheless, with grit and unwavering determination, I pressed on, knowing this maddening existence would soon end. I dedicated every penny I earned, every tip I received, and every ounce of effort to a single goal: Switzerland. I scrimped, saved and clung to every opportunity to amass enough resources for my liberation.

The long-awaited day arrived. Packing my belongings filled me with joy. I placed my treasured records into a shipping container and cradled my cherished cat, Cow, in my arms. I researched the airlines before I purchased my ticket to ensure she could fly with me in the cabin of the airline rather than be checked as baggage.

Switzerland summoned me with the promise of possibility. My previous experiences there left a permanent smile in me, and I wanted to make it my forever home. It symbolized a clean slate, an opportunity to leave the past behind and embrace a future filled with possibility. I envisioned a life where I could shed the weight of the past and the struggles and challenges that defined my journey thus far.

Excited and anxious, I embarked on my next chapter. I left behind the suffocating shadows of my former life. In that moment, I believed I was bidding farewell to the madness forever.

SWITZERLAND—MY FOREVER HOME?

Moving to Bern, the capital city of Switzerland, was a dream come true for me. I stepped off the train at the Hauptbahnhof. In one hand, I held my suitcase, filled with essentials for my new life in Bern. On my back, I carried a pack holding cherished mementos and the practical items I would need for the journey ahead. In my other hand I had a carrier that held my beloved Cow.

I scanned the bustling platform for a familiar face. And there, amidst the crowd, I spotted Danu along with Oli, my dear friends. Danu was also my soon to be roommate. With warm, expansive grins, they greeted me with a welcoming embrace. In true Swiss fashion, Danu bestowed a kiss on each cheek: right, left, then right again.

"Welcome back to Bern!" Danu exclaimed. "I'm so happy you're here. I'm thrilled to share my home with you."

Oli interjected, "Yeah, Delicia, we are so happy you are back! We've missed you very much!"

I smiled because I recognized the genuine warmth they exuded. "Thank you, both. I can't express how grateful I am."

Danu picked up my suitcase and motioned for me to follow him. We navigated through the bustling station and he shared his plans for our time together. We discussed the local attractions, hidden gems, and his favorite spots in Bern.

"I have to go back to work, but we can catch up later," Oli said as he headed back toward track ten.

Just outside of the train station, I marveled at the panoramic views—the snowcapped Bernese Alps, the picturesque old town, and the tranquil Aare River.

Danu watched my reaction and a proud smile crossed his face. "This is our new home," he said. "We are heading to my place in Liebefeld. You should try to get familiar, since you will be taking public transit."

We ventured off together and an odd feeling overcame me—I belonged. This entailed more than just a move to a new city; it was an opportunity to forge a deeper connection with Danu, Oli, Nadine, Sandy, Padu, and my many newfound friends. Additionally, I was looking forward to advancing my Swiss German skills that I'd learned in my early months here.

"I can't wait for you to settle in," Danu said. "I want to make sure you feel at home."

Filled with gratitude for Danu's support, I smiled.

My first time in Bern taught me the importance of slowing down, to appreciate the simple pleasures in life. With Oli, Danu and the gang, every moment was a gift. Whether it was strolling along the Aare River; hanging out at the Grosse Schanze; climbing up the medieval clock tower for a phenomenal view of the city or sipping a hot cup of tea while enjoying a joint atop the Reitschule.

The quest to secure a job and find a place to call my own proved daunting. The Swiss bureaucracy posed a unique set of hurdles that presented a catch-22. Without a permit, I couldn't find an apartment, and without a place to stay, I would not be able to obtain a permit. It was a never-ending maze without a clear solution.

I exhaustively scoured job boards and searched for any position I might have even a remote chance of getting hired for. However, each opportunity slipped through my fingers, as employers prioritized Swiss citizens or individuals with extensive local experience.

Slowly but surely, my persistence paid off. An ad in the local paper caught my eye—a farm was seeking a helper, and what made it even more enticing was it included a studio apartment. It seemed like the perfect opportunity since work and accommodation were both unattainable.

Upon arrival at the interview, a staunch German woman named Hilda greeted me. She stood tall and composed, radiating an air of no-nonsense professionalism. We exchanged greetings, and her firm handshake conveyed authority.

"Guten Morgen! You must be the applicant for the farm-helper position. I am Hilda, the farm owner. Please come in."

"A gruetze," I replied, trying to impress her with my Swiss German. She didn't find it amusing and continued.

"I trust you are well-prepared for this job. Have you worked with horses?"

"Well, I like horses, but I've never worked with them per se. I've had dogs before," I lied, knowing I could handle any dog and that it didn't take a genius to walk and feed dogs. "Regardless, I am certain I can fulfill this position, please give me an opportunity to prove myself."

"Hmm. We need someone with direct experience handling horses. It's a demanding responsibility. Are you confident in your ability to adapt and learn on the job?"

"Absolutely! I don't have direct experience with horses but I am a quick learner and I have a deep love for animals. I'm willing to put in the effort required. I won't let you down if you give me a chance."

"We appreciate the honesty and determination you've shown. We'll see if you can rise to the occasion. We value hard work, and you will have to prove yourself. If you're willing to take on the challenge, I'll give you a chance to show me what you're made of."

"Thank you, I appreciate the opportunity and I won't disappoint you."

"Very well. Tomorrow morning, you'll start with a thorough orientation and an introduction to our horses. We'll assess your abilities and make a final decision from there. Be prepared; this is your only chance."

"Yes, ma'am," I replied.

I left the room, but Hilda's curt and straightforward manner lingered in the air. Her words set the bar high and challenged me to prove my worth. With a determined spirit and a hunger to learn, I prepared myself for the opportunity to show her what I was made of.

The next morning, I arrived at the farm early. Hilda wasted no time and promptly set me to work. We began by training the horses, learning how to manage them, and building a bond of trust. Hilda walked me through the stables, pointing out where the supplies, food, tools and hay were kept.

Once the training session concluded, Hilda assigned me the task of cleaning the horse stalls. I embraced the responsibility with complete dedication, diligently scooping, ensuring a clean and comfortable environment for the majestic creatures. I finished the task, which brought me satisfaction, knowing I gave it my all.

Eager for my next assignment, I set off to find Hilda. I discovered her amidst a playful group of dogs, and her English sheepdog, Buddy, leapt toward me with his tail wagging furiously. The connection between us was instant, and Buddy's warm reception convinced me I'd made an impression on Hilda as well.

I believed this may have sealed the deal. It exhibited how much I loved animals.

"Hilda, I've finished cleaning the horse stalls. What would you like me to do next?"

"Ah, there you are. I thought you should be done by now. I was just going to come find you. Now, I need you to assist me with the dogs. There are tasks we need to address. Buddy seems to have taken quite a liking to you."

"I'm more than happy to help with the dogs. Buddy is such a friendly dog. I'm glad he likes me."

The day progressed with new tasks and responsibilities, and I embraced each one with enthusiasm.

At the end of the day, Hilda approached me and stated, "You did a decent job today. There are areas to improve, but I can provide training for you. I would like to offer you the position."

As we concluded our conversation, Hilda guided me to my new apartment, next to the horse stalls. We walked down a cobblestone pathway, and she handed me a set of keys.

"This is your new apartment. It may be small, but I hope you find it comfortable."

"Thank you, it's lovely. I really appreciate it."

Our conversation drew to a close, and Hilda reached into her pocket and pulled out another key, smaller but this key held great significance.

"Here is the key to the Vespa. Since our farm is situated so far outside the city limits, I am including the moped so you can get around town."

Now I had everything I needed: a job, a moped, and an apartment. Things were looking up.

"Thank you, I can't tell you how grateful I am that transportation is included."

Hilda nodded and walked away, leaving me in silence.

With the key in my hand, I understood the freedom it represented. It symbolized the ability to explore the vast countryside, run errands, and immerse myself in this rural setting while having a way to hang out with my friends at night.

I entered my new apartment and gratitude filled my heart. I knew working for someone as staunch as Hilda would not be easy, but I was willing to brave it as a steppingstone to my permanent residency in Switzerland.

From the moment I'd met her, it became clear Hilda embodied the stereotype often portrayed of German people in movies—a stern, hard, and cold individual, devoid of empathy and warmth. This contrasted sharply with the friendly encounters I'd experienced with other German people. She was different from most. She had a penchant for directing the nastiest of remarks toward me, treating me as if I were a societal dredge rather than a fellow human being. Faced with her unwarranted hostility, I struggled to maintain my composure.

This took a toll on me, both psychologically and physically. One afternoon, I was tending to the horses in the stables when Hilda approached.

"What are you doing? Those brushes are for grooming, not for playtime!" Her voice carried a sharpness that had a chilling effect on me.

"I'm sorry. I was just brushing them."

"They don't need your coddling! You're here to work, not to waste time pampering animals. Remember your place."

Her words stung, and I struggled to remain calm while confronted by her unwarranted hostility. She took enjoyment in belittling me and making me feel like an outsider.

"I understand the importance of my responsibilities here, and I assure you, I am dedicated to fulfilling them to the best of my abilities. It's important to me the animals are well cared for and nurtured."

"Well, you better learn quickly. We're not running a sanctuary for stray animals. You're here to work, and you'll be treated accordingly!"

Her harsh tone echoed throughout the stable and left a bitter aftertaste in the air. I wondered what led her to harbor such animosity toward me. Despite my efforts to prove my commitment and willingness to contribute, she saw me as nothing more than an unwelcome burden.

As days turned into weeks, her disdainful remarks, and callous treatment persisted.

I was grateful for the comfort that awaited me in Cow's constant companionship. Throughout our journey from the diverse landscapes of California to the less familiar terrain of Switzerland, Cow remained a steadfast presence. She offered comfort and familiarity in the ever-changing homes we'd traversed.

But Cow wasn't the only one who comforted me; In the gentle eyes and affectionate nuzzles of the animals I cared for, I discovered a refuge from the harshness I encountered daily from the boss lady. Whether a dog wagged its tail or a horse nudged my shoulder, their silent companionship conveyed a powerful message. They reminded me that compassion and connection both helped to alleviate my sadness, even if only a smidgeon.

In addition to enduring the daily onslaught of harsh words from my employer, I'd grappled with another intense weight—a homesickness that surpassed any previous experience imaginable.

I longed for the familiar, especially the presence of my mother. I missed the comforts of home—the savory taste of a perfectly crafted mac and cheese, the mouthwatering delight of greasy Mexican food—these simple pleasures remained elusive in Switzerland. This hunger enveloped me with an intensity I never anticipated.

The core of my being surprisingly needed the embrace of familiar surroundings, the contagious laughter of loved ones, and the everyday things that defined my identity as a California native.

While Hilda's actions and words chipped away at my spirit, I refused to let her define my experience in Switzerland. With each passing day, I grew stronger, determined to prove my worth to this stern woman and overcome the barriers imposed by her unkindness.

I recalled the day it began, a distressing chapter in my Swiss living experience that would be forever etched in my memory. I stood in the presence of Hilda, and a painful sensation settled deep within my bowel.

"Something is wrong," I mustered the courage to confide in her. I'd hoped for some semblance of understanding or guidance.

Her response was dismissive, a mere wave of her hand, as if my concerns were inconsequential.

Little did I know this day exhibited the beginning of an ordeal that would test my physical and emotional endurance for the rest of my life.

My intense homesickness didn't help. I was ill and alone with an uncaring stranger in a foreign country, far, far away from my mom. The pain in my abdomen wasn't just physical; it reflected the inner ache I felt.

One particular day, an unnerving change overcame my body. A relentless urge to defecate consumed me, and I spent an inordinate amount of time in the restroom. It wasn't just the frequency that alarmed me; it was the sheer volume and solidity of my stool. Something was wrong and my poop left me bewildered. I questioned the state of my health.

As the days wore on, it transformed from solid to liquid and the intense cramping exacerbated. Upon witnessing blood, my mind teemed with dire concern. The combination of physical pain, emotional distress and the realization that I needed immediate medical attention made the decision clear—I had to go home as soon as possible.

With the passing of each day, and the weight of Hilda's disdain, my poor health and my homesickness grew heavier. I was on the brink of emotional exhaustion. The time came for me to confront her.

No longer was I under the sway of the fear of losing my job. The urgency of my deteriorating health and the extreme longing for home left me with no other choice.

Inhaling deeply, I approached Hilda with a blend of resolve and apprehension. Besides notifying her of my departure, I readied myself to confront the way she treated me.

"Hilda, I have something to talk to you about. I don't like the way you have been treating me. I'm not trash, and you shouldn't treat anyone the way you treat me."

Hilda's steel gaze met mine. A flash of surprise flickered across her face before she composed herself with an air of superiority.

She retorted with a cold smirk. "You can't speak to me like that. Since you're always pining for your precious homeland. You should go back if it's so unbearable for you here."

Her callousness pierced through me, which exacerbated the emotional turmoil I felt. The pain of missing home became an unrelenting companion, and her persistent taunts only deepened my distress.

"Longing for my home doesn't erase the love I have for Switzerland. You weren't Swiss either before marrying your Swiss husband." My voice quivered with anger and sadness. "It doesn't make the hurt any less real when you spew your venom at me constantly."

Her expression remained indifferent, hardened by her own biases. It appeared that empathy did not fall within her realm of understanding.

"I don't need your power games or your belittling remarks," I continued. I mustered every ounce of energy I had left, met her gaze and spoke my truth.

"I'm going home!" I asserted firmly, my voice resolute.

The once-daunting presence of this woman was insignificant compared to the urgency of my situation. I'd reached the point where my physical and emotional well-being took precedence over any employment concerns.

Her silence spoke volumes, the air thick with tension and unspoken animosity. I turned away, no longer willing to subject myself to her cruelty. It was time to prioritize my well-being.

I accepted that my time in Switzerland had reached its end. My travels had taught me invaluable lessons; the most important might have been to stand up for myself. They bestowed upon me incredible memories and lifelong friendships, but now I had to return to the comforting embrace of home. I sought solace and recovery amidst cherished faces and familiar places.

Profound sadness consumed me as I packed my things to go back to California. Having to say goodbye to my friends was heart wrenching, but they understood how sick I was and they wanted me to get the help I'd so desperately needed. I experienced a complex blend of relief and anticipation, aware that returning home was the right choice for my well-being.

With gratitude and sadness, I closed this chapter.

My decision to move to Bern was one of the best choices I'd ever made. I learned that sometimes, the most rewarding experiences come from taking a leap into the unknown and embracing what lies on the other side, even if the end result isn't what we envisioned.

FINDING MY HIPPIE ROOTS

Upon my return from Switzerland, a hint of worry lingered. I didn't know what my future held. I arrived at LAX, and Gertrude was waiting for me with open arms. Her warm embrace welcomed me.

Unfortunately, while I was in Switzerland, the airline changed their policy. KLM now required that I either get a carrier far too small for my beloved cat or check her in as baggage. This broke my heart, but I had no other option. When we picked her up from baggage claim, she opened her mouth to meow, but no sound came out. After collecting Cow, we ventured off to Gertrude's house in Camarillo.

She went above and beyond to make a comfortable sleeping area for me. A pop-up metal-frame twin bed tucked in the corner and a modest dresser nearby greeted me as we walked in the garage. Her generous and kind gesture moved me.

Coming home alleviated the longing, but, regrettably, didn't ease the misery of the incessant gut pain in the slightest. Every minute, I suffered excruciating discomfort that left me dumbfounded. The unyielding sickness overtook me, and it was obvious that I urgently needed help.

Despite my desperation, the only choice was to persevere, as I did each time life presented me with monstrous challenges.

Years prior, long before my travels to Europe, a memorable trip to Santa Cruz with my mother sparked a significant idea. During this visit, the thought of attending college beckoned me. This lingered in my mind as a potential future endeavor.

Upon arrival, within minutes of entering the city, I fell in love.

Besides being awe-inspiring, I had a few friends there. Both Linda, and LR relocated to the mountains.

Something unique characterized this place. The small town, filled with hippies, sat nestled between the ocean and a redwood forest.

Despite my slim chances, because of my average GPA and SAT scores, UC Santa Cruz was the only institution I wanted to attend. I knew my best shot was to get in as a re-entry transfer student.

I planned to transfer to UC Santa Cruz during my time working for The Advocate. Immediately after high school, I'd enrolled at Los Angeles Valley College since it was the nearest school in proximity to my home. The likelihood of getting accepted from this school to a university was low. Instead, Santa Monica City College had the highest rate of transfer students into four-year universities. In order to increase my chances for admission, I switched schools halfway through the semester.

I'd hoped that my time in Switzerland would be valuable for my potential acceptance. I had a story to tell. My identity went beyond a simple GPA or SAT score. Part of my attraction to UCSC was their narrative-evaluation grading; I knew that if I was judged on the work and projects I completed as opposed to being just a test score, chances were, I could shine.

After I applied, anticipation consumed me as I awaited a reply. I realized that my year-long hiatus from school could have been an issue. This fueled my worries about potential denial. However, a sizable envelope in the mail signaled promising news. I held my breath and peeled back its corner edge. I unveiled the unfolded 8.5 x 11-inch paper adorned with UCSC letterhead. There, the words revealed themselves:

"Congratulations! We are pleased to offer you acceptance to the University of California, Santa Cruz, in the major of sociology. You are being placed on the wait list for your second major of legal studies."

Sadly, Gertrude was not there to join in my immediate shock and intense excitement. Unable to contain myself, I let out a cry of joy to the sky. The one who stood in the corner wearing a dunce cap in second grade was accepted into a university! I was so proud of myself. The light that shone from within emanated around me like the orange hue from a candle glow.

I combed through the classified ads for weeks, trying to secure a rental from afar. I left the sweltering heat of the San Fernando Valley behind and drove north on Interstate 5 to enjoy clean air, ocean, and mountains. This was the place I'd found most magnetizing on this planet thus far. I pondered what it would be like to live there. Linda and LR both raved about its awesomeness, and I'd witnessed this firsthand years ago. Now, I intended to make it my home, and I was beside myself.

Once I reached Santa Cruz, I pulled over in awe. Tears welled up as I marked off another item on my 'I made it' list. I not only succeeded in being independent of my mother, but I thrived in doing so. By the time I was twenty-three, I'd moved out on my own; had a successful job in accounting; completed my general education; moved to another country and now I'd made it to the place where I was supposed to stay forever. This was momentous since I'd already moved nineteen times in my twenty-three-year existence. Part of me questioned if I would ever find my roots and a place to call home.

I wiped the tears from my eyes, grabbed the list I'd made and began contacting people. Just to be sure I was covered, I secured a hotel for a couple of nights. After looking at a few places in town, I ventured outside the city limits in search of my new home. Rent in the mountains proved more affordable, and there was a particular place that piqued my interest.

I'd spoken to Fred, the current landlord, about a week prior, and he was actively showing the space, but promised to wait for me before deciding. Fred and I got along great on the phone, and this place sounded perfect. It was a converted garage. There was no bathroom, which was a huge deterrent. I would have to trek about one hundred yards to use the restroom and shower in the house.

The drive-up Highway 9 had a magical quality. It gave me the sensation of being a fairy buzzing through a forest. I found myself completely enthralled by the grandeur of the redwoods. Towering over the highway, the colossal trunks of the trees seemed to embrace the curves of the road.

One remarkable characteristic of a redwood tree is its durability. The bark contains tannins and other chemicals that make it resistant to insects, fungi and fire. This allows redwoods to thrive in the harsh environmental conditions of their native habitats. I felt a deep spiritual connection to the redwoods, particularly when I compared the majestic tree to the resilience in my own experiences and struggles. Much like myself, the redwood tree is a symbol of strength.

I knew I was headed home—to Boulder Creek, a small town nestled in the Santa Cruz Mountains, surrounded by these incredible trees. My drive past the main town continued about five miles to Teilh Drive. After making a left turn, I crossed a bridge and then made a right. I followed the winding road until I arrived. I was deep in the forest and relished every moment.

Fully aware I would have rented the studio sight unseen, I took a gander anyway. There wasn't much to it; it was a two-car garage that used to open from the front and was now sealed off. In that room, I had the ability to do anything I desired. The price was right, at only four hundred dollars a month.

It measured about four hundred square feet. The garage studio was cozy, yet ample for my needs. It became my sanctuary. A double bed nestled into the back corner, while a makeshift kitchenette occupied space beside the door. The living room was delineated by a couch, and opposite it, adjacent to the bed, sat an entertainment system that housed my television and stereo equipment.

Having to walk to the house in order to use the bathroom was a big issue. I was tremendously sick with intestinal problems, and my illness became worse and worse, no matter how many times I went to the doctor.

To say this was challenging would be an understatement. On several occasions, I almost didn't make it. My frequent nocturnal awakenings caused me to purchase a camping potty. I would find myself in the grips of excruciating agony and often would scream out in torment. It became a dreadful routine and repeated night after night, each one more unbearable than the last. Not grasping the underlying cause of my ailment, coupled with the incapacity of multiple physicians to provide a diagnosis, heightened my stress levels.

The initial days at UCSC seemed like a completely different world. As the start of the new quarter neared, a blend of excitement and nervousness built up. The picturesque campus hooked me from the start.

Upon arrival, the stench of eucalyptus mingled with the buzz of anticipation. I marveled at the natural grandiose surrounding me. With my map in hand, I began navigating the pathways, determined to familiarize myself with the layout and find the orientation events.

My first step was to seek out the professor responsible for admissions into the legal studies program. With only twenty spots available each year, I regrettably fell short but found myself on the waitlist. Law was my primary area of interest, fueled by my childhood aspirations of becoming a judge. I knew that pursuing a career as an attorney was the necessary first step. Therefore, making it into this major was my ultimate objective. I was willing to go to great measures to secure a place in this esteemed program.

At first, the campus looked like a maze with its numerous trees, hills, and valleys. Time passed, and I grew more familiar with the paths, shortcuts, and hidden nooks that became my everyday routes. Stevenson and Kresge, two of the college's oldest divisions, and the bustling Quarry Plaza became familiar landmarks.

The first meal I ate was at the kitchen commons, alongside the bookshop. They offered a daily special: a complete meal for five dollars. In an instant, I found myself back at the Reitschule in Switzerland. This just kept getting better and better! Although eating wasn't pleasurable to me any longer, since everything I ate caused a severe amount of pain, the experience was something I would never forget.

The cafeteria served buffet-style dining. The staff would serve you what you wanted after you made your choice. From my perspective, I couldn't see what was being offered. I inched through the line and attempted to peek my head around the people to see what was available.

I was still very much a carnivore and was expecting they would have rice, chicken and broccoli or something similar: simple, healthy, and balanced.

I asked, "So, what's the five-dollar deal?"

With a half smirk, the man behind the counter replied, "You get a choice of two sides and the main dish of the day."

"What is the dish of the day?" I inquired.

"Baked tofu," he responded.

He must have noticed the terror written all over my face. I was taken aback and asked, "you don't have any meat?"

"No, we are a vegetarian restaurant."

I grew up in Los Angeles, fueled by Breakfast Jacks from Jack-In-The-Box, and mostly meat and potatoes. I didn't know what to say. Therefore, I responded with a very polite, "I'll pass then, thank you."

"Have you ever tried tofu?" the server asked inquisitively.

With a furrowed brow and a puckered lip, I quipped, "No way!"

He chuckled a bit and said, "just try it."

I was in no mood to "just try it." Frankly, it looked disgusting, and I was still battling this mystery illness that plagued me. To introduce anything new into my system did not sound appetizing. However, I became daring after a little prompting. Once he said I could bring it back if I didn't like it, I was sold.

He scooped a heaping pile of brown rice on my plate, which I wasn't sure about either, then he continued with the broccoli and the tofu. Once plated, it actually looked good.

A wave of intrigue swept over me. This unique dish glistened with a golden-brown hue and emanated a tantalizing aroma. With a mix of anticipation and curiosity, I gingerly picked up a piece and smelled it. The texture was firm and lightly crispy on the outside. I brought it to my lips and a medley of seasonings hinted at the delightful fusion of flavors.

With a satisfying crunch, the outer layer revealed a pleasantly tender interior. Infused with a delicate balance of spices, herbs and aromatic notes, the magical powers of a savory marinade transformed the tofu. The flavors danced on my tongue, each bite unveiled a new dimension. The gentle tanginess mingled with a subtle sweetness, while hints of garlic and soy provided depth and richness. My taste buds were pleasantly surprised.

This experience was a gateway into a world of plant-based possibilities. It broadened my perspective on the endless combinations that could be made with the most basic of ingredients. The memory stayed in my mind long after this experience, and I ventured back to indulge in this delicious entrée time and time again.

This was a significant leap for me; How did I get from living in Bern, Switzerland, less than six months prior to being super sick and enrolled at a university? A university in an extraordinary town steeped with incredible energy, ocean waves, wonderful people, hippies, and the most amazing redwood forests

I'd ever seen? I realized how much I missed my home state while I was living abroad, yet it truly hit me at this moment. I adored California and everything about it, especially Santa Cruz! It doesn't matter where I am in the world: I will always come back to where I was born and my home forever, California!

From that moment onward, I fell in love with UCSC, my classes, my majors—including the coveted legal studies major I'd wormed my way into—and everything about college. I loved having the narrative evaluations; it encouraged and uplifted me every time I read a professor's notes about how talented or smart they perceived me to be. Although carrying a full load of classes while I dealt with my mystery illness proved more than challenging, I forged forward, enduring intense pain daily.

The memories of my time here, beginning with my initial dining experience, navigating through various challenges, and crafting meaningful projects, culminated in my unforgettable graduation ceremony. The banana slug, the beloved mascot of UCSC, which symbolized the spirit of my alma matter, will forever live on.

TRUSTWORTHY MONSTER #2

I returned to my homeland from Switzerland and was desperate to reconnect with family and friends. The homesickness was excruciating, unlike anything I'd ever encountered. I never expected to have such a deep emotional capacity to long for the presence of others.

Despite the jarring disclosure of Patrick's shocking revelation as a pedophile before I'd left, I made the choice to attempt forgiveness. I held a glimmer of hope that our conversations impacted him and illuminated him toward a different path. Perhaps, against all odds, my words resonated within him and sparked a change in his ways.

Regardless of his flaws, and they were big ones, I missed my brother and wanted to rekindle the relationship we'd had. I contacted Patrick soon after moving back to Santa Cruz.

Patrick lived in San Francisco, a mere hour's drive away from where I settled in Boulder Creek. Before I knew it, we revived our closeness and began spending time together once more. Notably, the fact that Patrick had no scheduled trips to Thailand led me to believe that our conversation might have made a difference.

During that time, Patrick was in a relationship with a woman named Charlotte. At first, she appeared pleasant. However, I noted her disingenuous and pretentious nature. Regardless, I was glad she was a part of Patrick's life. I'd hoped that she, too, had something to do with there being no foreseeable trips to Thailand in my brother's future.

One day in September 1994, Charlotte approached me and asked me to have a serious conversation. We sat down together on the couch, and her worried expression caught my attention.

"Delicia, I don't know what to do," she confessed, her voice filled with uncertainty.

"About what?" I inquired, curious about the reason behind her distress.

"I think I am pregnant. No, actually, I know I am pregnant," she revealed with intense concern.

Charlotte fabricated stories: she was someone who re-gifted used items and placed them in new Nordstroms boxes and then would brag about how expensive the gifts were. Therefore, I questioned the veracity of her words. Doubts lingered and I hesitantly asked, "Are you sure?"

"Yes, here, look," she replied and handed me a small plastic pregnancy test.

I glanced at the indicator and saw two pink lines which signaled a positive result. A mixture of surprise and skepticism swept over me. I pondered whether Charlotte was attempting to trap Patrick. I even considered the possibility she might have purchased a fake test or had asked someone to provide a urine sample.

At fifteen, Patrick lived through difficult and negative experiences on the streets, to some extent because Hazim put him up for adoption. This taught him the harsh realities of survival. At that moment, he developed an unstoppable determination that would inspire him to never desert his own child.

"Wow!" I exclaimed, my uncertainty still lingered.

"What should I do? Should I get an abortion? Should I keep it?" asked Charlotte.

"That's not my place to decide. You need to talk to Patrick," I insisted, trying to avoid getting entangled in their personal affairs.

"Yeah, I'm scared," Charlotte admitted, her voice trembled with anxiety.

"Just talk to him," I reiterated, reluctant to involve myself any further.

Months went by, and I made a conscious decision not to bring up the conversation with Charlotte or Patrick. I watched her belly grow larger with each passing month. By May 1995, her pregnancy reached its final stages, and she was ready to pop.

On May 7th, Charlotte was rushed to the hospital hoping to deliver her firstborn child. After she settled into her private room, her contractions came and went every few minutes. However, her cervix showed no signs of dilation.

The hospital stay lasted for two grueling days, and eventually, the doctors performed a c-section to bring Christopher into the world. Christopher's entry was far from easy. During the procedure, the doctors pulled out the tiny infant and they noticed that the umbilical cord was wrapped multiple times around his frail neck. His face was blue and unresponsive, and he struggled to take his first breath. Patrick, the producer, captured the intense moment on video. After the ordeal was over and I met my first nephew, love enveloped me.

From the moment Christopher entered my life, he and I shared a deep bond. Despite my illness, I made regular two-hour drives to visit my newborn nephew, my brother Patrick and Charlotte. The connection I'd felt with Christopher was instantaneous, and nothing would keep me from being a part of his life.

In March 1995, a couple of months before Christopher was born, Patrick's preoccupation with taking care of Charlotte kept us from celebrating my twenty-fourth birthday together. Instead, in June, Patrick visited me with one-month-old Christopher and we celebrated with a belated birthday dinner.

Patrick insisted on taking me to Gabriella Café, one of my favorite restaurants in Santa Cruz. He ordered bottle after bottle of wine. I wasn't paying much attention since he was driving and I knew he would get me home safe. This was my brother. I could trust him, right?

I fell asleep on the way back to Boulder Creek.

"Delicia, get up. Get up, we're here," Patrick cried out as he shook me.

I awoke slowly.

"Where are your keys?" he questioned.

"Pocket," was the only word I managed to get out before I passed out again.

"Delicia, get up. At least enough so I can carry you in."

Patrick grabbed me under my arm and held me up as I attempted to walk. I completely trusted him as he carried me into my apartment. He laid me down on the couch and ensured I was comfortable. I was incredibly dizzy, and I wished to escape the state of inebriation that took hold of me.

I woke up jarringly to words I'd never wanted to hear come out of my mouth, especially in the presence of my brother.

"Fuck me, fuck me, fuck me!" I screamed, waking up from a drunken dream state. The air was foggy, and it took me a second or two to orient myself.

My vision sharpened, and I noticed a massive weight pressing down on me. Gradually, I recognized the imposing figure as my brother, Patrick, attempting to "fuck me, fuck me, fuck me." The realization hit me hard and caused my stomach to churn violently. I involuntarily expelled a forceful stream of vomit, which covered his entire shirt. Fortunately, this occurred prior to his intended penetration, sparing me from what was about to transpire.

Utter shock and revulsion consumed me completely. I flashed back to the tiny office space and two officers in high school. "I'm sorry, ma'am, but he claims you said, 'Fuck me, fuck me, fuck me,' and his cousin is stating the same. We are going to have to drop the case." The words ran through me like tiny exploding embers of hot coal that flickered throughout my being. *Oh my gosh*, I thought to myself, *did I say that? Did I evoke the rape? Was it my fault it happened?* So many questions ran through my mind, and feelings of guilt saturated my soul.

The familiar wave of repugnance enveloped me and left me baffled by my own actions. *Why did I keep allowing myself to get intoxicated and place my trust in others? When would I finally learn from my mistakes?* This was beyond comprehension and left me bewildered: *How on earth did things escalate to this point?* Countless thoughts raced through my mind, while Patrick attempted to wipe his exposed body of the vomit I had expelled.

I scoured the room, and my eyes fell upon my nephew's car seat tucked away in the corner. A surge of urgency propelled me forward, and I rushed to make my way over to check on him. Thankfully, he was sound asleep, unaware of the vile circumstances that surrounded him.

I cast a gaze filled with abhorrence and contempt toward Patrick, my voice hushed so I wouldn't disturb my slumbering nephew. With controlled restraint, I directed my words at him, my tone dripping with disdain: "get the fuck out of my house. You're never welcome back here."

Patrick grabbed his jacket and slipped out of the room while he carried my sleeping nephew in his arms. He muttered a brief "bye" under his breath.

When I was left alone, self-disgust encased me.

A wave of despair overcame me as the stench in the room grew unbearable. I realized it was too late to disturb the other occupants of the house. I resigned myself to wallow in my filth until the early hours of the next morning. I sat in the dark and lonely room, while memories flickered—a younger me, being raped at seventeen, then the jarring return to the present.

For what felt like an eternity, I'd harbored an internal cocktail of disgust and shame. These chapters happened when I was seventeen and twenty-four, respectively. Now, at the age of fifty-three, after writing this chapter, editing, re-editing, and re-reading it several times, these simple words repeated over and over in my mind. It. Wasn't. Your. Fault.

I went to bed that night not thinking much of it, but was awakened in the wee hours of the morning, curious as to why? Why wasn't it my fault? How did my body know that but my mind bashed my thoughts and self-worth throughout the years?

It finally dawned on me! How was it humanly possible for someone to get so intoxicated that they could be unconscious one moment and wake up screaming obscenities the next?

At last, it became evident: It was impossible! The notion that a body, in the depths of intoxication, could transition from unconsciousness to screaming "fuck me, fuck me, fuck me" without external influence is preposterous. It struck me with chilling clarity: these men violated my body prior to my awakening. They attempted to rouse me from a drunken stupor which left me screaming. Without their interference, I would have remained undisturbed, lost in the oblivion of intoxication.

Besides my internal despair, the weight of society's blame pressed down upon me like an iron fist, but I refuse to carry it any longer. For every soul who has felt the crushing burden of guilt and doubt from abuse, hear me now: You are never alone, and it's not your fault.

Let us cast off the cloak of victimhood and rise above. Let our scars transform into symbols of resilience. Each experience telling a story of strength and fortitude. Together, we can shatter the silence, blazing a trail lit by our shared courage and invincible spirits.

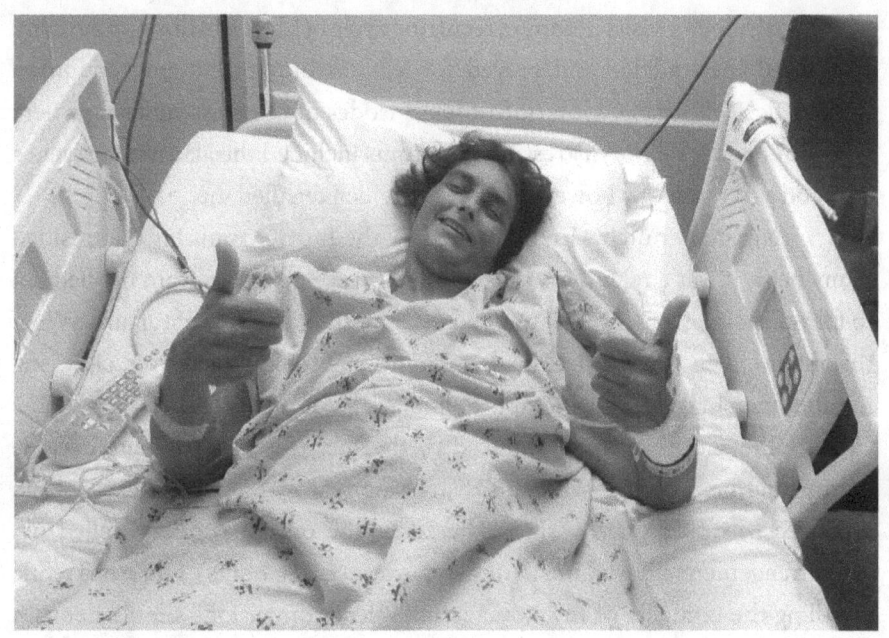

WHY DOES MY BODY HATE ME?

Throughout my time at UCSC, I found myself in a familiar predicament of self-financing my education. Simultaneously, I navigated the demanding terrain of employment while I shouldered twelve to fifteen quarterly units. My dedication persisted, even as I confronted the mystery of an undiagnosed illness that tormented my digestion incessantly.

My gut issues were like something out of a true crime drama, with twists and turns at every corner. The relentless pain took over my life. This turned into a never-ending cycle of anguish and exasperation.

Desperate for relief, I faithfully ingested every prescription given to me, regardless of the toll they took on my already ailing body.

My doctor visits became a recurring cycle of hope and disappointment. I followed their advice and prayed for a breakthrough, but my condition worsened. Nights turned into torturous episodes of ceaseless suffering where I'd cry out in agony. My distressing symptoms included the alarming presence of blood and pus in my bowel movements, which terrified me.

Night after night, I was plagued by the horrific monster that resided in my belly. It was a relentless torment that forced me to rise from my bed ten to fifty-plus times a night, as if trapped in a nightmarish cycle of torture. When this intense pain would seize me, I would find myself doubled over, clutching my abdomen in desperate attempts to find any semblance of relief.

The act of vomiting, induced by the sheer intensity of pain, became a grim routine. To cope with this distressing reality, I kept a bucket within arm's reach, strategically positioned next to the portable toilet I relied on. This arrangement allowed me to undergo excruciating bouts of diarrhea while expelling the contents of my stomach in violent convulsions simultaneously. The experience was surreal and disheartening, my body turned against me in a harsh and unforgiving manner.

Throughout this nightmarish ordeal, I clutched to any small comforts, like the presence of the bucket, a macabre symbol of my daily existence. It was a cruel reminder of the immense difficulties I confronted, a constant companion during the tortuous nights when I was in agony.

Amidst my suffering, thoughts of my uncle and his battle with his horrible disease flooded my mind. Memories of watching him change his colostomy bag lingered in my psyche. During this time, my uncle confided in me, he revealed the unbearable suffering he dealt with daily. I was aware of the devastating toll it took on him. The thought of facing the same affliction filled me with paralyzing anxiety.

Days dragged relentlessly into weeks, and weeks melded into months. Time lost its shape and blurred into an indistinguishable continuum. With the passage of each moment, the toll of my illness manifested in undeniable ways. Helplessly, I watched as my physical form withered away, shedding copious amounts of weight. The reflection in the mirror revealed a gaunt figure, a mere shadow of the vibrant person I once was.

In addition to my physical body deteriorating, the lack of sleep I endured because of this illness was unfathomable. It left me in a perpetual state of exhaustion.

In the midst of this suffering and sleeplessness, I forged ahead. I worked at my part-time job at Santa Cruz Biotechnology and attended UCSC. Though fatigued and worn, each day became evidence of my internal strength, as I withstood what felt like endless anguish.

My work life became entangled with the relentless grip of my illness. Time became my captor, and I found myself imprisoned within the walls of the bathroom. The cries of agonizing torment echoed through the public restroom and unmistakably reached the ears of my concerned colleagues.

Observant co-workers, who had witnessed the drastic changes in my appearance, voiced their concerns. Since I worked within a medical establishment, many of my colleagues had insights and experiences to share, and their genuine concern compelled them to offer suggestions and ideas. In the absence of definitive answers from the medical professionals I'd consulted, their well-intentioned input offered a glimmer of possibility.

Upon exiting the restroom stall one day, my co-worker awaited me with an empathetic look.

"Hey, have you ever considered it might be Crohn's disease?" she suggested with genuine concern.

I was certain she saw the mix of curiosity and confusion that swept across my face.

"Crohn's disease?" I asked, my tone reflected a glimmer of hope for a potential answer, although I knew that wasn't the answer I wanted.

"Well, it's considered a sister disease to Ulcerative Colitis," she explained, her voice gentle yet informative.

Dread overcame me, and the world around me slowed down to a crawl; Since Ulcerative Colitis was precisely what my uncle suffered from. Her voice persisted and morphed into the distant and unintelligible murmur of a "Peanuts" teacher. These words repeated continuously in my head: "sister disease to Ulcerative Colitis." I'd already researched the variations of Ulcerative

Colitis, and I knew how much worse Crohn's disease was. The mere thought of it filled me with dread. My mind spiraled into catastrophic thoughts.

Not noticing, she continued, "Both conditions fall under the umbrella of inflammatory bowel disease. While they have similarities, Crohn's Disease can affect any part of the digestive tract, from the mouth to the anus. Whereas Ulcerative Colitis primarily affects the colon and rectum," she said in a flat, scientific tone.

Her words took hold, and anxiety overcame me. *Was it possible that she was right? Was Crohn's Disease a likelihood?* The frightening nature of this seized me and left me with an urgent need to find answers.

When I got home, I fervently delved deeper into research and looked up symptoms and information about Crohn's Disease. With each page I turned, my fears became more pronounced and daunting.

Several months passed since the incident with Patrick, and an awkward silence hung between us. In August 1995, his girlfriend Charlotte, arranged a small birthday gathering. I, very hesitantly, decided to attend. Before I'd made my decision, I set a clear boundary. I sternly warned Patrick that if he dared to come within fifteen feet of me, I wouldn't hold back my anger. And that I'd make sure everyone knew what he had done to me.

My mother also attended the party and noticed a change in her beloved daughter. Filled with concern, she made the immediate decision to accompany me back home that night.

As the sky grew darker, my declining health became more apparent to her.

"Delicia, what's your address? Just in case we need to call an ambulance tonight."

"Honestly, Mom, every night is like this. It's become the norm for me. It's been happening for a year and a half," I replied wearily.

"A year and a half?" Her voice raised several octaves. "Why didn't you tell me earlier? I had no clue things were this bad for you."

"I didn't want to burden you, Mom. You are dealing with your own stuff; you don't need to deal with mine on top of everything else. Honestly, I just didn't want to worry you. I've been going to the doctor, taking the medications, but nothing is helping. They have no idea what's wrong with me."

That night was an agonizing blur. I muddled through, much like I did every night, longing for relief. I'd reached a critical point, and the next day, my mother took me to the Kaiser Permanente health facility in San Jose. We arrived at the familiar office of Dr. Thennemann, the physician I was seeing in search of answers to my mysterious ailment.

He entered the room, reviewed my chart, and stated without looking at me, "These symptoms are deeply concerning, but I'm still trying to determine the underlying cause."

Positioned on the examination table, my body weak and bruised, I awaited the doctor's response as he glanced in my direction.

He took my temperature and proclaimed, "Your fever is alarmingly high at one hundred and three point four. You have jaundice and are extremely dehydrated, young lady. This appears serious, but I don't believe hospitalization is necessary."

I was crushed by the thought of having to endure another day of suffering. But then, my mother, a force of nature, sprang into action. She possessed a determined spirit, ready to advocate for my well-being.

I watched as my mother's face turned a crimson red. Calmly, she turned and commanded, "May I have a word with you outside?"

Mom left the door open a crack, and I overheard their conversation. My mother did most of the talking; Dr. Thennemann didn't seem to say much.

"Dr. Thennemann, I respect your expertise, but I implore you to reconsider. Look at her—she's in agony. We need answers, and we need them now. I won't accept anything less than her immediate admission to the hospital. You didn't see her last night; she was in the most amount of pain I'd ever seen her in. This is unacceptable. Admit her!" she implored.

Dr. Thennemann was talking in such a low tone that I couldn't discern his response.

They emerged from the hallway. Both wore expressions that revealed a shift. Dr. Thennemann's displayed a blend of reluctance.

"I've reconsidered. Given the urgency and the decline in your condition, I'll arrange for immediate admission. Don't worry, young lady, we will sort this out."

Relief set in. The efforts of my mother proved successful. I glanced at Mom; a mixture of admiration and gratitude welled up inside me. Her fierce love triumphed and ensured I would receive the medical attention that would hopefully set me on the path to recovery.

The nurse rolled me in a wheelchair through the hospital's corridors. Along the ride, I smelled the scent of sterility and felt the apprehension in my bones. Each step brought me closer to the pivotal moment, where answers and relief might emerge. The nurse guided me into the operating room, where the chaotic surroundings heightened my anticipation.

She approached me with compassion and witnessed my agony with every passing minute.

"The doctor will perform a colonoscopy to investigate the problem. It's a procedure where he inserts a flexible tube with a tiny camera into your rectum to have a look at your colon. This will help us gather more information and get some answers."

Her words carried a mix of reassurance and hope.

Dr. Thennemann entered the room with a syringe in hand, ready to administer a powerful dose of Demerol. The drug coursed through my veins and a wave of warmth and tranquility swathed me, reminiscent of the calming haze of being stoned. *This isn't so bad*, I thought to myself. The pain dulled, which allowed me to drift into a state of slight bliss, briefly forgetting the discomfort that had plagued me for so long.

With a gentle touch, he inserted a rubber hose into my rectum. This granted me a surreal view of my own insides. The vivid display of my internal organs captivated me and awakened a mixture of curiosity and morbid intrigue. I found myself fixated on the screen, watching the intricate workings of my body.

Amidst the mesmerizing spectacle, the doctor's voice jolted me out of my fascination.

"This looks like Crohn's Disease, young lady," Dr. Thennemann proclaimed with arrogance.

My heart sank, and a surge of anguish flooded my being. I cried out in desperation and terror.

"Noooooo!" The fear exploded within me.

In the confines of the operating room, an impending doom consumed me. As Dr. Thennemann continued, I hoped his diagnosis would prove inaccurate.

Immediately sobering up from the Demerol, I'd hoped that I was having a nightmare. I said, "Dr. Thennemann, please tell me you're mistaken. It can't be Crohn's. It just can't be!"

"I'm sorry, young lady, but the signs are quite indicative of Crohn's disease. All of the evidence points in that direction."

Terror filled every crevasse of my being as the reality of a life entangled with the challenges and uncertainties of Crohn's disease began to settle in. Helplessness submerged me.

A combination of frustration and anguish surged within me. My struggles seemed insurmountable and never-ending. Fate dealt me a cruel hand, leaving me to question the injustices that befell me.

This was too much! When will this suffering ever end? Maybe I was a serial killer in a past life or something!

Amidst the horrific and life-changing news, my quirky sense of humor remained unscathed. I held on to it like a lifeline, a glimmer of light within the darkness. I was briefly situated on the fifth floor while I awaited the decision about my further treatment.

"Good news, we're moving you to a different floor," the nurse cried out as she entered the room.

"So, where are we headed now?" I asked, curious about the significance of the move.

"Well, you're currently on the cardiac floor; therefore, we'll be moving you."

They'd upped the Demerol dosage to help alleviate my pain. A drug-induced grin stretched across my face.

"Are you taking me to the poop floor?" I teased.

The nurse chuckled, her laughter interjected with the gravity of it all. Our shared humor formed a brief connection, a slight pause from the challenges that surrounded us.

As my body battled the relentless onslaught of pain and digestive turmoil, the medical team devised a plan. They decided to administer total parenteral nutrition (TPN), a form of nourishment delivered directly into my bloodstream, bypassing digestion altogether. This liquid lifeline, a concoction of essential nutrients, promised to give relief to my exhausted body.

A team of nurses and specialists gathered around. With meticulous precision, they prepared the equipment and medications for the TPN infusion. A mixture of anticipation and cautious optimism filled the room.

Both my mother and I were warned about how dangerous this procedure was. The doctor's insertion of the central line into my main artery vein might have fatal effects. Luckily, the procedure went smoothly for me.

My body was so inflamed that it took about two weeks on the TPN for any sort of improvement to kick in. In the interim, unbearable suffering afflicted me continually. My bowel movements emitted a stench that permeated the air. Intense guilt consumed me since I'd subjected my hospital roommate, who was in for an unexplained headache, to my moans of agony and foul stench.

The dignity I once held regarding my bathroom practices vanished entirely. Medical attachments prevented me from reaching the shared restroom, which left me exposed and vulnerable. I used the commode next to my bed, which forced me to relieve myself in front of a stranger. She was only separated from me by a thin, sheer curtain. At first, the embarrassment was devastating, but as time went on, I cared less about it. Unfortunately, this gradual disregard for privacy had a significant impact on the newfound self-worth and self-esteem I'd found during my travels to Europe.

The TPN infusion, coupled with high IV doses of prednisone, provided a hiatus amidst the unpredictable nature of this disease.

During those moments, I found relief in the stillness, allowing my body to rest and my mind to reflect. While my bowels were granted a break, my spirit grew stronger.

It had been almost three full weeks, and I wanted to put my toes in the grass and touch the earth with my bare feet. I'd been begging the nurses but they were either unable or unwilling to take me outside. I felt trapped, as if I were in a cold prison cell.

From the age of seven through my early teenage years, a close family friend subjected me to continual molestation. Isaac, Trustworthy Monster #1, who proceeded my brother as my childhood molester, had always been a constant presence in my life. I met Isaac when I wandered down an alleyway by myself. At seven, our relationship began as an innocent friendship on my part, and unfortunately, ended up being one of the most abusive relationships I have experienced.

Despite the abuse, in my teenage and young adult years, I continued to communicate with him. The deep desire to have a father figure in my life was still something I'd longed for, and for me, Isaac was the closest thing to it.

I harbored a well spring of shame over the love and closeness that I felt for Isaac. This was the reason that I never told my mom what he was doing to me. I knew she would forbid me to see Isaac or worse, have him thrown in jail, and that terrified me to no end.

As a child, I worshipped him, because beyond our relationship, I felt worthless. I clutched onto his love with desperation, like a fading star that struggled to shine. Regardless of the abuse I'd endured.

Being violated when I was twelve years old, I had reached a breaking point and I mustered the courage to take a stand. My mother allowed me to spend the weekend with Isaac and his son, David.

While sleeping at their house, oblivious to the turmoil that awaited me, a heavy weight pressed down upon me and startled me awake. Isaac was attempting to insert his erect penis into me and violate me in the most reprehensible way. Enraged, I refused to be a victim any longer. Something within me snapped and ignited a fire that surged through my veins.

Isaac, a triple black belt in karate, had wielded his martial arts prowess as a symbol of power and dominance. Yet the fury that engulfed me upon waking up to his despicable act overshadowed any fear I had. In a split second, I propelled both my legs forward, forcefully striking his stomach, which sent him flying several feet backward. He collided with the bedroom wall. The impact reverberated through the room, both physically and emotionally.

I arose from the floor, every fiber of my being aflame with righteous anger. I expanded my small frame and stood tall like a giant before him. Closing the distance with just inches separating us, I unleashed a primal scream that pierced the air. My voice, amplified by a torrent of emotions, rang out with a declaration that I'd hoped would remain in Isaac's consciousness forever.

"And don't you ever touch me again, you sick, perverted motherfucker!"

The room trembled with the weight of my words and the intensity of my defiance. Isaac appeared dazed. He gazed at me with shock and fear once he realized the severity of his actions.

The final echoes of my outburst faded into the air and a steely resolve settled within me. I vowed to protect myself, to allow no one to harm me in such a deplorable manner again. With Isaac sprawled on the floor, I gathered my belongings, fueled by a newfound empowerment and a burning desire to escape the suffocating atmosphere. I marched the entire three miles home with determination in every step.

The scars of that haunting encounter would forever remind me of the power I summoned. This was the pivotal moment that marked the beginning of my path to independence and freedom from my first molester.

Isaac had been respectful since I took a stand for myself, and I did whatever I could to shield him from the judgments of others. Isaac made me feel loved, seen and heard. Unlike the rest of the planet, to Isaac, what I said mattered and my opinion meant something. Or so I believed. Because of this father-like relationship I thought we'd had, protecting Isaac became second nature to me.

Upon learning about my hospitalization, Isaac drove up from Southern California to visit me. When he arrived, I braced myself for a familiar conversation, one with a simple "hello" and "how are you?" However, what unfolded caught me off guard.

Isaac walked into the room, bearing a considerable expression of concern.

"How are you feeling? I'm sorry that you're so sick," he murmured. "I needed to see you."

With conflicting emotions, I managed to force a weak smile. Isaac was both my abuser and a confidant, a paradox I still struggled to comprehend. At this point I was twenty-four, and Isaac hadn't behaved inappropriately towards me for over twelve years. Yet his presence still comforted me and made me anxious.

He settled into a chair by my bedside. The air crackled with tension as we met each other's gaze.

Isaac spoke, his voice hinted at remorse. "I have to talk to you. I want to apologize… for the times I abused you, for the pain and damage I might have caused."

His words cut through the fog of my thoughts. Isaac, the one who'd caused me so much suffering, was finally acknowledging his actions. I never expected an apology.

"Why now, Isaac?" I asked, my voice a faint whisper. "Why apologize after all these years?"

Physical pain became my nemesis, and the emotions of the past bore heavily on my soul.

Isaac's eyes glistened with regret as he reached out to hold my hand.

"I'm so sad to see you sick. Seeing you here, in this hospital bed, I just feel so awful! I'm afraid that it's my fault, or at least partly my fault that you are sick. I think I hurt you as a child and I am deeply sorry for that. I really do love you and I'm so afraid the things I did to you when you were a kid are affecting you now. I have done so much studying on how trauma and abuse can impact your health. If I contributed to this in any way…" he said, choking back tears.

Filled with disbelief and confusion, emotions overcame me. Isaac's remorse appeared genuine, but was it possible to find it in myself to grant him this reprieve?

"I… I don't know if I can forgive you," I admitted, my voice quivered. "The pain runs deep, Isaac."

His grip on my hand tightened, "I know, and I don't expect forgiveness. I just want you to know that I understand the depth of the hurt I caused and I'm sorry."

A heavy silence descended upon us. With the enormity of the past and the uncertain future filling the room. The choice to forgive or not remained mine, a burden, and a blessing that I carried alone.

In that fragile moment, I looked into Isaac's eyes and searched for a glimmer of redemption. Despite the scars he'd caused, which lived within me, I longed for healing, for a chance to move forward.

"I...I forgive you, Isaac," I whispered as tears cascaded down my cheeks. "In my heart, I forgive you, but there is no way I could ever forget the things you did to me."

His eyes filled with tears. I made it clear to him that my forgiveness didn't erase the past. My intention was to free myself from the suffocating grip and open the path for my healing and growth.

The road to recovery from the abuse would be long. At least Isaac's apology allowed me to take the first step toward the pathway to light.

Choosing forgiveness, in my mind, did not absolve Isaac of his actions. Instead, I hoped forgiveness would allow me to release the extreme resentment, anger and self-shame I'd harbored for so many years.

Isaac stood up and exited the room. I was uncertain whether he would return or if our conversation overwhelmed him, and I considered he might need some fresh air.

To my surprise, Isaac reentered, wheelchair in hand, and declared, "let's go," with a smile.

"Go where?" I inquired, intrigued by his sudden change in demeanor.

"The nurse said I can take you to put your toes in the grass. Let's go."

"Really?" I swelled with jubilation, momentarily forgetting the intensity that filled the room just minutes prior. Isaac wheeled me outside and I settled down in the grass, sensing its softness against my bare feet. I gazed up at the sun with gratitude. This was a central step toward reclaiming my health. The next part was showing the nurses that I was ready to go home and care for myself.

The juxtaposition of Isaac's and my relationship was heavy. On one hand, I detested him for the abuse he inflicted upon me, and on the other, he was my savior and the one I always depended on.

There were many earth-shattering conversations I had once I was lucid enough to have them. When I started to recover, I called my friends. Although Nile and I spoke almost every day, he wouldn't make the time to visit me. This hurt, since I needed my brother, but he wasn't willing to dive five hours to see me. Although he would make time to call every couple of days to check on me, his business was top priority for him. This confirmed what I already knew; I ranked fairly low on his list of priorities.

My friend Marc was going through a rough patch in life. He'd moved a few years prior to San Diego for college. While there, his addictive personality got the best of him, and the last I'd heard, he was using meth and living out of trash cans. I was worried about Marc, yet there was nothing I could do to help, especially not from a hospital bed.

I contacted his parents, and they told me he was okay. His dad gave me a number where I might reach him. I nervously dialed and a girl answered. The background noise almost drowned out her voice.

"Is Marc there?" I shouted. I'd hoped she understood me over the blaring music.

She appeared clueless and asked, "what?"

"Is Marc there?" I yelled louder which clearly annoyed my hospital roommate.

"Hold on." She put the phone down.

I waited for what felt like an eternity. I hoped and prayed to hear his voice.

"Hello?" he said in a chipper voice.

"Marc, is that you?"

"Delicia, how are you? Someone told me you were sick. Are you okay?" he asked, worried.

"Well, I'm in the hospital. I wasn't okay, but I'm doing better now. They've had me on a feeding tube through my vein for a couple of weeks, which gave my bowels a break."

"Oh my, honey, I'm so sorry. Is there anything I can do?"

"Just tell me you are okay, Marc. That is all I need to know. The rumors I've been hearing aren't good."

"I'm okay, but I'm not okay. I have been trying to start my business. I dumpster dive; then I am posting what I find online and selling it. This is how I've been surviving. My parents refuse to help me anymore; they know I am using."

"Oh, Marc, that's heartbreaking."

His brain might have been affected by meth because he casually embraced this as his life's path and portrayed that everything was fine and devoid of problems.

It was incredibly tough for me to handle when I found out that Marc was addicted to methamphetamine. I had heard about many people's lives being completely destroyed because of that drug. My only option was to hope a miracle would happen so that I could get my friend back.

I hadn't seen my best friend, Jason, in a while. I'd been so sick, and he never talked about how he was doing when we chatted. He prioritized my well-being over his own. Now that I was on the mend, I called but wasn't able to reach him.

I contacted Danny to check on him and ask if he had any information on Jason's whereabouts.

"Oh, you didn't hear?"

"Hear what?"

"Jason is in the hospital too."

"What? Why? What happened? Is he okay?"

"He is okay for now. I'm not sure how to tell you this or if I should even be the one telling you this, but he's your best friend and you need to know."

"Know what?" Nervously, I waited.

"Well," he began with hesitation in his voice.

"Well, what?" my impatient self cried out.

"Jason was just diagnosed with full-blown AIDS."

The receiver dropped to the floor and shattered. Stunned, I'd hoped that I hadn't heard him correctly. I began to push the nurse's button so I could request a new phone.

After what felt like forever, maintenance came. I dialed Danny's number to pick up where we left off.

"Sorry, Danny, I dropped the phone. What did you say?" I was hopeful that I misinterpreted what he had said.

"Jason has full-blown AIDS."

"What does that mean?"

"It means there isn't much they can do for him. He's never been tested and his immune system is barely there. He has pneumococcal pneumonia, which is something a lot of people with AIDS die from."

I was beside myself. My best friend was dying. I was helpless and wasn't even able to visit him since I was so sick myself.

I flashed back to our conversation at The Palms, where I pleaded on my knees for him to get tested so something like this wouldn't happen. My heart shattered; I had no idea how long the doctors were giving him. I was sick, and he was sick. And besides living six hours apart, I wasn't sure how I would cope. The only thing I knew was that I had to pick my emotions up off the floor and be strong for Jason.

Toward the tail end of my visit, the nurse who originally moved me from the cardiac floor to the poop floor disappeared. I didn't see her again until a few weeks later when she stopped by my room.

"Oh, hello," She greeted me. A mix of surprise and familiarity filled her tone. Perhaps she never expected our paths to cross again.

"You're still here?" she joked. "I was hoping you'd be long gone by now."

Slightly amused, I smiled and nodded. It touched me that she'd even remembered me.

"I'm afraid so. The poop floor is still my current residence. Although I feel much better than I did the last time I saw you."

We exchanged a knowing chuckle, our eyes met with a gentle understanding.

She held something in her hands reminiscent of a notebook. She handed it to me, and a smile crossed the corners of her mouth. Her eyes filled with warmth and empathy.

"What's this?" I questioned with enthusiasm.

"It's for you; open it."

"For me?" Perplexed, I opened the indigo blue spiral notebook, and discovered a heartfelt message inscribed on the first page—an expression of her compassion and connection.

In that precious moment, she shared with me a glimpse into her own life. She revealed she was a mother of four and had battled Crohn's disease herself. She was someone who intimately understood the challenges that came with childbirth. And yet, in her graciousness, she acknowledged the battle I faced with Crohn's was an especially difficult one, which surpassed the hardships of giving birth. Her words, like delicate brushstrokes on a canvas, painted a portrait of empathy and kindness.

I hold the memory of this angel dear. Her journal has now become a treasured keepsake—a reminder of the camaraderie that one can discover in unexpected encounters with strangers. In the face of my struggles and trauma, she embodied a beacon of joy and a source of inspiration. Regardless of my suffering, I discovered that if I nurtured my wishes and worked diligently, I too, could uncover a radiant light.

This was another pivotal moment where I discovered the power within myself to shape my narrative, to rise above and reclaim my joy. I understood that no matter what I'd undergone, I had the capacity to kindle the flame within, to illuminate the path toward healing and growth.

In the wake of my hospitalization, my journey toward healing followed a path filled with medications, each one designed to relieve my unbearable suffering. Prednisone became a steadfast companion, joined by a chorus of other medications like 6-Mercaptopurine, Flagyl, sulfasalazine and countless others. With unwavering determination, I pursued every avenue to find relief and reclaim a life free from misery.

Yet, despite my tireless efforts, the discomfort persisted, an ever-present reminder of the lingering battle within my body. Each day proved my resilience as I navigated through the depths of distress, seeking some semblance of normalcy.

A few months after I returned home from being hospitalized, Fred moved out of the main house, and I took over as "the landlord." Because I remained severely ill, having my own bathroom was of utmost importance, given my life-altering diagnosis.

Alongside grappling with my digestive troubles, one of my initial job experiences in Santa Cruz involved working in sales for a software development company. Back then, the detrimental effects of cradling a phone between one's neck and shoulder while typing were unknown. This persistent pain took me out of work for months on workers compensation then turned into short-term disability.

After countless visits to doctors and a battery of medical tests, the truth behind my second mystery illness began to unravel. Holding the phone against my neck while I typed had consequences far more severe than I'd ever imagined. Like a comedic hoax in a tragic play, this simple gesture turned into a source of relentless agony.

Days blurred into weeks. The sterile environments of hospitals and imaging centers became daunting routines. A plethora of procedures including X-rays, CT scans and MRIs followed suit. Each procedure or test held a desperate plea for answers and a hopeful path toward relief.

I awaited my scheduled appointment to discuss the previous test results. As the date neared, my anticipation grew. Hopefully, whatever my doctor said would unravel the mysteries behind my immobilizing neck pain.

I embarked on the drive down Highway 9 to Watsonville. I recalled the countless times I'd traveled this scenic route and marveled at the breathtaking vistas and picturesque redwoods. The winding road had always been a delightful escape that offered a diversion from the demands of everyday life. But now, with each turn, a searing jolt shot through my neck, eclipsing any trace of radiance the surroundings offered. The exquisite sights I once marveled at transformed into mere peripheral distractions, scarcely registering amidst the unbearable pain that coursed through my body.

I arrived in Watsonville and sought refuge in the doctor's office, hopeful I'd find answers and relief. The waiting room became an oasis of anticipation, a space where minutes stretched into an eternity. I crouched in the chair, and the persistent throbbing intensified. It's rhythm synchronized with the ticking of the clock on the wall. Each pulse echoed in tandem with the passing seconds, and created an unsettling pattern that only amplified my mounting anxiety.

After what seemed like forever, the nursing assistant led me into the doctor's office. Within just a few minutes, Dr. Talty arrived. Her white coat emanated both professionalism and compassion.

"Hi, Delicia, how are you feeling today?"

"Still in a buttload of pain. My body is riddled with nothing but pain. My depression is getting worse every day because of it."

"Well, at least I have a few answers for you today," she remarked as she pulled out the x-rays and positioned them against the light board. With a flick of a switch, the room dimmed, casting an ethereal glow upon the images that held the secrets to my anguish.

She pointed to my cervical spine. I sat in awe, a mixture of fascination and trepidation coursed through my veins.

"What you have is degenerative disc disease," Dr. Talty explained. "This condition breaks down the discs that are the cushions between your vertebrae. This is what has been causing your discomfort."

As the x-rays shed their revealing light, the severity of my ailment sank in. A veil of uncertainty loomed over the road ahead. Once more, a shadow descended that shrouded my future and compelled me to confront the daunting prospect of another lifelong ailment.

Her words hung heavy with implications. The fragility of my youth became apparent, as the invincibility I once possessed gave way to the vulnerability of a betrayed body. After years of agonizing torment, my body now faced the additional challenge of a separate disease affecting a different area. The weight of this added affliction was disheartening, especially considering my youthful age of twenty-five. A flood of questions rushed to the forefront of my mind, which intertwined with my fear. *How would this shape my life as I aged? Would pain forever dominate my existence?*

The uncertainties crushed me, their weight pressed upon me like an unwelcome burden.

"What are my options for treatment?" I asked in a morose tone.

"There is no cure. However, there are several treatment options we can explore. First, we begin with conservative measures, such as pain management techniques, physical therapy, and lifestyle modifications. Since we have been vigilant in doing these things and nothing has been helpful, I'd suggest we take the next step."

"Which is?" I inquired with desperation.

"There are more advanced interventions. One option is epidural steroid injections. This can help reduce inflammation and provide temporary relief. Unfortunately, surgical interventions are not an option since this is in your cervical spine. If it were on your lower spine, surgery would be an option.

That might change in the future, but for now, our best bet is injecting the steroids."

"How?"

"I'm not going to lie; it's not an easy procedure. We take a needle about a foot long and stick it in through the front of your neck. Then, we push it through to the back and inject the steroids."

"Sounds painful," I responded.

"We give you some local anesthesia so you won't feel it; you will be out for the procedure."

"Well, if you think it will help. I'll do anything at this point."

"Okay, let's get it set up; they are a few months out."

"That's okay. I am still dealing with these other issues. I'm not only coming here and doing physical therapy for my neck and hand therapy for Carpal Tunnel. I've also been driving over the hill to see my Kaiser docs for Crohn's and I'm taking so many medications. Nothing is working. They are just making me sicker. I have to figure out how to stop this. Between my neck and my gut, sometimes I think I'd rather be dead."

"Oh, come on, you know you are young. You will figure this out, and it will get better," she said, attempting to give me encouragement.

"I really hope you're right."

I left the office without even a tiny spark of optimism.

Relief was elusive. The pain persisted and was unrelenting and all-consuming. It became the unwelcome guest that robbed me of the simplest joys and confined me to the surroundings of my home. The couch was my sanctuary, the array of medications my only solace.

Days turned into weeks, weeks into months, and I found myself suspended in a timeless limbo of suffering, again. OxyContin, with its potent grip, offered fleeting moments of relief, while self-administered shots of Demerol in my thigh became a desperate act. I became intimately familiar with the world of pain management, and navigated the delicate balance between finding relief and avoiding the perils of dependency. I was aware of my addictive personality and I had a long-term addiction to weed, I was determined not to become reliant on medication. The fear of developing another dependency weighed on my mind and prompted me to approach these drugs with the utmost conscientiousness.

Amidst the haze of physical agony, another battle waged on. My intestinal suffering, a relentless companion that never ceased to remind me of its presence. My body served as a constant reminder of the ongoing battles from within.

The eighteen months that followed became a blur, a hazy memory filled with moments of despair and determination. But even in the darkest nights, glimmers of hope emerged, faint sparks hinted at the possibility of healing and renewal. I clung to those sparks and fanned them as best as possible, for they were my lifeline in a sea of suffering.

The specter of degenerative disc disease persisted, a steadfast companion in my journey. While the steroid injection provided temporary relief, it was a mere interlude in a larger narrative of recurring flare-ups. Each episode served as a poignant reminder that this affliction would continue to demand my attention.

The memory of that time was evidence of the incredible power of the human spirit. A reminder of the depths of suffering we can endure and the bravery we can summon when we are pushed to our limits.

I finally had my diagnoses. The cervical spine issues were no longer a mystery, and neither was the Crohn's. However, the never-ending suffering overtook my life.

Desperately, I sought relief and expected each new medication would be the answer. Instead, they only brought me disappointment and shattered hope. Rather than easing my discomfort, they exacerbated my symptoms, and made me sicker and more defeated.

I explored alternative therapies, adjusted my lifestyle, and sought advice from medical professionals, urgently seeking a breakthrough. But the pain, like an unwelcome companion, remained steadfast, it refused to relinquish its grip on my life. The reality was frustrating, a constant struggle with temporary victories and frequent setbacks.

I refused to succumb to despair. Drawing upon reservoirs of my inner-strength, I learned to listen to my body, to understand its needs and limitations, and to cultivate self-compassion during an uncompromising condition.

Through this journey, I discovered healing was not always about complete eradication of pain, but rather about finding moments of respite, small victories that punctuated the struggle. It became a process of acceptance, of learning to coexist with the agony while I refused to let it define my life.

In the darkest moments, I held onto hope. During the times when my symptoms would ease, it revealed a glimpse into a future where joy and comfort existed. I surrounded myself with the support of loved ones who offered understanding, empathy and encouragement. Their presence became a beacon of optimism, reminding me I was not alone in this laborious journey.

Though the road ahead remained uncertain, I embraced the mantra of perseverance. I believed that there were still possibilities to explore, treatments to attempt, and moments of relief to discover.

And so, with tenacity and a fierce determination to live a life defined by more than just suffering, I moved forward. I embraced each day as an opportunity to find the inner-strength, create joy and uncover the power that would carry me through the most challenging of times.

FRIEND OR FOE?

From an early age, cannabis has intertwined itself with my life, and together we have weathered the storms of my existence. At the tender age of eight, I first encountered its embrace, unaware of the tremendous role it would come to play in my world. Over the years, pot has served as my steadfast companion, and has guided me through moments of both tranquility and turmoil.

We lived a short stint in Hawaii during my teenage years. Here, the days seemed to stretch endlessly and boredom consumed me. Weed became a refuge from the tedium. It provided an escape, a portal into a world of carefree exploration.

But beyond the surface, it brought a deeper purpose. It became a means of shielding myself from the haunting memories of a childhood marred by unspeakable horrors. Its gentle embrace dulled the edges of pain. Pot offered a smidgeon of relief not only from my smothering gut and neck pain, but also the nightmares and traumas that burrowed themselves into the core of my being.

A few months after being diagnosed with Crohn's, I was fortunate to be in the main house. I indulged in every inch of my new space, including my very own private restroom. In the confines of my new room lay a sanctuary that remained untouched for far too long—the perfect sauna.

The warmth of its wooden walls called to me and enticed me to unveil its true potential. An idea took root within me, a daring experiment that piqued my curiosity: growing weed. With a hint of covert excitement, I embarked on a journey to transform my idle oasis into a flourishing garden.

I'd planted the few seeds I stumbled upon in my last baggie of weed. Little did I know those humble beginnings would evolve into an unforgettable segment of my life, that intertwined nature's mysteries with my audacity. Excitement filled me when they sprouted. Within a few weeks, three tall, spindly, anemic plants began to grow. They were for my personal use. I had limited income during my disability. Pot helped my pain, and I aspired to grow my own for financial as well as organic purposes.

My new roommate, Eugenia, who'd lived in my house for about six months was behind on rent. She occupied one of the downstairs rooms in the main house. Since my cash wasn't flowing, I refused to let her dig herself deeper into financial debt with me.

I needed to get away, and a few months prior, I'd made plans to attend the Michigan Womyn's Music Festival. It was necessary for me to end this nonsense with Eugenia before I left.

I approached her and said, "Eugenia, we need to talk about your rent. It's been three months since you paid, and I'm getting worried."

Her tone steeped in annoyance, Eugenia called out from behind her closed bedroom door, "look, I told you I'm having financial difficulties. I can't pay the rent right now, and I don't know when I'll be able to."

Eugenia was only nineteen-years-old and although I was hesitant to rent to her, I decided to give it a go. However, in this moment, her immature nature was brazen.

I sighed and tried to maintain a calm demeanor. "Eugenia, avoiding the issue won't make it go away. We need to address this now, before I leave tomorrow. It's super important to get this resolved."

She scoffed contemptuously. "And what solution do you expect me to find? I don't have the money, and it's not going to magically appear."

"I understand times are tough," I attempted to connect with her on a rational level. "But as a landlord, I have my own financial obligations to meet. I rely on your rent. We have to figure this out."

Without opening her door, Eugenia responded, "you should have thought about that before renting to someone like me. I'm not going to pay you anything."

Surprised by her response, I struggled to remain composed. "Eugenia, this is a serious matter. By refusing to pay, you're breaching our lease agreement."

I heard the smirk in her voice as she boldly stated, "go ahead, take me to court. It'll just be a waste of time for both of us. I have no assets for you to claim, so good luck getting anything out of me."

I took a deep breath and realized the gravity of the circumstances. "Eugenia, I hope it doesn't come to that. Please think about it; Let's try to work together to find a resolution."

She laughed. "Why would I do that? I have no intention of cooperating with you. You're just another greedy landlord trying to take advantage of people like me."

She screamed, "I've made up my mind! I'm not paying, and there's nothing you can do to change it!"

Further discussion was pointless and getting angry would only inflict harm upon myself. I realized I would need to pursue legal counsel to ensure the protection of my rights as a landlord.

"Eugenia, I have no choice but to consult with an attorney and start legal proceedings if you continue to refuse payment. I'd rather not have to evict you."

"Do what you need to do. I'm not scared of your threats."

I left the hallway, and disappointment lingered. Reflecting on my tendency to trust others too quickly, I questioned whether this revealed a flaw in my judgement or simply a string of unfortunate circumstances. The process of checking references was supposed to ensure reliability, but it fell short this time around.

The next morning, before I left for Michigan, I gave her an ultimatum. "I'm leaving Eugenia. I expect you will have the rent when I'm back or I will start the eviction process."

She responded with a simple and condescending, "whatever!"

After a long plane ride, I arrived at my destination. I hopped onto a small shuttle bus that brought me to the festival. Excitement and introspection filled the atmosphere inside the bus. Women sat scattered throughout the vehicle, lost in their own thoughts. I contemplated the transformative experiences that awaited me.

As we reached the festival grounds, the bus doors opened, and we stepped out, ready to embark on our individual paths within the collective space. The reality of being in the middle of nowhere dawned on me, and I appreciated the break it provided from the outside world and my own problems.

Surrounded by pickup trucks, RVs and a sea of diverse women, a feeling of community permeated the air. The unmistakable scent of patchouli wafted through the atmosphere, which added to the ambiance. Music resonated from the festival's speakers and boosted my spirits.

Friend or Foe?

I headed off in search of my campsite and pitched my tent. I introduced myself to the ladies around me, and they greeted me with welcoming smiles.

The women in my immediate camp were amiable. However, as time passed, I felt unwelcomed. Despite the crowd of women, there was a palpable sense of exclusion in the air. Cliques had formed, which made it difficult to join these established circles or start conversations.

Amidst the grip of sickness and pain, an unexpected discomfort arose: the presence of others, particularly at large gatherings, left me uneasy. I find it peculiar to admit that the presence of hundreds of women, especially considering that I am a lesbian, felt unsettling. The discomfort I experienced while being around these ladies made me question where I could find a sense of ease and comfort. Upon deeper reflection, I realized it wasn't about gender or sexual orientation, but rather the unease I felt in my own skin when in the presence of others.

The walls I'd built, born from a history of abandonment, obscured my ability to connect, especially in large social gatherings. I grappled with the complexities of human connection and the effects that lingered from my past traumas. It was an ongoing journey of self-discovery that forced me to dismantle the barriers I'd unknowingly erected and to embrace the potential for genuine connection with others.

Suddenly, someone rapped on my tent. Bewildered as to who it was, I crawled over and unzipped the door.

I'd been so uncomfortable, and I thought perhaps someone had noticed. *Maybe, they were concerned and came to check on me?* At this time, cell phones were not readily available. I was astonished to discover that it was the camp director.

"Hi, are you Delicia?" she asked.

"Yes, why?" I inquired.

"You have a phone call from home."

"Is something wrong? Did something happen to my mom?" I asked in a panic.

"I'm not sure. She said it is an emergency, and she needs to talk with you immediately."

I grabbed my backpack and followed her to the tiny electric golf cart. We rode about a half of a mile until we reached a makeshift office in an RV.

Perplexed and frightened, I grabbed the phone with urgency.

"Hello?" I questioned.

"Hi, it's Eugenia."

"What's up? Why are you calling me here?"

"You need to come home!"

"Why?" I asked.

"Because the cops were just here."

"What? Why?" I said with confusion.

"It's your plants."

"My plants?" I questioned with extreme bewilderment. "My plants in the sauna? What about them? Why would I need to come home for my plants?"

"The DEA just raided the house, and they have issued a warrant for your arrest."

"Excuse me?" I asserted as my eyes bulged out like a pug in heat.

How would the cops even know about my plants? I wondered.

"They told me you have three days to turn yourself in."

I needed to get back to the airport as quickly as possible. Everyone had already arrived. The buses were parked and weren't moving for at least five days!

The director took me back to camp and I packed my things while she contacted a cab.

On my way back to the airport, I reflected on my fleeting time at the festival. I'd hoped this would be a space of acceptance and sisterhood, but it left me feeling like an outsider.

I questioned if this perception of being unwelcomed stemmed from something within. *Had the traumas I'd endured throughout my life taken such a toll on my sense of self that it impacted my ability to experience acceptance from others? Why was I able to overcome these challenges while in Switzerland? Yet in my homeland, being in a large crowd felt unbearable.* This ignited an intense desire to delve deeper into my journey of healing and self-discovery.

As soon as I found a payphone, I called my mother. She was always the first person I would reach out to in times like these.

"Hey, Mom. It's me. How's it going?"

"I thought you were in Michigan?" she responded.

"I am, but I am on my way home now."

"What? Why? You just got there."

"Mom, I need to talk to you about something serious."

"What is going on? You sound worried. Is everything okay?"

"Well, Mom, something happened today and I need your help. I am not sure how to tell you this, so I'll just come out and say it: The DEA raided my house today, and they want to arrest me."

"What? The DEA? Why? What happened? Does this have something to do with your mari-j-uana?"

"Yes, Mom. They found the three plants I tried to grow. When I left, they were babies, and they didn't even look good. I have no idea how this happened or why they want to arrest me. It must be a mistake. I should have been more careful, Mom. I'm really sorry."

"Why in the world were you growing that stuff? I can't believe this happened. Call me when you land. In the meantime, I will contact some attorneys to see if they can help."

"It's fine, Mom, don't worry about it. I will figure it out when I get home. I need to speak to an attorney before I volunteer myself to be arrested. They confiscated the plants and searched the whole house. I feel so stupid. I was just spending so much money I didn't have on weed, and it helped me with my pain. I never meant to cause any trouble; I was just trying to, I don't know"

"I'm just glad you're safe. We'll deal with this together. Call me when you get home. I have a few people I can reach out to. Hopefully, they can help."

"Thanks Mom. Your support means the world to me. I appreciate you always being in my corner."

"I'm your mother; there is no other option than for me to support you. Try not to worry; it will only hurt your stomach. Let's focus on finding the right legal counsel and we can work through this. I love you, and I'm here for you, always."

"I love you too, Mom. Thank you for understanding and being there for me."

Upon my arrival home, I consulted with an attorney. She advised me: "one hundred thousand percent, do not turn yourself in because then it will be a mark on your record. If they want to arrest you, they will. I guarantee you, for something like this, the police wouldn't waste their time coming back."

I heeded her advice. Thankfully, they never came.

The prospect of returning to work filled me with dread. I was uncertain what my boss's reaction would be. This made me anxious about potential negative consequences. The fear of losing my job loomed over me, since pot was still very much illegal and I often found myself skilled at catastrophizing situations.

I stepped into my boss's office, my heart pounded and my palms dampened with perspiration. The weight of the recent DEA bust bore down on my shoulders, and I struggled to find the right words. Chris, a powerful woman with an air of authority, glanced up from her orderly desk and noticed my unease.

"Hey, Delicia," she said, her voice tinged with curiosity. "Is something the matter? You seem a bit off."

I tried to steady myself. It was time to be honest and disclose the truth about what happened in Michigan.

"Well," I began, my voice trembled slightly. "I need to tell you something."

"I can see something is troubling you; what is it?" she replied with concern.

"Something happened while I was in Michigan. You know I smoke weed to help with my pain, right?"

"Yes, I knew that. But what does that have to do with anything here at work?" she questioned.

"Well, I was growing three tiny plants, and somehow the sheriff found out about it. The DEA raided my house and now, they want to arrest me."

A flicker of surprise crossed her face, but it transformed into an expression of concern and understanding. I watched the gears turn in her mind as she processed this information.

"The DEA?" she asked, her voice low and measured. "I see. How did this happen?"

I mustered up the courage to explain the series of events that led to this predicament.

"It was a mistake on my part," I confessed, my voice laden with regret. "I didn't fully grasp the consequences of my actions. I thought nothing would happen. They were three small plants. It says in the report that they found 'three tall, spindly, anemic plants.' I'm really sorry, Chris, and I truly hope this won't cause you any trouble."

Chris leaned back in her chair and displayed serious contemplation. I wasn't certain what she'd thought.

The gravity of the situation hung in the air, and I awaited her response.

"Thank you for being honest with me," she said, her voice filled with a surprising warmth. "I understand mistakes happen, but we must also face the consequences. Have you sought legal counsel?"

I shook my head. "Not yet," I admitted, my voice filled with apprehension. "I've been trying to research and find the right attorney, but I haven't made much progress."

Her gaze softened, and to my astonishment, she reached into the desk drawer and pulled out her checkbook.

"I'd planned to give you a bonus for Christmas, but now I will just make it an early bonus. Well, it's very early. I don't think you will get into trouble for this if you have the right legal counsel, and I want to help you," she said with genuine compassion. "Here is a thousand dollars to help you pay for the attorney. Let me talk to my husband and see if there are any good criminal lawyers we know that might be able to help. Don't worry, we will work together to find someone who can get you off. I mean, it's ridiculous they spend my taxpayer dollars to bust someone like you growing three tiny plants for your own personal medical use. Ludicrous!"

I was stunned. My eyes widened in disbelief. Everyone knew Chris was strict about rules. At this time, scientific research into the medical applications of cannabis was in its preliminary stages, but the emerging findings were irrefutably positive.

Emotion overwhelmed me and tears filled my eyes. My shoulders felt lighter. To my surprise, my boss showed a supportive and understanding outlook that I never anticipated.

"I don't know what to say," I stammered, my voice choked with gratitude. "Thank you. Your kindness and support mean the world to me."

She nodded, a faint smile graced her lips as she handed me the check.

"We'll face this challenge together, and I'll be here to support you every step of the way."

With renewed hope and gratitude, I left her office. I now knew that despite the difficult road ahead, I had an ally in my corner.

We found an attorney in San Jose who exuded a remarkable level of confidence in his ability to defend me against this so-called "crime." Despite the circumstances, his expertise instilled a semblance of hope within me. My mother made the courageous decision to take out a second mortgage on her house. With these funds, she contributed the remaining four thousand dollars required. Mom knew I would pay her back and she wasn't too concerned. With the necessary funds secured, I hired an attorney.

I was desperate for relief from the extreme torment of Crohn's disease and my neck pain. Regardless of my efforts and despite having exhausted all avenues of medical advice, excruciating pain persisted and it profoundly affected my life, daily.

While I gathered support for my case, I reached out to my Internal Medicine doctor for help. In a candid conversation with him, I confided about my use and how it provided some measure of relief. I recounted the DEA's intrusion and the seizure of my plants. With sincerity, I asked if he would consider providing a letter which expressed his professional belief or opinion that it possibly helped to alleviate my pain.

Despite the repercussions it could have had on his career, he went above and beyond for me. At the time, doctors who advocated for cannabis in any way normally lost their license. My doctor took a crucial step and crafted a note for me. The note, which I received with the utmost gratitude, stated: "My patient, Delicia Niami, firmly believes marijuana assists her in managing her Crohn's disease."

Armed with this note from my doctor, I shared it with my attorney. I expected a positive outcome.

"Well, this is quite promising. With this note from your doctor, we have a sound piece of evidence in our favor," he boasted with confidence.

A wave of reassurance consumed me, only to be tempered by my attorney's next statement.

"However, we need to be aware of the challenges we might face. You see, the district attorney in Santa Cruz has a notorious reputation with these cases. She holds a deep-seated animosity toward it."

I raised an eyebrow, and a mix of curiosity and concern crept into my voice.

"What do you mean by 'animosity'?"

"She believes marijuana is the devil incarnate and likens it to PCP and other strong hallucinogens. She's irrational and extreme when it comes to pot."

I chuckled at the comparison, although it was far from amusing.

"So, you're saying she's completely opposed to it? Even in cases like mine, where it's for medical purposes?"

"That appears to be the case, but this will help a lot. The Santa Cruz DA's office has a reputation for relentlessly prosecuting these offenses, regardless of the circumstances. It's an uphill battle, but we'll do everything we can to navigate this. Don't worry, you chose the right attorney. If anyone can get you off from this, I can. Even in Santa Cruz County. We'll build a strong defense."

It didn't matter if it was just a few measly weak plants like mine, incapable of producing any significant yield. The district attorney had a fierce determination to make an example out of anyone involved in cultivation. Her approach was merciless, and sought to impose severe penalties. She even advocated for imprisonment. The prospect of facing prison time scared the crap out of me. The weight of the already daunting legal battle I confronted increased with this unsettling and harsh reality.

I prepared for months and doomsday finally arrived. I walked down the stark white, chilly, endless hallway. Upon glancing at the schedule posted on the wall, my eyes scanned the list until I found: "NIAMI vs. SANTA CRUZ COUNTY." I noted the room number and headed in that direction. It was a few minutes shy of 8:00 a.m., the designated start time for court proceedings.

I navigated the corridor, and thoughts whirled through my mind, but my attention was diverted when I spotted the district attorney—a staunch woman who wore a baby blue power suit. Curiously, she neither acknowledged my presence nor made eye contact. I wondered, *shouldn't she be in the courtroom right now?*

Just as the questions began to mount, my attorney emerged from somewhere in the bustling hallway. He grasped my arm and prompted me to follow him. He provided no immediate explanation. We descended the stairs in silence. I followed him to the cafeteria. Confusion consumed my thoughts. *What was happening?*

Once inside the cafeteria, my attorney purchased a bottle of water for me before we settled at a nearby table.

"She dropped the case."

My jaw fell to the floor in disbelief. I was so surprised by the sudden revelation. My mind raced, I tried to process what I'd heard. My attorney continued, shedding light on the pivotal factor that led to this surprising turn of events.

"The note your doctor provided was the reason why the case was dropped."

I surprised Chris as I bounced in the door to work earlier than expected.

"So, what happened? Why are you back so soon?" she inquired.

"Well, they dropped the case, because of the note from my doctor."

"I think the phone call I made to Janet had something to do with it."

"Who's Janet?" I responded with curiosity.

"Oh, the DA. She is such a stickler. But I called her and told her what I thought."

"You know her?" I asked, surprised, my eyes widened as I did a double take.

"Yes, long story, but she's an old friend. More of an acquaintance now. Anyway, I called to inform her that there are better ways to spend my tax dollars. I also told her I was quite angry they would waste their time and money on someone like you. You are not a big-time drug dealer; you are a hard-working person who has been riddled with ailments and from such a young age. It's ludicrous, and I let her know I was upset, and she shouldn't be wasting taxpayer dollars on people like you."

"You what?" My mouth hung open, as if I were trying to catch something in midair. "Oh my, Chris, thank you! Thank you! Thank you! Maybe that's why she dropped the case before court even started. Perchance, with your call and my doctor's note, she realized I wasn't a threat. Thank you! How can I ever repay you?" I proclaimed.

"Don't worry, I'm just glad it worked out the way it did. You didn't deserve this."

Her kindness, empathy and generosity left me astounded. I was thankful that I'd been blessed with such an incredible boss, and someone I considered a genuine friend.

Driven by a burning desire for answers to uncover the truth about the informant who caused the DEA raid, I embarked on a merciless quest.

I followed the trail of clues, and each piece of the puzzle brought me closer to the core. Contradictions in people's actions and peculiar conversations ignited my suspicions and hinted at a betrayal that lurked in the shadows.

I confronted various individuals along the way. While I searched for answers I had no idea the key to this mystery was closer than I imagined.

One evening, on the precipice of evicting my roommate, I found myself engaged in a casual conversation with her boyfriend. The atmosphere was frigid, charged with unspoken tension.

"You know, it's crazy how this happened," I said, while I tried to keep my voice steady.

He glanced my way with a hint of unease, and his eyes darted away.

"Yeah, it's a real mess. I can't believe someone would do that to you."

His response seemed off, noticeable in his lack of eye contact and a slight change in his behavior. Clearly, he was hiding something.

"I've been thinking a lot about it," I said, cautiously. "And the more I think, the more it seems like someone close to me was responsible."

He fidgeted in his seat, his tension mounted. "What are you talking about?"

"You know, the informant who tipped off the DEA. It's just too coincidental it happened right after I left for Michigan. It's as if they knew I'd be gone. Plus, there were only a handful of people that even knew about my plants."

He squirmed and looked nervously around the room. "I don't know, why are you asking me? All I know is that you are kicking my girlfriend out on the street!" His voice raised several octaves.

"What does that have anything to do with this? She hasn't paid rent for almost four months, and she told me that she wasn't going to. What am I supposed to do? What would you do if you were in my shoes?"

"Whatever, you know she was going to pay you back," he responded with a snarky tone.

I knew this was my last opportunity to confront him.

"The pieces don't add up, and the evidence points toward you. The inconsistencies, the conversations I've overheard. Everything points to you being the informant."

He paled, and I saw a mixture of guilt and fear written across his face.

"It wasn't fucking me; how could you ever even say that? You're such a bitch!"

He stomped off to Eugenia's room in a huff.

I marched upstairs and slammed my bedroom door so he would think I was no longer within earshot. I silently opened my door and snuck back downstairs, I came close enough so I could hear his conversation.

"Listen, Eugenia, I'm sorry. I didn't mean for things to go this far. I was desperate, and I thought the only way to protect you was to get the DEA involved."

I busted open the door and screamed, "So it was you! And for what? To protect her? Protect her from what?" I demanded, my voice fused with anger and confusion.

There was nothing to say at this point; I had caught him red-handed.

"Get the fuck out of my house right now!" I screamed at the top of my lungs.

His face flushed crimson with embarrassment, and he gathered his belongings and made for the door. Meanwhile, I paced the living room, and tried to quell the torrent of rage that surged through me. Violent thoughts danced at the fringes of my mind, which tempted me to act on my anger. All I wanted to do was to unleash my fury and let it manifest in an act of brutal retribution. Yet, I realized if I let myself succumb to such impulses, it would only perpetuate the cycle of pain and destruction. I fought to regain control of my emotions, determined to rise above the urge for vengeance.

Instead of stirring the pot any more by confronting Eugenia, I avoided her entirely until she moved out the following morning.

Thankfully, I closed this chapter, and the experience served as another catalyst for growth. It taught me to be careful in judging someone's character and how easily trust can be destroyed. Despite Chris's kindness, it made me lose trust in humanity once more.

The next set of roommates more than made up for the previous betrayal. We had many amazing and fantastic memories together and have remained friends to this day.

UNCHARTED HEARTACHE

Massive life changes occurred while I lived in Boulder Creek, that shaped the trajectory of my path in the most unexpected ways. Amidst the serenity of the redwood forests and the gentle flow of the creek, I confronted challenges that would test my resilience and redefine my sense of self.

I'd reached my wit's end. After countless doctor visits and medications that failed to provide relief, it became clear to me that I'd have to take matters into my own hands.

The chronic pain in my neck and gut became the drive that persuaded me to embark on a quest for answers. Embracing a new way of living became imperative, bound by extreme dietary restrictions and ongoing medical treatments. With a newfound respect for the fragility of my health, I plunged into the world of self-help literature. I voraciously read every book by Jordan Rubin on gut health and delved into Deepak Chopra's works on spiritual nourishment. Desperate to find answers amidst life's chaos, I sought to regain control of my fate.

But life's lessons didn't stop there. The DEA raid on my spindly plants I'd attempted to grow covertly in my sauna resulted in a tumultuous legal ordeal. It was a powerful symbol, that represented the consequences of choices made for personal relief while being bound by societal norms.

Just when I'd thought the swells of transformation had settled, an email from an unfamiliar sender shattered my world. Out of nowhere, a message from my long-lost father, Hazim, arrived, after twenty-three years of abandonment.

A simple e-greeting card unearthed questions that I'd pushed to the back of my mind. The unexpected message appeared on my screen and memories of my early trauma flooded my thoughts like a torrential downpour.

Hazim's name flickered in my mind like a fluorescent light bulb in a never-ending hallway. This cast an eerie glow on the memories I'd long tried to bury.

Despite the trauma inflicted by his actions, I stood firm and confronted the memories that threatened to consume me. I acknowledged the wounds, but I refused to let them define me or dictate my future. The journey toward healing persisted and I was determined to reclaim my narrative and navigate my path. A path I'd hoped would cast away the dark shadows of my past.

Now, as a twenty-eight-year-old responsible adult, there was no room in my life for someone who'd hurt me so severely. The void left by his absence shaped my journey in ways I'd never imagined. I pondered the thought thousands of times: *If Hazim had been around, would I have ever met Isaac, Trustworthy Monster #1?*

Months went by, and my tenacity had a hold on me. I needed to find the answers to these long-standing questions. I re-opened Hazim's email.

When I clicked on the provided link, it transported me to a website called "Blue Mountain," where an animated greeting card awaited. Colors danced on the screen and a heartfelt message played out before my eyes. He appeared eager to connect, but I remained skeptical.

I stared at the screen for what felt like hours before I replied:

Hi Hazim,

I was surprised to hear from you after twenty-three years! I would like to get to know my father; however, I am owed some explanations before I make a final decision on whether I want to start a relationship with you or not. There are also some things about my lifestyle that need to be known and accepted before I agree to meet with you. I don't want, nor do I need, to be hurt by you again. You hurt me very badly and were never there for me. I lived my life without a father…and for what?

The first thing I need to know is where have you been for the last twenty-three years? I don't mean location because I know you have been in California. I mean, why have you been absent from my life for so long with no letters, no birthday cards, no NOTHING? Please don't put the blame on my mom, she has never said anything bad about you. In fact, she'd always told us that if you wanted to find us, it was easy. Which, as I have discovered later in life, is absolutely true. There are not too many people with the last name of Niami, and we have always been listed. Wakim found me, as you know. So, first and foremost, I deserve an explanation of where you have been all my life and why you deprived me of my right to know my biological father?

We should take this one step at a time, and I would appreciate communication only via email. I am not completely comfortable with this yet. I am glad you contacted me, and perhaps this can work out after a lot of explaining.

PS Why is your email address abunameer? I learned from Wakim that in the Arabic tradition you name your email address after your firstborn child. Shouldn't it be abupatrick, considering he is your eldest son?

Your daughter, Delicia

I felt a weight of apprehension and anticipation. I sent the email and sought answers but never expected a connection. I checked my inbox for years, but no response came. He disappeared, yet again. This left me, once more, with a lingering feeling of emptiness and being unlovable.

In times like these, I felt fortunate to have Cow by my side, my beloved companion. She'd traveled with me near and far. Cow even accompanied me on my life-changing second try at a new life in Switzerland. She enjoyed her time there on the farm. I found it quite entertaining to watch her roll in the hay and play with the horses.

Our move to Boulder Creek instilled a security that allowed me to grant Cow the freedom to wander, reminiscent of her days on the farm. Daily, when I arrived, the sounds of meows would greet me. Cow awaited her snuggles and love and would often beckon me out of my car.

Whenever I came home, if she wasn't right next to me, she was busy catching birds and mice or frolicking amongst the redwoods. Cow loved it here. The minute I walked in the door, if not sooner, she would jump, leap, or bound into my arms. It was seldom necessary for me to call her name.

One afternoon after finishing my daily errands, I arrived home and Cow was nowhere to be found. Terror consumed me. *Where is she?* No matter how much I called, she never came.

In my fevered searched for my loving companion, the echoes of my voice resonated alongside the fear that swelled inside me. Something was critically wrong.

I rushed to the street, and I thought the worst. Once I noticed it was unobstructed, relief set in, since she never ventured beyond our two cross streets. I inspected her usual hiding spots, but she remained elusive. I walked along the driveway to the other side of my car next to the trash cans.

Just off the dirt road, I spotted a small black-and-white ball on the ground. My knees buckled beneath me, and my heart cracked like a shattered window. My baby lay just off the street, and I didn't know if she was alive or dead.

I approached with caution. When I knew for certain it was Cow, I swiftly made my way to her. I knelt down next to her and felt her body. It was stiff; rigor mortis had already set in.

In a panic, I turned her over and thought about giving her CPR. This was my first experience with the death of something I'd held profoundly close. My only other gut-wrenching experience with mortality happened when Cow's five precious kittens were killed by fleas.

Tears streamed down my cheeks, and I scooped Cow into my arms. I sobbed uncontrollably. My best friend and longtime companion was gone.

I let out a howl to the sky that shook the fierce redwoods to their roots. I sprinted back to the main house. My mind reeled, and I had no idea what to do. Instinctively, I called my mother.

Unable to speak from the pain, anguish and tears, I sobbed. I tried my best to utter words.

"Mom!" I cried out.

She always knew when something was wrong.

"What? What, baby? What is it?"

"Cow! Cow is dead!" I struggled to get out the words.

Within milliseconds, she said, "I'm on my way."

I held my stiff cat in my arms for hours. I sat on the back porch and rocked her until my warmth made her body soft again. I'd never felt anything this painful in my life. Grief completely consumed me.

Mom arrived in two and a half hours from her home in Colfax, a small town north of Sacramento. Though the drive normally took at least three hours, she rushed in the front door and called out my name long before I'd expected.

She heard my cries and approached me. I sobbed with my cat still cradled in my arms. Although my roommates were home, nobody else knew what to do.

Mom grabbed a towel and pried Cow's lifeless body from my arms. She set her in a small bed she'd made from a blanket, then embraced me. Her longing to help was futile. I'd just lost what felt like a child to me; in an instant, she was gone.

"I'm so, so, so sorry, honey," Mom repeated as she held me tight.

We sat in silence for a long time while I stared at my cat's lifeless body.

"We have to call the vet."

"Why, Mom? She is dead!" I wailed as my emotions overcame me.

"Do you want to bury her here?"

"No, I want to know what happened. She was lying on the side of the driveway with one drop of blood next to her mouth. Other than that, she looked fine. I'm so confused."

"Will the vet be able to help figure it out?"

"I want them to do an autopsy."

"I'm not sure they can do that on animals," she responded.

"Of course they can, Mom. I need to know what happened."

Once the vet arrived, she promised to have Cow's body back to me within a few days.

Days passed, and my grief grew. I missed my baby; I was dying inside without her. I found myself completely alone after Mom left. Despite having roommates, there was nothing that could fill the void.

After waiting for what felt like weeks, I heard from the vet.

"It appears she was hit by something large. The impact caused internal bleeding."

I had answers, but it didn't help the pain I experienced on such a profound level. The bond Cow and I shared was one-of-a-kind.

Cow's death was the primary factor that prompted me to move out of Boulder Creek. The thought of remaining in the place where we'd created countless memories, and where I lost her, shattered me emotionally; my heart couldn't bear it.

I found a fantastic two-bedroom triplex available in Scotts Valley and knew I had to fill the other room quickly. I approached my friend, Linda, to see if she wanted to move. Luckily, she did. I secured the place for us, and she moved in with me the following month.

Although I ached daily for Cow, I knew the time had come to move on. Within a few weeks, I ventured down to the Santa Cruz County SPCA and found my next feline companion, Blossom. She was also a black-and-white tabby with a fierce attitude.

Jason and I remained close from afar. Once he was diagnosed with AIDS, he relied on a plethora of experimental medications, that appeared to worsen his condition. He had difficulty walking, and he was confined to a wheelchair. Both Jason and I acknowledged that his time was short, but we maintained extraordinary hope for the medication—or at least I did.

One night, while we chatted, he confided in me.

"You know, all of this medication is just making me sicker. Nothing is helping. I think I've decided just to stop taking everything. I feel like I'm slowly being poisoned."

"But, Jason, you have to keep taking the medication or you will die."

"D., I'm going to die anyway, so why not go out feeling good instead of being sick all of the time?"

"Oh, J., please don't talk like that. New medication is always being invented."

"Are you kidding? This is the gay men's disease. Nobody cares about us faggots!"

"Come on, be positive. Please."

"Well, I just wanted you to be one of the first to know. I hope you can support me in my decision."

"Are you serious?" I asked with a bit of selfish disdain. I knew this would be a death sentence for Jason, my closest companion on the planet.

"Yes. You don't understand how sick I've been. I throw up all day. I can't walk, I barely weigh anything, I can't eat… I'm miserable. I think if I stop the medication, I'll feel better."

"And kill yourself," I mumbled under my breath.

"I'm sorry, but it's my life and it's my decision."

I realized I was being selfish and that my real problem was the fear of losing him. In reality, it was his choice.

"Okay, J. I love you so, so much. You are my heart, you know? All I want is to offer my support. I hate that we're so far apart, and we are both so sick; I can't even help you right now because I'm dealing with Crohn's and neck issues. Honestly, I couldn't drive that far even if I wanted to."

"I know, and it sucks."

"Well, I am here from afar, and I love you more than the stars and the moon."

"I love you too," he said. "I'm sorry, and I know it's disappointing, but it's the best thing for me."

"It is what it is. Just know that I'll always be here for you."

This decimated my soul. Jason's choice to stop his medication felt like a death sentence. His decision came immediately after I experienced profound devastation over losing Cow. The concept of human mortality was completely foreign to me, especially when it came to my best friend. The uncertainty of how I would cope consumed me. I didn't want him to suffer from the side effects of his medications, but the thought of losing him wasn't something I could fathom. Jason was my "framily," and it would have been impossible for me to not be supportive of him, whatever his choice, even if it meant death.

A few months passed, and Jason and I spoke often. His health deteriorated, but I still held onto hope.

He now nursed a nagging cough that wasn't going away on top of everything else. At least life was a bit more bearable for him now that he stopped taking his medications. The challenge lied in the fact that his immunity had reached a dangerously low level, and he needed to maintain a state of vigilance.

After a few days of not speaking with him, I became worried. LR maintained a close bond with Jason as well and I assumed she would have information about his whereabouts, so I called her.

"Hey, LR? Have you talked to Jason?"

"Not in a couple of days. Why?"

"Me either, I'm just a little worried," I responded. "I am going to call his dad and see if he has talked to him. His phone just rings and rings, no answering machine. It's weird."

"Good idea. Please keep me posted."

I hung up and tried Jason's dad's number. "Hi John, it's Delicia. Have you talked to Jason lately?" I asked.

"Oh," he responded. "I thought his mom called you, she didn't?"

"No, what is it?" My anticipation grew, afraid something might have happened to him.

"Well, he is in the hospital again."

"For what this time?"

"It's pneumococcal pneumonia or something like that."

"Is it serious?"

"Well, kiddo, I hate to tell you this, but this time he's in hospice."

Tears filled my eyes and intense pain penetrated my soul in a way I'd never felt before. It was like someone was shoving cotton balls down my throat, silencing my words. My body was in shock.

"Delicia, are you there?" John asked.

I coughed in order to catch a breath of air. I mustered out a few words.

"Where is he?"

"He's in Los Angeles at Carl Bean House on West Adams."

"How long are they saying he has?"

"They don't know. They don't think it will be too long."

"Oh my gosh, I'm so sorry, John. I'm here if you need anything."

"I'm okay. Don't worry about me. Worry about Jason. And, hey kiddo, thank you for being so good to my son. You're really something special to him. I want you to know I appreciate the love you've shared."

"I'm going to book a flight down because I can't drive with my neck pain."

"Okay, I'd get here as soon as you can."

Without delay, I called Jason at the facility. I could hear the frailty in his voice, even though he was ecstatic that I reached him.

"Jason, I'm coming down to see you. I will be there in two days."

"You don't have to. I mean, I'd love to see you, but no big deal. I know how sick you've been." He acted as if he weren't dying.

"It's okay," I played along. "I miss you so much and need to see your beautiful face."

"Cool, see you in a couple of days," he said, then hung up.

After our goodbyes, I called LR.

My arrival at the Burbank Airport was different this time. The visit wasn't motivated by happiness or family connections. Rather, it was to say goodbye to my dearest friend in the world. I reminisced about some of the amazing times we'd shared. My eyes filled with tears as I recalled some cherished moments.

We stood strong against our bullies at school; He introduced me to gay town and the bars in Los Angeles; so many adventures. We saw each other through thick and thin. No matter what, Jason and I had each other's backs. He was someone I could always count on. He'd never belittle or abandon me. I had a voice when I was with him. My opinion mattered. There wasn't anything Jason and I couldn't do, so long as we faced it together.

I stood in line for my car rental, and a myriad of thoughts filled my mind. I was overcome with fear in addition to sadness. It wasn't just the uncertainty that gripped me, but the stark reality that Jason would be the first person I knew who would die. There were some kids from high school we lost to drunk driving, but they were merely acquaintances. In comparison, this was my best friend, and he owned half my heart. Frankly, I wasn't sure how I would live without him. I'd just lost Cow. How was it possible that I could lose Jason only a few short months later?

On my way to hospice, I stopped by Baskin-Robbins. He had little time left and one of Jason's all-time favorite things was "Daiquiri Ice" ice cream.

I, personally, found the flavor to be peculiar. However, I made a quick detour to grab a pint.

Jason was overjoyed to see me when I arrived, and I gave a hug to both his mom and dad. For the first time since I'd known Jason, his parents were together in the same room. It was odd, but it made this so much more real.

I gave him a gentle hug. It was evident to me that he weighed around eighty pounds or so. He hadn't been eating, yet he was enthusiastic about the ice cream. He tried a bite, but his body was being consumed by the disease from the inside, which resulted in mouth ulcers. Therefore, anything he ate caused him pain, even cold ice cream.

My heartache intensified. I knew this was it. This was, most certainly, the last time I'd ever see his sweet face.

After I visited Jason for several hours and we shared some intimate and heartfelt conversations, I hugged him for the last time, and tears streamed down my cheeks.

"I love you, Jason," I said and smiled as I walked out the door.

"Love you too…" He barely got his words out before he nodded off to sleep.

His dad called me only a few days later to inform me that Jason had passed. All I could do was cry. I cried and cried and cried. I cried like I'd never cried before. Other than Cow, I'd never faced the loss of someone close, and it was gut-wrenching.

Jason always said things come in threes, and I pondered the thought. *I'd lost Cow and now I'd lost him.* I sure hoped he wasn't right. I wasn't confident in my ability to deal with a third occurrence of this magnitude.

Not My Circus

APRIL 16, 2001

In 2001, about a year after Linda and I moved to our Scotts Valley triplex, Mom and I were supposed to take a vacation together for her spring break. My mother was a special education teacher at Lincoln High School in Lincoln, California. We postponed the trip since neither my mom nor I had money to spend on a vacation.

A few years prior, Nile purchased tickets for Mom and me to go to Jamaica together. This served as our first real vacation since I became an adult. Mom and I always lived paycheck to paycheck.

We had a remarkably close relationship. Of course, she got on my nerves, as most moms do, but she was my rock. Whenever I needed advice or

I wanted to bounce something off of someone, I'd call my mom. If I was sad, lonely, happy, or overwhelmed, I'd call my mom. Mom knew everything about me, including the fact that I remained a steadfast pot smoker.

Often, we'd talk on the phone and I'd smoke my weed. Mom would always remark, "Stop smoking that shit while you are on the phone with your mother!"

"Sorry, Mom," I'd say, and then I'd put down the pipe.

Neither of us had been to Jamaica before. To me, Jamaica meant one thing: high times. I was over the moon to be going to the country where Bob Marley was born and the religion of Jah flourished. It seemed like a dream. I made it a point to talk to her about this before our trip.

"Mom, I know you don't like me to smoke, but when we are in Jamaica, we have to find some pot for me. It's Jamaica, you know… when in Rome."

"I don't know if that's such a good idea honey. I think we should just stay at the resort and enjoy the activities there. According to what I've heard, Negril can be dangerous."

"Oh, Mom, don't be silly. It's no more dangerous than here."

"I dunno, honey."

"My neighbor told me about this place called Mrs. Brown's. It's in downtown Negril and you can get pot brownies and joints there. Can we go please, Mom?" I begged.

"We'll see."

Once we arrived, I pressured my mother for permission to venture out on my own to see Mrs. Brown's. After I continuously pestered her, she agreed to come along with me. Mom established connections with everyone she encountered during our trip. She made friends with some Jamaican guys on the beach, who climbed up a tree to cut down a fresh coconut for her. Then, I watched her dance like I'd never imagined. Mom also got a complete head of cornrows braided by a girl on that same beach.

April 16, 2001

The highly anticipated day came: We set off for Mrs. Brown's, where my authentic Jamaican experience awaited.

Along the way, we ran into several people, some friendly, others not. Mom was oblivious. I began to worry about our safety when two guys approached us.

I'd had my fair share of dealing with men when I'd traveled to Greece, and giant red caution flags waved above their heads.

Mom chatted away with them like they were long-lost friends, while I freaked out internally.

"Mom, we have to go, we are late for our appointment," I pushed.

"What are you babbling about?" she quipped. "I'm making friends here," Mom said as she giggled.

"Mom, really, we have to go now," I stressed.

"But we was jus gonna treat yo muther to a nice Jamaican-style lunch," one guy said.

"Thank you, but we are on our way to eat now, and we have to go," I sternly stated, then I grabbed Mom's hand and pulled her toward me.

"Eh... where you goin'? Come back, we was just gettin' started," the other guy shouted as we hurried away.

"What's your problem?" Mom asked as she yanked her hand free from mine.

"Mom, those guys were dangerous. Believe me, they didn't want to just have lunch with you."

"Don't be ridiculous, honey," she replied. "They were just nice guys trying to show us a fun time. Why do you have to be so uptight?"

"Mom, just come on. We have to get there before they close."

We approached Mrs. Brown's, about five blocks down the street.

"Welcome to Mrs. Brown's, where you can get whatcha want when you want," he said.

"Thank you," I replied as he showed us the way in.

There was regular food on the menu as well—coconut rice, jerk chicken and other delicious options. My eyes were drawn to the "special cakes" on the menu.

"What are these 'special cakes' you got here?" I asked the nice man behind the counter.

"Dey are special to Jamaica, and Mrs. Brown make them herself with herbal butter."

He was coy about it. I found out, fairly quickly, that the legal status of weed wasn't what I'd thought it would be here.

"Great, I will take one of those, please."

"Can I get you any ting else, ma'am?" he asked.

Mom interjected, "make it two, please."

"What? Mom!" I squealed.

"When in Rome, right?" she replied.

"Alright, Mom, awesome!"

It both shocked and made me proud that my mom was willing to try a pot brownie. She had smoked weed in college, but that kept her high for three days—and she hated it. I always thought it had to have been laced, as I'd never experienced staying high that long from weed.

We decided to wait until the next day to eat our brownies and have a fun experience together.

The next morning, I woke a bit earlier than Mom did and headed down to the buffet for breakfast. I enjoyed my bagel and scrambled eggs when she approached the table. Mom positioned herself beside me and remained silent.

"Mom, did you want to get some food? The waffles are great."

"Maybe later, honey."

"What are you going to do today? You already have your bathing suit on?" I inquired.

"I'm going snorkeling with a group."

"Oh, cool, have fun." My plan was to do my own thing during the day and then reunite with her for dinner. This was our normal routine thus far while on vacation.

"I have a question for you, though," she said in a clandestine whisper.

April 16, 2001

"What is it?" I whispered back.

"How long does it take for that 'cake' stuff to affect you?"

I reared my head back and my eyes popped out of my head like a firefly.

"Why, Mom? What did you do?"

"Oh, nothing. I ate it for breakfast, so I was just wondering."

"The whole thing?" I strained to keep my voice down.

"Yeah, why?" she responded nonchalantly.

"Mom, it could take hours to work. You weren't supposed to eat the whole thing, only a bite! You shouldn't go snorkeling. We can stay here and I'll make sure you will be okay."

"Oh, don't be ridiculous, I will be fine. I don't feel anything," she said as she got up from the table and sauntered off for her trip.

"Mom, be careful," I shouted as she walked away.

This concerned me. It was difficult to ascertain the quantity of THC in a brownie and the intensity of its impact.

I waited anxiously for my mother to arrive back at the hotel. Relief set in once I realized she was okay. Fear turned into wonderment and a bit of excitement.

"So, how was it?" I probed.

"Well," she said, "I don't know if it was the sun or the ocean or what. I'd be talking to people, and in the middle of my conversation, I'd completely forget what I was saying. It was odd—I'd draw a complete blank. Over and over again."

"Mom, you were stoned," I responded.

"No, I don't think I was stoned. It wasn't anything like I'd felt in college."

"Whatever you smoked in college must have been laced with something, Mom. Weed isn't that strong."

"No, it was fine. I am starving though, and exhausted. I just want to eat everything at the buffet and sleep for hours."

"Yeah, Mom, you're stoned," I mumbled as I chuckled my way to the buffet. This experience with my mom bonded us unlike I ever imagined. I felt disappointed she didn't wait for me, but, on the plus side, I now believed that she understood me a little better after her "special cake" experience.

My academic years unfolded, and I worked diligently and graduated as a double major in both sociology and legal studies. The legal studies major required me to complete a thesis to obtain my degree. As a result, I spent a substantial amount of time composing an intricate thesis on *The Concept of Evil in Murder.*

Once I completed my thesis, I was allowed to walk for graduation. My commencement ceremony was in June 2000. Mom, Ron, Nile, Patrick, Issac, Gertrude, Tommy and my entire family came to celebrate with me. This was one time Nile prioritized me, and I was grateful.

During this time, Nile was vice president of a motion picture distribution company owned by Marvin, his Big Brother from Big Brothers Big Sisters of America. Nile jet-set the world and produced film after film. *The Watcher*, which starred Keanu Reeves, was the first film, out of the thirteen he'd made, that found success. This film was released into theaters in September 2000.

Nile made a name for himself. He was flying high on the one percent band wagon, while Mom and I both struggled. I'd just claimed bankruptcy, and Mom had difficulty paying her taxes. Nile was kind enough to send us on vacation to Jamaica together a few years prior, but neither of us wanted to ask for his help again. We were both too proud and didn't want to deal with the incessant way he threw any kindness he expended toward us back in our faces.

We also knew our financial burdens were of no concern to him. Nile lived his mega-indulgent life while we struggled. Both mom and I felt like he'd earned his money. That gave him the right to spend it however he wanted; we had done nothing to help in his get-rich endeavor. This allowed me to justify his behavior in my mind. Mom and I both thought it best to take our vacation in the summer, when we hopefully, could afford it—on our own.

April 16, 2001

I had a Southwest Airlines' free ticket voucher coming up for expiration and used it to take a solo vacation instead of the trip mom and I had planned. I needed a quick getaway. In order to reach Maine on Southwest Airlines, I had to fly into New Hampshire, the nearest airport. From New Hampshire, I rented a car to get me to Maine. I drove so that I could see the entire lower half of the state.

I'd never driven on the East Coast before, and I discovered that getting lost wasn't too difficult. Somehow, I ended up in Massachusetts. I took this trip before Google Maps existed, and cell phones were still a mind-boggling phenomenon. I pulled out the folded map I'd picked up from the DMV prior to my trip. Upon exiting the freeway in Boston, I parked and figured out my bearings. Finally, I was headed in the right direction, north.

Once I arrived in Maine, I loved it. The food tasted incredible, especially the affordable lobster. The people I met were extremely amiable, and I made a few new friends along the way. I traveled from Portsmouth, New Hampshire, to Eastport, Maine and back again.

Maine was a very welcoming place for the LGBTQ+ community. I researched some local lesbian bars and visited one along the way. The moment I walked in, I felt accepted. Even though nobody knew my name, it felt like I'd walked onto the set of *Cheers*. The people were warm and received me with smiles and hellos. The experience greatly differed from the Michigan Womyn's Music Festival I had attended years prior.

I met two amazing women that day and stayed with them for the evening. We talked about life in California and everything in between. Oddly enough, I felt comfortable. They made me feel secure even though we were strangers. A constant fear played in the back of my mind. I always anticipated something negative would inevitably happen. This level of comfort with strangers wasn't something I'd experienced often.

The reception I received in Maine had a familiar vibe. It reminded me of my time in Switzerland.

This trip immensely improved my self-esteem. I was anxious to go back to Santa Cruz and embrace this newfound self-love.

After I stopped for gas, I realized it was Easter Sunday. While the sun dawned on the West Coast, it was too early to call my mom.

When we landed in Kansas City, I was one of the few passengers who didn't have to exit the plane. This was a brief layover en route to San Jose, California.

Once they allowed cell phone usage, I called my mother. The phone rang several times before she answered in a very sulky tone.

"Hi, Mama, happy Easter!" I expressed with enthusiasm.

"Happy Easter," she said in an Eeyore-like manner.

"Mom, what's wrong?" I inquired. I could hear the sadness in her voice.

"Nothing," she stated.

"Mom, you don't sound well. Is everything okay?" I asked again with concern.

We only had a few minutes to talk, and I tried to lighten the mood.

"Mom, I'm in Kansas City. The plane stopped to let people off and I didn't have to change flights. I'm calling you from the runway, isn't that cool? I should be in San Jose later tonight."

"Great," she responded drearily.

"Mom, what's wrong?" I asked again.

"Nothing, I'll talk to you when you are home, okay, honey?"

I heard a profound sorrow in her voice, and my heart broke. I wasn't certain, but I had a suspicion about the potential problem. Mom and I were best friends and we talked about everything. A few days before I left, she shared with me some serious intimacy problems she and my stepfather were having. I knew she was sad about a lot of things, but she longed for her husband to be attracted to her. Mom didn't feel desired by him, and she needed some affection and love.

I'd made some suggestions to her about romantic things to try, like a bubble bath with candles, rose petals, or getting dressed up.

"Did you try the stuff with Ron?" I asked.

"Yes, but nothing worked," she sulked.

"Don't give up, Mom."

"It's okay, honey, I will talk with you when you get home, okay?"

"Sure, okay, Mama. Happy Easter. I love you."

Mom and I never hung up the phone without an "I love you." Before my brother and I were kidnapped and taken to Baghdad for a year, Mom never told us "I love you." Nor did she give us many hugs or kisses. While we were gone, she saw a psychologist. The therapist emphasized the importance of expressing love verbally and physically upon our return. Mom took this matter to heart. After my brother and I were back in California; I can't recall a time she didn't express her love when we said goodbye, either over the phone or in person.

Yet, on this particular day, she offered no response.

"Mom... I love you," I said, slower and louder, to make sure she heard me.

"Okay, honey, call me when you get home," she replied.

Completely puzzled, I said again, clearly and methodically, "Mom, I love you!"

Finally, she said, "I love you too, baby. Please let me know you get home safely."

"Okay, will do."

We ended the call, and the rest of the day appeared uneventful. I arrived home just after midnight and knew Mom usually woke up early for school. I chose not to wake her on the final day of her spring break. Instead, I decided to try her the following day.

I didn't think much about this sunny sixteenth day of April 2001. Much like any other day, I headed to work. It was a Monday, and I knew Mom would be at school. Therefore, I figured it was best to try her later.

When I arrived home, I called my mom. Her answering machine emitted an odd sound, as if submerged in water. Mom's "Chatty Cathy" message was her attempt to sound as sweet as her childhood doll, but now it was extremely distorted.

Something felt off. There was a shiver in my bones.

Linda had tropical fish and always took amazing care of them. We chatted while she cleaned her fish tank. We discussed the breathtaking scenery of Maine when my phone rang.

With caller ID, I easily recognized the caller as my aunt.

"Hi, auntie," I said. "How's it going?"

She didn't answer my question or even acknowledge my presence. Instead, she asked, "do you have a roommate?"

Bewildered, I responded, "Yes, why?"

"Is she there?" my aunt replied.

"Umm, yes, but what is happening, auntie?" I demanded.

"Can I please talk to your roommate?" She responded gravely.

"What? Why?" I questioned with confusion.

"Please, Delicia. Can I please just talk to your roommate?" she asked again in a monotone voice.

I held my phone out to Linda, who was elbow-deep in fish sludge, and I stated with a confused look, "she wants to talk to you."

"Huh?" Linda responded. "Okay, let me go wash this fish gunk off my hands."

"Hold on, Auntie, she is washing her hands."

April 16, 2001

"I'll hold," again in a blasé voice, without inquiring about me or saying anything. She sat in silence while she waited for Linda.

I found this entire conversation strange. I handed the phone to Linda when she came back into the living room. Linda grabbed it, then walked into the restroom and shut the door.

I settled on the back of the couch, baffled. *What in the world is this about?* I'd wondered.

About a minute and a half later, Linda returned with a deadpan look on her face and handed me the phone again. I found myself perplexed and uncertain about anything at that moment; but I knew something giant had happened.

I reached for the phone and placed it to my ear. With extreme trepidation, I spoke. "Heeellooo?"

"Are you sitting down?" My aunt questioned.

"Why? What is going on?" I responded with a bit more irritation.

"A homeless man broke into your mother's house last night, and beat her to death."

"What? Shut the fuck up. Fuck you. Why would you say something like that?" At that moment, I heard my brother's voice in the background, and that was the crushing blow. I knew my mother was gone.

Nile grabbed the phone from my aunt's hand, and exclaimed, "Delicia, Delicia, Delicia!" I heard the anguish in his voice.

"Nile, what's going on?"

"Delicia, what auntie said happened. You need to get on a plane now and come down here."

"What? Are you kidding me? Mom's dead? Mom's dead? Shut the fuck up, why are you doing this to me? How could you say something like that? You're an asshole!"

"Delicia, please, we are all having a tough time with this. I booked you a flight on American Airlines. It leaves in an hour. Can you make it?"

"You're kidding! This can't be real. This can't be happening!"

"Delicia, listen to me. I need you to get on a plane and come to LA immediately. Can you get to the airport in an hour?" Nile asked.

"Yes!" I cried out and abruptly hung up the phone. My mind was in a complete daze. I couldn't believe this. This wasn't true!

Linda noticed my astonishment, ran to my room and put together a duffle bag of clothes. She grabbed my hand and pulled me out the door.

"Come on, Delicia, let's go. If you want to make the flight, we need to go now."

We drove to the airport. Disbelief and anger was all I felt. *Could this be true? This couldn't have been true. My mother was so strong. Someone beat her to death? Was this all a ploy? Perhaps Mom left and faked her death because she was so sad?*

That is what I'd hoped. It was far-fetched. But, when someone close to you dies in such a sudden and tragic manner, you reach to the farthest corners of your mind to find any possible alternative imaginable.

I'd never felt so numb. There were no words. *Why would they lie to me?* I wondered. *How can they do this to me? Why would they say such horrible things about my mother?* Varied thoughts raced through my mind, like a scratched vinyl record that repeated endlessly.

Upon arrival, my emotions shifted from disbelief to fear. Nothing could stop the madness in my head.

It took us about forty minutes to get to the airport. Therefore, I had fifteen short minutes to check in and get on the plane. Nile was a big shot by this time and got pretty much anything he wanted, whenever he wanted.

Before I'd hung up the phone with Nile, he'd explicitly stated, "I talked to the airline, and they understand what happened and are holding the plane for you. Don't worry, I promise you will get on the plane."

The lady at the front counter checked me in promptly and I rushed through security. Luckily, the airport was deserted.

It took a while to make my way from security to gate twenty-three, where my plane was scheduled to depart. I ran as fast as possible. I had to make it onto that plane. The next plane to Los Angeles didn't leave for hours.

I rushed for the gate and observed a few individuals and the attendant closing the jetway door.

April 16, 2001

"Wait!" I cried out and sprinted toward the door that closed right before my eyes.

"Please don't shut the door! I have to get on the plane!" I shouted in a panic.

She obviously heard my screams, but she purposely closed the door.

In an extremely haughty tone, she said, "I'm sorry, boarding is closed."

At the worst moment in my entire life, I pleaded with as much grace as possible; "Ma'am, my mother was just murdered, and I have to go to LA to see my brother and aunt. I can't sit here for hours by myself right now dealing with this."

She responded like a robot, "Sorry but once the door is shut, we cannot open it. You're going to have to wait for the next flight."

"Are you kidding me?" I screamed. "I just told you my mother was murdered—murdered!"

In a cold robotic tone, she reiterated, "I can't open the door once it's closed, ma'am."

I was so upset and dumbfounded. I couldn't believe the power trip this woman was on. She made a noticeable effort to wreck my nerves even more than they already were. And at the worst possible moment in my life.

Without much thought, I blurted out, "Well I certainly hope your mom doesn't get beaten to death, and you get stuck in an airport by some power-hungry bitch like you."

While I awaited the next flight to Los Angeles, I called Patrick with the horrific news. Three hours dragged on as I pondered how my mother was savagely killed. *My mommy, my best friend, my confidant, my rock... gone! This can't be...*

Nile and my aunt waited for me at LAX. Supposedly, we were going to figure out how to deal with this tragedy together, as a family.

After several grueling hours, I arrived and was greeted by my brother and aunt. We went to Nile and his wife's house to regroup, since they lived closest to LAX.

Upon arrival, Nile led me to the kitchen, where he opened a drawer that revealed a tray with a few joints.

"I figured you would want to smoke, so we have some."

"No, I'm okay. I need to deal with this sober. It doesn't seem real."

My response shocked me.

That night, I slept in their living room. Nile and his wife never kept their house locked. I was terrified the entire night. I felt uneasy about requesting permission from Nile to lock the doors. His house was fifteen thousand square feet. There were far too many doors to sneak around and lock. Nile often accused me of being dramatic and overreacting whenever I tried to ensure my safety in his presence. Therefore, I locked the sliding glass door and any others near me, but I knew the rest of the house was literally, an open door.

I'd been terrified of sleeping next to patio type doors since my chilling encounter with Richard Ramirez, the "Night Stalker." Ramirez, the Southern California serial killer, invaded our home through the sliding glass door when I was thirteen and jerked off in front of me. This happened just prior to his first kill, and I'm not sure why he spared my life, but I am sure grateful he did.

The following night, I thought I'd be more comfortable at my aunt's house. She'd already offered to let me stay with her, so I accepted. I hoped that we could support one another, considering the enormous loss we'd both faced.

In addition to dealing with her sister's death, two days prior to my mother's demise, my uncle left my aunt. According to my aunt, things were going smoothly between them. She had no idea why he would leave and she believed they were a happy couple. His departure shocked her. I was sad for my aunt; I wanted to be there for her and hoped she would do the same for me.

Unfortunately, and much to my dismay, my stay was not supportive or loving. In fact, it was the total opposite. She treated me with a cold and calculated demeanor. I did my best to give her the benefit of the doubt. Nonetheless, I struggled to find ways to handle my intense emotions. Internally, I held a mix of anger, disbelief, sadness, grief and disappointment. It felt like I'd lost my mind and I desperately needed to confide in someone. I've never been a fan of talk therapy. However, at this moment, I recognized the need to speak to someone before I exploded—or even worse, imploded!

I searched through the phone book for the local Kaiser Permanente, grabbed the phone, and dialed.

"Who are you calling?" My aunt yelled as she descended the stairs.

"I'm gonna call Kaiser because I need to talk to somebody. I'm going crazy right now; I have a million thoughts and feelings."

"Good luck," she replied in a snarky tone while she rolled her eyes back into her head. "You're not going to be able to get in. I called two days ago when Dennis left me, and they wouldn't give me an appointment."

It puzzled me that she would equate her husband leaving with my mother's brutal murder. Regardless of how she treated me, I knew it was vital for me to make the call. To my aunt's chagrin, I managed to get an appointment. It was in an hour, and I needed a ride.

"Auntie, I got an appointment. Can you please take me to Kaiser?" I asked.

"No, I will not give you a ride! I want you to get the fuck out of my house!" she replied.

Complete and utter shock overcame me! I was speechless.

My aunt lamented, "you are trying to take the place of the Laurie Niami drama queen in this family, and you are always trying to one-up me."

I wasn't sure whether I'd kept my jaw from hitting the floor or not. At that moment, all I wanted to do was to leave. I, once again, felt unloved and completely unwanted.

She'd kicked me out because I wanted to get some therapy the day after my mother was killed! Anytime I tried to take care of myself in this lifetime, I wasn't allowed to do so without some family member disowning me. This wasn't the first time I'd felt abandoned and unloved by my family, nor would it be the last.

I found a park down the street from my aunt's house and held my duffle bag while I waited for Gertrude to arrive.

It was unfathomable to me that simply because I wanted to see a therapist, I became the family's new drama queen. My aunt made it worse when she claimed I tried to take my slain mother's place and that everything I'd done was a deliberate attempt to "one-up" her. To top it off, she kicked me out—onto the streets, three hundred miles from home, with no mode of transportation!

After this horrific trip I'd taken in order to be "consoled" by family, I wanted to get back to Santa Cruz where I actually felt loved.

Sadly, I was only home for about a day before my stepfather, Ron, asked me to come and help him.

"I need your help, Delicia. I am stuck on the couch with this cast, and my emotions are all over the place. Could you come help me sort through some of your mother's things?"

Ron recently had hip replacement surgery, and his entire right leg remained in a cast.

"Of course, Ron," I replied, without a second thought about myself or what my needs were. Instead, I packed another bag and hit the road.

The drive was one of horror and anguish. *How would I handle it once I arrived at my mother's house and she wasn't there?* I stayed strong for Ron. This was the only way to get through it. *Why exactly am I doing this for him when he hasn't ever really done anything for me?* So many unanswered questions flooded my mind. I needed answers, so I continued onward.

Mom and Ron lived about a half mile away from their closest neighbor. I maneuvered the desolate dirt road, and clouds of dust enveloped my car. I pulled over as I was on the verge of arriving at my mother's house, the one she had customized for herself. Mom strategically oriented her office bedroom toward the train tracks, which allowed her to watch it pass by. She'd found pinwheels that were rainbow colored and about five feet tall and placed them by the tracks to catch the wind without toppling over.

April 16, 2001

Whenever a train passed, Mom would run outside, and wave to the strangers who passed by; she'd watch with delight as the pinwheels spun in circles. Occasionally, I was fortunate enough to be on the phone with her during these moments. These glimpses into my mother's world allowed me to view a more carefree side of her. It was like a time-machine that brought my mother back to her joyful eight-year-old self.

Mom suffered from asthma from the time she was small. Because of her severe allergies, she wasn't able to own pets since they made it hard for her to breathe. When I was seven, I got a puppy. The dog was a black Labrador, so I decided to call him Blackie. I kept this puppy for about three days before Mom got too sick and we found him a new home.

When my mother moved to Sacramento, she befriended her neighbor's dog and miraculously wasn't allergic to him. Mom fell in love, and when her neighbor got sick, she offered to take the dog in.

Fast-forward a few years and several homes later: My mother, who was deathly allergic to dogs, now possessed not one, not two, but six dogs—no asthma inhaler needed! Mom's dogs meant everything to her. They were fantastic watchdogs, and whenever anyone approached the house, they'd bark like crazy. At times, it was quite scary.

The prior year, for Mother's Day 2000, I surprised Mom and arrived with a bouquet of balloons and flowers. While I visited, someone got lost and ventured up to Mom and Ron's house for directions. Theirs was the only house within a half mile. There were few alternatives for help. Ron fumed with anger when the car approached. The dogs barreled outside and barked while they jumped on the car doors. This intimidated the ladies, who were evidently just lost.

"Mom, what is going on?" I inquired with curiosity.

"Just leave it," she snapped.

"Huh? What do you mean, Mom? Ron is being so cruel to those ladies. Clearly, they are just lost."

"Just leave it," she said again. "He has been like this lately. He is so rude and mean to anyone and everyone. Frankly, I am getting tired of it."

Ron and I were cordial to each other but never had a close relationship, so I just let it go.

My mind reeled, as the memories flooded back. The swirls of dust on the road enveloped my car and it felt suffocating, like I couldn't breathe. I wasn't sure how I'd continue. I reminded myself I needed to push forward to support my stepfather.

I told myself to take calm, deep breaths. Although I'd never experienced a panic attack, the act of breathing seemed to have prevented what felt like the onset of one.

Once I regained my composure after a few minutes, I carried on up the dirt road.

Yellow police tape surrounded the house. It read in giant block letters: "CRIME SCENE DO NOT CROSS." It was too real for me now. I somberly paced around their house, my anxiety heightened with every step. The dogs were incessant barkers. They saw it was me and didn't approach. Instead, they lay on the porch, and were clearly depressed.

Ron yelled from inside the house, "Delicia, is that you?"

He was in the process of recovery from his week-long hospitalization following the attack. My mother's killer, Jay Conrad Johnson, not only took her life but also faced charges of attempted murder on my stepfather. Upon his hospital admission, Ron's scalp was detached from his skull. If he hadn't been such a large man, he likely wouldn't have made it.

"Yeah, just give me a minute," I yelled from the front as I paced back and forth near the crime scene tape. I didn't want to pass the police tape. I had no desire to go inside the house and see where my mother was bludgeoned. But I had to forge ahead, just like everything else I'd dealt with prior to this point. This was just another tragedy I had to deal with.

Holding back my tears, I knelt beneath the crime scene tape, I stepped onto the concrete path that led to Mom and Ron's residence. I felt a powerful presence. A heavy weight pressed down on my shoulders. It wasn't merely the tears that pooled or the stress and anxiety I felt. It was a presence beyond this existence. I sensed that my mom hadn't crossed over yet. I'm not sure how I knew this, but I knew.

I walked into the living room, where the crime took place, my stepfather sat on the couch. His leg was elevated and a large gauze bandage covered almost his entire head and face. Red splotches indicated where the stitches were.

Making an effort to stay calm, I said, "hi, Ron, how are you doing?" in the most empathetic tone I could muster.

He was as depressed as the dogs. He'd just lost his wife and partner of seventeen years and witnessed the violent killing himself.

I approached and gave him a gentle hug.

"Have a seat," he implored as he gestured to the space on the couch next to him.

I noticed a large patch of carpet was missing from the floor. It was approximately two-foot square. I stared at the patch and observed the dark-colored stains exposed on the concrete that resembled old blood.

"What is this?" I asked earnestly.

"That is where your mother was killed," he replied with a morose tone.

"What the hell, Ron? Why is this just cut out, and what are the stains? Is that her blood? I can't sit here anymore." Hastily, I left.

I got into my car and slammed the door. I struggled to recall how to breathe. A few minutes later, Ron hobbled out the door with his walker.

I stepped out of the car to help him. I knew I had to handle this, since he didn't have anyone other than my mother. He had two daughters from a previous marriage. The closest one lived in Reno, the other in Los Angeles. Neither of them were involved in his life. My mother and I were all this man had, and as much as I wanted to melt into molten lava, that was not an option. I remained strong knowing that this was what my mother would have wanted, I felt compelled to support and help Ron as much as possible.

I avoided sitting in that spot on the couch until about four days into my stay. An unseen force guided me to the concrete patch stained with my mother's blood. I gazed at it for what seemed like an eternity.

It felt like ages before I found my voice. "What happened?"

"Well," Ron began, "I was watching Imus in the Morning and had just gotten my coffee. It was about 5 a.m. I heard someone trying to get in the back door. Obviously, it wasn't easy for me to move, so I paused the TV. The dogs weren't barking, and I thought maybe I was just hearing things."

I listened intently to his words.

"Suddenly I saw a man in the house, and he was holding a stick. He rushed over to me and beat me on the head. I called out, 'Laurie, help me!'—and he kept hitting me. I covered my head, but he just kept beating me. I cried out again, a bit louder, since your mother was sleeping: 'Laurie, there is someone in the house! Please help me!'

"Your mother came out from the bedroom. She was rubbing her eyes in an attempt to discern what was happening. Once she saw him beating me, she ran toward us and jumped on his back. She hit him with her fists and tried to get him off of me. He turned around and cold-cocked her, I think he knocked her out with one punch. He hit her in the face, and she went flying. She hit her head on the ground and she was knocked out."

"I watched him pick up the wooden TV tray and smash it on her face. Then he ripped the lamp out of the wall, wrapped the cord around his hands as he came toward me. 'God sent me to kill you motherfuckers,' he proclaimed and I knew he wanted to kill me. Something came over me and I was able to get to him and pull his jacket over his head. That's when he ran out of the house. I crawled over to your mother, and had to hold my scalp on my head. I prayed she was okay. When I reached her, I knew she was dead."

"What?" I was more riddled with questions now than I was prior to his account of the crimes. "Wait a minute, did you know this guy? How did he find

April 16, 2001

this place? This makes no sense. Why would he pick this house to come into randomly, and why didn't the dogs bark?"

It sounded way too strange.

"I can't answer those questions; I don't know," he replied. "All I know is that after he left, I immediately called 9-1-1. And that my wife died right in front of me." Tears welled up as he spoke of the incident.

"So, who was this guy? How did they catch him?"

"Apparently after he left here, he walked three miles down the hill to a pay phone and called his mother. Then the detectives said that he walked to the convenience store and was behaving oddly, which is why the cashier contacted the sheriff. He already left by the time they arrived, but witnesses reported seeing him headed across the bridge to Rosie's Diner. They arrested him while he was having breakfast."

"What the fuck? Are you joking me? This son of a bitch killed my mother then walked to a pay phone and called his mother? Then goes to buy cigarettes and have breakfast? What the hell?" The entire account left me both enraged and baffled.

"Are you sure you didn't know him, Ron? Did you have a fight with him or something? I know how you get."

"What?" He quipped. "Absolutely not. I didn't know him. I've never seen him before in my life."

A surge of anger overcame me. "I swear, Ron, if I ever find out you had anything to do with my mother's death, I will kill you with my bare hands. I don't give a shit how big and strong you seem."

I needed to leave—immediately. I paced in circles around the house and pondered how this happened. Perhaps I'd never know, but I was tenacious and I needed to find out.

I left without a word to Ron, certain this made him wonder if I'd return or not. I drove, and my anger fumed like an erupting volcano. The need for answers burned within me, and I wanted them now! I wasn't sure where I was going or why, but I had to unravel this mystery. *Why would a stranger enter my mother's house in such a remote location and beat her to death?*

Nothing made sense. With no specific destination in mind, I drove aimlessly. I entered the main town and turned left over the same bridge where my mother's killer walked about a week prior. I noticed the convenience store Ron referred to, and I stopped.

In my boxy white Volvo 240 GL, parked on the side of the road, I was determined to solve this case. I reflected on this goal and questioned my sanity. I gathered my composure and formulated a plan: I would see if the cashier who alerted the sheriff was working. Without her intervention and informing the authorities about Mr. Johnson's peculiar behavior, he might have remained at large and unpunished. I may have never found out who killed my mother. I sat in wonderment and imagined the additional fear I'd have if he wasn't behind bars. Hoping to catch her at work, I made the decision to express my gratitude.

With trepidation, I swung open the double doors and entered the store. The counter was enclosed with thick plexiglass, for the protection of the workers. Next to the cash register were various cigarettes behind a thick plastic shield.

I approached the cashier and inquired, "um, hi. I'm curious if you know who was on duty the morning of April 16th, a week ago on Monday?"

"I was, honey, why?"

"Um, were you the one who called the police on my mother's murderer?" I blurted out without much thought.

"Yep, that was me. One second, I'm gonna get her to take over. I wanna talk to you."

I held open my palm and put my hand through the slot in the plexiglass. "Thank you for helping to catch my mother's killer," I proclaimed.

"Oh, honey, I'm so sorry I couldn't have done more. One sec, I want to tell you something."

"Um, okay?" I questioned. "About what?"

"One sec," she said as she urgently beckoned her co-worker.

She came around to the other side of the counter and grabbed my hand. "Let's go outside, I want to talk to you."

I followed without hesitation, eager to learn what she had to say about my mom.

April 16, 2001

We stood in the parking lot and she hugged me tight.

"I'm so sorry, honey. I wish there was more I could have done."

"What do you mean?" I asked with curiosity.

"Do you believe in psychic ability?" she asked a bit shyly.

"I do, why? Do you know something? Did you see something?" I was in agony and wondered what she wanted to say.

"I have prophetic visions," she began, "a few nights before this happened, I had a vision, and I knew something horrible was going to happen."

"What, specifically are you referring to?"

"I saw a very violent crime happen, but I couldn't tell who the victim would be. I knew when that man walked into the store with blood on his forehead, trying to grab those cigarettes, that it'd happened. He sent a chill up my spine and I knew someone had died. I just wish I could have stopped it. It's horrible for me to see these things, know they will happen, and not be able to do anything."

This blew my mind. On one hand, I was so grateful because without her, my mother's killer may still be roaming the streets uncaptured. On the other, she told me that she'd had a premonition but couldn't stop it. It was hard and, frankly, too much to take in. I politely thanked her and headed back to my mom's place, even though I'd knew I'd be miserable.

INTROSPECTION

I'd spent about a week with Ron, and I still hadn't talked to a therapist. It was essential for me to get help for my overall wellness, and I needed to do it urgently.

My mom was gone! I couldn't wrap my head around it. Deep down, I still hoped I would wake up from this nightmare.

I combed the internet for anything that might help me make sense of this crazy world I lived in. Nestled above the cliffs of Big Sur, I came across the renowned Esalen Institute. I scrolled through the website until I saw a workshop that spoke to me. Unfortunately, it was a high price tag, and in addition to my financial constraints, the cost made it out of my reach. This was one time I had to swallow my pride and ask Nile for money.

He understood my duress, and generously offered to pay for the beginning of my newfound in-depth exploration I called "healing."

The path to Esalen felt like a therapeutic journey in itself; the trees surrounded me as I drove alongside the Pacific Ocean amidst the redwoods.

When I arrived, a guard greeted me and checked my ID to make sure I was a registered guest. If you were not vetted, you weren't allowed in. This gave me a much needed feeling of security. Once authorized, the gates lifted, and I drove onto the sacred land.

I parked and found the office to check-in. Prices soared if you wanted to stay alone, so I chose to stay in a room with two bunk beds. This meant I had to sleep with three women I did not know. The presence of unfamiliar individuals following the event heightened my anxiety significantly.

The staff greeted me and gave me a tour. The dining area was our first stop. I found the food options to be impressive, mainly because they were organic and grown on the land. After my first tofu experience at UCSC, I began to explore more produce, and specifically organic and local vegetables at the various farmers markets'. On Thanksgiving of 2000, I decided to stop eating meat altogether. I ate fish but was mostly vegetarian at this point, technically, a pescatarian.

After lunch, they guided me to my cabin. Only one of my roommates had arrived thus far. Guida was an Italian woman who lived in Los Angeles. She sought out internal harmony as much as I did. We introduced ourselves and chatted about what drew us both to Esalen.

"I work in a world of men, and it is always so hectic and crazy. I just needed a getaway to clear my head," Guida stated. "What about you?" she asked.

"Well, my mom was just killed, and I am trying to find my space in this world again without her."

"Oh my gosh, I am so sorry, my dear." Guida approached me with her arms open wide.

I gave her a half-hearted hug. I'm not comfortable hugging strangers. At this moment, with what I felt, or didn't feel, I lacked the desire to hug anyone. However, she reached out and offered a helping hand, and I reluctantly accepted.

The other two ladies arrived within a half hour. We chatted about life and what brought us to this point. The camaraderie we discovered was extraordinary.

The workshop changed my life. Our instructor, Glenn, went above and beyond to make everyone feel welcomed. The class participants and the women I shared the room with were amazing. It was nothing short of a miracle that the people I had crossed paths with helped reignite my self-worth and lovability.

Despite the darkness that plagued me, this workshop sparked my journey to happiness. I knew deep down I had to heal and regain my self-worth.

I found comfort in the shared experiences of others who also faced heartbreak and loss. This was especially true for the women I shared the cabin with. We became close through group discussions and activities. I opened up about my feelings and fears and was able to reach my vulnerable side. I realized I wasn't alone. It helped me to understand that trauma hit hard for everyone on a variety of levels.

Everyone's trauma was real and just as frightening as the next person's. The empathy and support I received from the workshop made me feel understood and loved. I struggled with being vulnerable, and this kind of support was unfamiliar to me. Accepting it had been an immense challenge. I wrestled with the deep scars in my soul.

One of the pivotal moments of the workshop for me was when they tasked me with identifying my positive qualities and strengths. At first, it seemed like an impossible task, since the excessive grief and other trauma throughout my life clouded my perception. However, with guidance and inspiration, I recognized the courage from within. It also dawned on me that I had the ability to empathize with others, something I'd thought I lost along the way.

I harbored a burning passion and a resolute determination within me to rebuild my life. Once again, I picked up the pieces and moved on, no matter how difficult it proved to be. The act of compiling a list of positive attributes, regardless of how small they appeared, was life-changing.

Throughout the week, I also learned techniques to challenge my negative self-talk and replace it with compassion. This concept never occurred to me before the workshop. I'd hoped that this simple and logical practice could conquer the never-ending feelings of loneliness and emptiness that resided within me. My pain was being perpetuated by blaming myself and holding onto the belief that I was unlovable. I needed to reframe my thoughts and attempt to speak to myself with kindness and understanding. My self-esteem had been bashed on so many occasions. I had to remove the echo in my mind and replace it with supportive and caring mantras.

As my week-long journey at Esalen came to a close, I felt a deep gratitude for the transformative experiences I'd undergone. The closing ceremony provided a space for reflection and integration. This allowed me to appreciate the personal growth and connections I'd cultivated during my time there.

I took with me a revitalized self-awareness and a set of tools to further my development beyond the workshop. The memories and connections I made served as a reminder of the transformative power of self-exploration and deep human connection.

Before I attended the workshop, I'd prioritized exhibiting kindness to others over extending the same consideration to myself. This highlighted the need for me to consciously shift that focus and try to cultivate self-kindness.

During that week at Esalen, I not only regained a feeling of being loveable, but also discovered a renewed purpose in life. I realized that the loss I'd experienced was enormous, and though my mother's life ended, mine had not. I knew she would want me to live my life to the fullest and be the happiest I could be.

Upon my arrival home, I continued my healing journey. I sought a plethora of support, which included friends, grief counseling and writing groups. I invested a significant amount of time in therapy and I nurtured and built my "framily," my personal network of longtime friends who lift me up during my darkest moments.

My personal growth was greatly influenced by the self-help books I read and I made it a point to read as many as possible. People would laugh when they would see my bookshelf lined with nothing but books like *The Maker's Diet, From Crappy to Happy* and *Reclaiming Your Inner Child*. I also dedicated time to activities that brought me joy, such as painting, hiking, and writing. These outlets allowed me to express emotions and find a bit of enjoyment in life.

EVERLASTING LOVE?

During my time at Esalen, one thing I attempted to manifest for myself was love. I wrote out a list of specific qualities I wanted in a partner in my journal. Positioned on a rock, I gazed at the Pacific Ocean and indulged in the aroma of the sea, while I immersed myself in the sound of the waves breaking thirty feet beneath me.

I pondered the thought of love while I stared into the vastness. It had been fifteen years since my last committed relationship. Although I dated a bit here and there, there was never anything serious. I wondered and seriously doubted that love would ever be an option. I daydreamed about meeting the perfect person and what it might be like, and I put it into the universe. With pen in hand, I attempted to write.

This was my first go at writing since my mother's death, and I was afraid but I knew I had to start somewhere. My pen touched the paper, and the words "I AM ANGRY" came out. My hand pressed so hard that I tore three pages into the journal. My intention for this exercise was not to focus on my anger. Therefore, I pushed it aside for the moment. I knew my mom would want me to find love and do whatever I needed to make it happen.

I removed my sandals and sank my toes into the rich brown earth. The energy here was powerful. Once again, I tried to set my anger aside and focus on my path to love. I placed the pen on the paper and wrote: "what I want in a FUCK I'M ANGRY" appeared as my pen tore through additional pages of the journal.

Despite my best efforts, I realized I needed to take a few moments and write about my anger. Otherwise, I would end up with nothing but a shredded journal.

After I released a smidgeon of the rage, I was able to finally focus. Again I wrote:

1. I want someone who is beautiful inside and out.
2. Someone who is kind and treats me with respect.
3. Someone who is into me as much or more than I am them.
4. Someone who values what I need and has a desire to make me happy.
5. Someone who is independent and will let me have my "me time."
6. Someone who I can feel free and playful with, both sexually and otherwise.
7. Someone who is honest and emotionally intelligent.

Once the list was complete, I closed that chapter and let the universe know I was leaving it in their hands.

Before my mother's death, I worked at a company called Rainmaker Systems in Scotts Valley. Just before she was killed, I was one of the top sales reps. In fact, I was the first salesperson to make it into the Presidents Club for the year 2000. This was the most amazing Presidents Club I'd ever attended.

The company rented out an entire Windstar luxury cruise liner, and the only people on it were Rainmaker employees and their guests. I brought one of my closest friends at the time, Elise. She and I met while we worked at Santa Cruz Biotechnology, and we became fast friends. She was with me every step of the way from when I was diagnosed with Crohn's, through Cow and Jason's death and so much more. She was my closest confidante at the time.

While on board, each of us were gifted a thousand dollars to spend on anything we wanted. An open bar and free twenty-four-hour room service were part of the package as well. I felt like I'd died and gone to heaven.

I was a valued employee at Rainmaker and remained one of the top sales reps for the rest of 2000. After my mother's demise, I took several months off to handle logistics and attempt to grieve. I worked again in August 2001, four months after my mother passed.

Upon my return, I found that the managers, positions and departments underwent significant changes. My supervisor transferred me from HP printer-support renewals to Norton-support renewals.

My new manager, Frankie, walked me to my cubicle. It was at the opposite end of the building from where I'd worked before. I arrived in the Norton department, and I saw the most stunning woman I'd seen thus far in my lifetime. My heart was aflutter, I was googly-eyed, and I was dying to know what her story was. I asked around about her, but was too shy to introduce myself and I was quite certain she was straight anyway and wouldn't be interested.

A few weeks passed, and I still couldn't muster up the courage to say hello. I worked with East Coast folks, so I came in at 6:00 a.m. and left at 3:00 p.m. One afternoon, around 2:45 p.m., my email notification chimed. I clicked into my inbox to see who the message was from.

The from line read: "Vanessa P." Subject: "Heard you were interested."

Curious and scared, I opened the email and read: "Hiya, heard you were interested. Feel free to give me a call sometime." She left her phone number and signed the email "XOXO Vanessa."

My heart skipped a beat and my jaw dropped to the floor—it was the girl! The one I was so interested in, yet fear kept me from approaching. No one had ever reached out to me like that, and despite my anxiety, I had to follow through.

I called her that night, and we talked for hours. This was the beginning of something I'd never experienced. I felt something that was foreign; it wasn't the same as when I was in love with Cindi, my high school girlfriend. Something was different; we were connected on such a deep level.

Vanessa and I grew our relationship via phone for a few weeks. We talked endlessly into the night. At times, I even fell asleep and woke up the next morning on the same phone call.

Vanessa had a six-year-old daughter, Ruby. Ruby was about the same age as my nephew, Christopher, who would spend the summers with me. I was excited for them to meet. Ruby and I also bonded on a deep level, and she began to love me as her "Mama D."

During Vanessa's and my courting period, I planned a trip to the San Francisco Opera. Live opera was a new experience for both Vanessa and me. After a carefully planned date, I presented my idea to her. First, we would shop for gorgeous dresses, as if we were going to prom. Then, an amazing dinner at one of the best restaurants in San Francisco. Afterward, the main event.

When date night came, Vanessa and I watched part of the performance, but weren't able to keep our hands off each other. We were still very much in the honeymoon phase of our relationship. This was such a problem that we left at intermission.

On the ride home, I did things in a car I'd never even imagined. Vanessa's legs perched high out of the sunroof, my hands in places they should have never been, while I drove eighty miles per hour down the freeway. This was a passion unlike I'd ever felt before. *How did I find someone I felt free with?*

What happened to my inhibitions? Vanessa made them dissipate like the fog on a summer's morning.

Vanessa, Ruby, and I had many adventures at our favorite local destination, Big Sur. Ironically, this was the same place where, in my mind, it all began—with the list I'd made and released to the universe. Some of my most memorable moments were our drives through the windy redwoods along the coast. We loved Fernwood Resorts, where charming cabins tucked away amidst towering trees greeted us. Playing games late into the night brought us closer as a family and formed deeper connections.

Almost every weekend, Vanessa, Ruby, and I would venture out to some new locale.

I had no memory of ever going to Yosemite before, so when Vanessa approached me with the idea of renting a cabin for the weekend, I found it irresistible.

On the public transportation in Yosemite, we, once again, couldn't keep our hands off each other. It was as if we were the only ones in our world, except for Ruby.

Sadly, I met Vanessa at the wrong time. I shouldn't have been with anyone. Taking the necessary time to mourn would have been more appropriate.

Following the chain of tumultuous events, Linda opted for her own space and relocated within a few months. This paved the way for Vanessa and me to embark on cohabitation. Despite the swift timing of this crucial decision, it resonated with us. However, Vanessa's apprehensions about her aunt's declining health made her wary of how my grieving process might affect Ruby's welfare. Each attempt at processing my grief was met with resistance, even within the confines of my own home. Consequently, I found myself unable to properly mourn the loss of my mother.

I remember a time when Vanessa specifically told me I wasn't allowed to experience the deep anguish I felt because Ruby was in the house. Frustrated with being stifled, I retreated to my tiny backyard, which was only about six feet wide with a hillside and a retaining wall. I let out a piercing scream unlike anything this neighborhood had ever heard. The deafening noise was so loud it scared Vanessa—enough to cause her to pack a bag and leave.

I called to find out where they went, and she replied, "You were scary, so we left."

"I was scary? You don't let me grieve for my mother, who was murdered!" I screamed with rage. "Sorry, but I had to let it out. You have stifled me for long enough! You can't tell me I'm not allowed to mourn, especially not in my house!"

I was furious and indifferent to their potential return. Even the strangers I'd met at Esalen encouraged me to grieve. My girlfriend's lack of support for my emotions was difficult and hurtful. She was devoid of respect for me, my personal boundaries, and my feelings, or so it appeared. I'd invited Vanessa into my home, and now she made me feel stifled. The entire relationship began to feel wrong. Massive red flags waved, but I disregarded them.

Eventually Vanessa and Ruby came back, after she realized I had a right to mourn. We set boundaries so that I had my personal space, and Ruby and Vanessa wouldn't experience any burden from my anguish.

Other than the red flags, our relationship was great. We discussed expanding our family. I already had Blossom, my replacement cat for Cow, but we talked about getting a new friend for her.

When we informed Ruby about our desire to add a new addition to the family, she was overjoyed. Waiting for the weekend was tortuous, since we knew we were going to find our new baby at the shelter. When we arrived, we filled out some paperwork before they escorted us to the cat room. With multiple options available, I deferred to Vanessa and Ruby's choice for a new kitty.

A tiny grey kitten caught Vanessa's eye. She approached the cage and exclaimed, "It's her. I want that one."

"We don't know her temperament. She's super cute though, so let's have a visit," I insisted.

I sought out the shelter personnel to let them know we were interested. We wanted to share a few moments with the tiny kitten to make sure she was the right cat for us.

In an instant, I saw Vanessa melt. I knew she was our new cat.

We took her home, but Blossom wasn't happy. This once very affectionate cat turned into a terror. She'd hiss and stretch her back to the sky. *Uh-oh*, I thought. I sure hoped we could make it work.

We tried for months, but our cats did not get along. We just let them agree to disagree and tried our best to move forward with the cohesive family unit we had created.

"What's her name?" I asked Vanessa not long after we'd brought our new kitty home.

"I dunno. Ruby, what do you think?"

"Whatever you want, mama," Ruby replied. "She is special."

"What about Six?" Vanessa suggested.

"Six?" I asked with one eyebrow raised. "What kind of a name is that?"

"Six months later... they got a cat," Vanessa smirked.

"Six it is!"

Despite our conflicts about my grief, our relationship was by far the greatest I'd had thus far. At thirty, I was acutely aware of the time that had passed and I longed for a life partner. I was certain Vanessa was the woman I wanted to share my life with. From the time I was little, I daydreamed about my grand proposal.

For weeks on end, I found myself lost in contemplation. I explored countless scenarios and envisioned how I would propose. A search for the perfect ring was also at the forefront of my mind. I knew Vanessa wanted a princess-cut diamond, so I had some saving to do.

The events that surrounded my mom's murder led me to quit weed for several months. Since I was fourteen, I'd indulged in smoking daily. Despite the constant pain in my neck and gut, facing my emotions was important right now. Quitting was a monumental step for me. I understood that to grieve appropriately, I needed to allow myself to embrace my emotions without the numbing effects of substances.

After she moved in, it became evident that Vanessa had a penchant for alcohol. She would drink a half of a handle or more of Southern Comfort mixed with Dr. Pepper practically every night. As our relationship progressed, I came to realize she bore a vicious battle from within. One fateful evening, Vanessa expressed a desire to explore additional substances and pleaded with me to get some weed.

She was well aware of my tumultuous history with pot and the challenges I'd faced in attempting to quit. In the two years that led up to my mother's passing, I made daily promises to myself that I would abstain from smoking. Sadly, I was addicted to cannabis. Every day, when I'd wake, I craved weed and would give in to the urge.

It surprised and unsettled me that Vanessa placed me in this position.

"I don't think it's a good idea," I replied with vigor.

"Please, please, please," she persisted, relentless as she begged. She was oblivious to the fragility of my mental and emotional state.

"No, Vanessa. I am an addict, and I need to deal right now, not push my feelings down."

"Please!" she badgered me with no regard for my circumstances.

"Fine, I'll go," I reluctantly conceded. Annoyance and frustration overcame me. Being manipulated made me feel incredibly uneasy.

For the first time in about a year, I attempted to contact various dealers and procure weed. *How did I end up here?* I wondered. Here I was, striving to take care of myself and maintain sobriety. Now, because of Vanessa, I searched for the very drug that tugged at my heartstrings daily.

I began to wonder if Vanessa was just trying to control and use me, or if our connection was genuine. An internal battle of emotions stirred within me. To compound matters, Vanessa still stifled the grief I grappled with, which forced me to suppress my despair.

I embarked on this errand, and my cell phone rang incessantly. Vanessa called me every thirty seconds. She'd impatiently ask, "Did you get it yet?"

My annoyance toward her skyrocketed.

I found an eighth of weed and returned to the house, armed with a pipe and lighter. Once Ruby went to bed, I indulged in my first hit in almost a year. The familiar sensations of numbness and relaxation permeated me. I felt the release of the tension in my back that I hadn't realized existed. It was astonishing how rapidly my vice resurfaced, reclaiming its hold on me.

Our relationship underwent a significant transformation following this pivotal moment. Instead of embarking on exciting weekend adventures, the minute Ruby would head to bed, we'd spend our time in the makeshift office in the garage. Vanessa and I indulged in smoking weed and drinking alcohol. We also immersed ourselves in computer games like RollerCoaster Tycoon. It was a noticeable shift, but surprisingly, I accepted it. My love for Vanessa never wavered. One of my primary focuses was to ensure both Vanessa's and Ruby's happiness. In doing this, I overlooked my own needs and desires and lost sight of myself amidst the dynamic of our new routine.

One evening, the scent of skunk lingered in the air and I engaged in a conversation with Vanessa about our altered lifestyle. I took a deep inhale from the pipe and exhaled slowly. The smoke swirled and dissipated into the room.

"You know, babe, I never thought we'd end up spending our evenings like this," I remarked, a hint of nostalgia in my voice.

Vanessa's eyes glazed over. She nodded in agreement. "Yeah, me either. But it's okay, as long as we're together."

Even in the midst of our intoxication from the potent combination of weed and alcohol, we shared many moments of laughter and amazing conversations. Our experiences brought temporary joy that allowed us to escape the harsh realities of life, if only for a little while.

One night, when I was high as a kite and Vanessa was drunk as usual, an urge overcame me to "just do it." With a surge of determination, I grabbed a piece of wire that was next to the keyboard on the desk and wrapped it into a circle. I leapt out of my chair and approached Vanessa, who sat across from me. I spun her chair around to face me and dropped to one knee, my heart pounded with nervous anticipation.

"Vanessa, you have brought more happiness into my life than I ever thought possible," I began, my voice filled with sincerity. "I can't imagine my life without you. Despite the challenges we've faced, I know together we can conquer anything. I'd planned to wait for the perfect moment, but I can't wait any more. I love you, and I want to spend my life with you. Vanessa, will you marry me?"

I extended the simple wire ring toward her; a radiant smile illuminated her face as she rose to her feet. She lifted me up in an ecstatic embrace. "Yes, yes, yes! Of course, I will marry you!" she exclaimed joyfully.

I burst with elation. Vanessa ran into the house, straight to Ruby's room, eager to share the news.

"Look, Rue, Mama is getting married! Mama D and I are going to get married!" Vanessa exclaimed, her excitement contagious. Ruby's eyes widened with delight as she twirled around and reveled in the joyous announcement. I recognized their happiness, as well as my own, something I hadn't experienced many times before.

The makeshift ring wasn't the grand gesture I dreamt of, but it held the symbol of our love and the promise of our future as a family. Even though gay marriage wasn't yet legal, we planned on a commitment ceremony and hoped that someday we would have a real wedding.

After the proposal, something triggered a downward spiral in Vanessa. It was unclear whether her family's lack of acceptance, specifically her mother's, played a part in this change. Regardless, our relationship deteriorated rapidly, soiled by escalating arguments and frequent conflicts. The once-bright future we envisioned together took a dark turn.

It was only a few short weeks before I found myself bewildered by a series of events. Even with the challenges we'd faced, I held onto the belief that our engagement meant something.

One evening, as we retreated to our familiar routine in the garage, Vanessa dropped a bombshell.

"Hey, D? Ruby and I are going to move back to our apartment in Capitola. I'm not breaking up with you or anything; I just think we need some space." Her words left me dumbfounded.

Confusion and frustration surged. The fact that Vanessa kept her apartment in Capitola despite our engagement felt like a betrayal to our commitment. Her decision to retreat to her own space raised doubts about her true intentions and dedication.

"But we're engaged," I stammered. "I don't get why you even kept your apartment. It feels like a betrayal."

"I know," she replied in an evasive tone. "I just think it's what's best for us right now."

Her vague response only deepened my bewilderment. The uncertainty and emotional distance that had grown between us was daunting. I questioned whether our engagement lost its meaning or if it ever had any significance for her to begin with.

"What does that mean? You are moving back to Capitola but you are not leaving me? Sounds like a contradictory statement."

"There is nothing more to say. This is what I am doing. I've already decided."

Our space, once a source of connection and fun memories, now felt like a breeding ground for the cracks in our relationship. The uncertainties that surrounded our future together loomed ominously. This left me with the painful realization that the love we'd once shared was slipping through my fingers.

Within the next two weeks, the living room was filled with boxes of Vanessa's and Ruby's things. Their departure was imminent. I realized I, too, needed to find a place of my own.

When Vanessa arrived with the moving van and her mother, I attempted to slip out unnoticed. That is until I spotted the cat carrier in Vanessa's hand. At which point, I approached her.

"Excuse me, what is the cat carrier for?"

"It's for Six, what else would it be for?" She exclaimed with a snarky tone.

"Listen Vanessa, you can leave, please do. But you are not taking Six! I paid for that cat and she belongs to me! My name is on the paperwork. I'll sit here all day while you move your shit out to make sure you don't take my cat with you!"

"But I picked her!" She whined.

"I don't give a shit! I paid for her and she is my cat. She likes me more than she likes you anyway. Whose lap is she always on? Mine! You are crazy if you think you are taking her!"

"Fine, you paid for her so you keep her. I don't care."

"I know you don't, that is exactly why I am keeping her. I do care!" I responded.

Vanessa and Ruby began moving their boxes out, while Six, Blossom, and I remained in the bedroom and waited for her negative energy to leave my home.

In the subsequent weeks, I witnessed a side of Vanessa I never saw before—a mean and cruel spirit that appeared entirely out of character. The transition from her declarations about not wanting to leave me to the way she treated me, as a complete annoyance, was abrupt and confusing. Her lack of communication left me even more perplexed. We hadn't officially broken up, yet she displayed a complete disinterest in engaging with me. She refused to even talk on the phone.

When we managed to have a discussion, she exhibited intentional rudeness and mean-spiritedness. She took pleasure in taunting me with the encounters she'd had with men. She emphasized her current dating escapades and deliberately rubbed them in my face. *I thought she wasn't breaking up with me?* Her words and actions were definitely not aligned.

The feelings of confusion and hurt consumed me. The foundation of trust and love we built crumbled beneath me, which left me grasping for answers. *How did we go from meeting eight months prior to planning a future together, only to end up in this spiteful and hurtful dynamic?* The emotional roller coaster I'd experienced made me question my worth and the authenticity of our relationship.

Despite the turmoil and pain, I clung to the belief that the love we once had might be revived. However, with each instance of Vanessa's indifference and callousness, doubt crept into my heart.

Her consistent disregard and dismissiveness left me questioning again the sincerity of the promises she had made. Our vows became hollow echoes, crushed under the weight of her hurtful actions. This realization was heartbreaking.

In spite of the pain, I remained unwilling to let go. I clung to a glimmer of hope, longing for a resolution that would rekindle what we'd lost. Unfortunately, the opportunity never presented itself to me. Instead, the avoidance and abandonment I felt from Vanessa stung on a multitude of levels. It decimated my soul to no end. I sought out someone I connected with who would allow me to be myself. Just when I thought I'd found it—it was gone.

Over time, I accepted the painful truth and stopped attempting to contact Vanessa. I realized I would never get the answers I deserved. It became clear she moved on, and it was a difficult pill to swallow. Despite my awareness of the necessity to let go, the attempt to release my love for her proved to be an ongoing struggle for many years to come.

Regardless of the occasional longing for what I'd thought we had, I remained focused on my healing and growth. My optimism remained intact for the potential of new love and possibilities. Because Vanessa didn't provide me any reasons for her leaving, this made it extremely difficult to let go. I gradually learned to do just that and accept that some connections are lessons rather than enduring love stories.

As the years unfolded, I discovered love can come in unexpected ways. The capacity to experience deep connections with others still existed, regardless of how many times I was abandoned. I nurtured the flicker of hope that one day I would find a love that would surpass even the depths of what I'd shared with Vanessa. I embarked on my next chapter, excited to embrace the joys that awaited me.

UNBREAKABLE BONDS

Even though I'd lived in Santa Cruz County for eight years, I never made it up to Bonny Doon. However, when I stumbled upon a Craigslist ad that read, "Small cottage for rent," I was intrigued. The appeal of this unexplored territory called to me.

"Hello, my name is Delicia, and I am inquiring about the cottage for rent."

"Hi," a man said in a gruff tone. "Do you want to come look at the place?" he asked immediately, as if he had no interest in my background.

"Um, sure. But don't you want to know anything about me?"

"Nah, I'll ask you when you are here if I need to know more."

His answer shocked me a bit, but I thought I should check the place out.

I drove through Scotts Valley and down into Felton. I then drove up the captivating drive on Felton Empire Road. The winding road meandered through the towering redwood forest, much like my drive on Highway 9 when I'd lived in Boulder Creek.

I arrived in Bonny Doon, and its rustic charm captivated me. The countryside exuded a peaceful serenity with rolling hills that dotted the landscape amongst the tall redwoods. I instantly connected with the relaxed and artistic atmosphere. Local stores were non-existent, only trees, houses and an unparalleled energy.

The diminutive size of the cottage surprised me. The humble abode measured around five hundred square feet. Tiny but mighty, it featured a functional kitchen, an adorable bathroom with a half-sized bathtub, a comfortable living room, and a minuscule bedroom that barely fit my double bed. To maneuver around the bedroom was a challenge. I'd have to enter and exit from the foot of the bed because of the lack of space on either side.

While I explored the cottage, I appreciated its pleasant energy and practicality. The layout maximized every inch with thoughtful design. The calm on the mountain was crucial for me at this moment in my life.

The gruff man, who I came to know as Doug, turned out to be a kind person. We continued our discussion at his residence, adjacent to the cottage. During our meeting, surprisingly, Doug didn't pry or inquire about any past rental details. I'd thought it odd, since he and I had just met and he was considering leasing the cottage to me.

Instead, we engaged in a heartfelt dialog about life. We talked about how quiet it was up on the mountain. Also, about his aviaries with cockatiels and lovebirds, and his collection of clocks that covered nearly every inch of wall space. The conversation moved to the quilts he made by hand when I noticed the varied sizes of Fabergé-style eggs. He told me how each one was meticulously crafted with a special window or door that opened into a different world altogether. Some had family photos with tiny intricate frames; others were constructed with different holiday themes. I always loved miniatures myself and was in awe of this man and the craftsmanship he possessed.

With a genuine smile, Doug stated, "If you want the place, it's yours."

Taken aback by his implicit trust, I wondered if he needed references or further information. "Do you want me to fill out an application or anything?"

"No, I go by my gut, and I like you, Da-lee-shee-a, or is it delicious?" he chuckled.

His comment caused emotions from my past to stir within me, but I hoped he meant nothing by it. Despite such comments, I felt at ease with Doug. I knew destiny brought me to Bonny Doon and to my new little cottage—soon to be my sanctuary amidst the peacefulness of this delightful town.

Doug proved to be an individual of remarkable qualities; however, like a coin with two sides, he also had a crass aspect to his personality. His old-school mentality offered a unique perspective. Admittedly, in today's society, his use of terminology that harkened back to an era of overt racial inequality would be considered insensitive by most. However, I got to know Doug better, and I realized that this was his way of being playful. He used it to tease and endear, without ill intent.

Doug had the rare quality of being brutally honest, a trait I find increasingly scarce in our world today. This unfiltered authenticity resonated with me because I, too, believed in speaking my mind candidly. However, I've observed that not everyone appreciated this straightforwardness. Our shared understanding for frankness created a strong bond between us.

My tranquil haven took a sudden turn when I received distressing news about my brother Patrick. He fell gravely ill, diagnosed with lymphoma carcinoma, a blood cancer. To make matters more complicated, Patrick was the primary caregiver for my nephew, Christopher, who was now seven.

Charlotte and Patrick shared custody of Christopher for the first five years of his life. Given the strained state of my relationship with Patrick, I relied on Charlotte as the primary point of contact to communicate with Christopher during his early years. Patrick and I hadn't spoken since his birthday party just before I was diagnosed and hospitalized with Crohn's Disease. It took nearly five years, and the murder of my mother, before the ice between us finally broke.

Although I was speaking with him again, the trust we once had was severely shattered by the incident that occurred back in Boulder Creek. I couldn't stand idly by when I knew they needed help. By this time, Charlotte gave complete custody of Christopher to Patrick and rarely took the time to see her son.

Although Nile and Patrick weren't close, he reached out to Nile for financial help. Patrick was undergoing an alternative treatment several months prior. Much like me, he was a naturalist and wanted to avoid chemotherapy if possible. Nile graciously paid for this. However, this natural form of medicine was not strong enough to combat his cancer.

Despite the relationship between us, whenever my brother needed me, I would gladly step in to care for Christopher. One significant weekend, I arrived at their place to collect my nephew, only to find my brother's condition alarming. The sight that greeted me was a grim reflection of his deteriorating health. Dried feces with traces of blood stained the carpet, and an overpowering stench filled the air. Stacks of unwashed dishes with layers of mold thriving on their surfaces cluttered the kitchen. In addition to the disarray, haphazardly scattered porno movies were found on what remained visible of their coffee table. Even the white toilet transformed into a sickly grayish-black hue.

The pain in my chest worsened when I noticed a long burn mark that stretched across my nephew's stomach. Concerned, I asked, "Christopher, how did you get burned?"

"Um, so check it out. I went to the store and bought some food. I came back and cooked it by myself, and I got burned. But look, auntie, I did it myself!" My independent seven-year-old nephew touted.

His innocent response revealed a shocking reality—he had been forced to fend for himself, to navigate the perils of this treacherous environment. Filled with worry, frustration and love for my nephew as well as my brother, I pleaded with Patrick to seek medical attention.

"Patrick, you're not well. You need to go to the hospital. Please, think about Christopher and the danger he's in."

My deperation grew and so did Patrick's anger. He adamantly resisted my pleas and stood firm in his refusal.

"I don't need anyone's help! I'll be fine," he barked.

"Patrick, I don't want to do this, but if you won't take care of yourself, I'll have to call 9-1-1."

"You wouldn't dare!" His words came out in a feeble whisper.

I watched Patrick struggle, both physically and emotionally, and it crushed me. I loved my brother but he was being so stubborn and I recognized that he was on the verge of death.

Enraged, I confronted him with unflinching honesty.

"Listen, Patrick, you are being ridiculous. Why are you choosing to die? Please just let me call an ambulance so they can see what's going on with you. If you are going to subject yourself to death that's your prerogative but I refuse to leave my nephew in this godforsaken place any longer. It's dangerous! What the fuck Patrick, why are you refusing to let me call an ambulance or go to the hospital. Whatever, you are an adult and I can't force you. But I'm taking Christopher!"

I recognized the urgency, and I knew that immediate action was necessary to protect Christopher's well-being. Taking hold of his belongings, I swiftly led my nephew away from the chaotic scene.

On the drive home I called Nile at once. I was desperate and didn't know what to do, so I pleaded for his help.

The following day, Nile drove from Los Angeles to San Francisco. Upon arrival, he'd observed the same horrible surroundings I had the day prior. He also noted the pornographic movies boldly laid out around the living room that mixed in with the kid's movies. Nile, who was now a father himself and the most meticulously clean person in our family, was disgusted, to say the least.

Once he saw the state of Patrick's apartment, Nile called me immediately. He was furious and screamed at the top of his lungs, "What kind of horrible person are you? Who sees someone as sick as Patrick and just leaves?"

"Excuse me?" I asked, bewildered. "I'm the one who called you! I'm the one who told you he needed help. He refused to let me get him to the hospital, call an ambulance or do anything. He was furious. I wasn't going to leave Christopher and I didn't know what else to do, so I took him."

Nile interrupted me and continued to berate me. "You are a horrific, vile, disgusting human being. How in the fuck could you leave him like that?"

"Nile, I left with Christopher because Patrick refused to go to the hospital or let me call an ambulance. He got super angry and threatened me when I tried."

"Whatever. Nobody in his condition could threaten you," Nile said, fuming. "You're horrible. I'm taking him to the hospital now!"

He hung up. Besides feeling confused, I was angry. By this point, I had been admitted into the hospital on at least five occasions due to Crohn's disease, and Nile still hadn't found time to come visit me. Not once!

Where did I stand on Nile's list of priorities? The question haunted me and triggered intense self-reflection. Nile only recently formed a connection with Patrick. They met when Nile was eighteen, and the relationship between them was strained at best. Yet, when Patrick needed someone, Nile dropped everything and drove six hours from Los Angeles. Meanwhile, amidst this display of care and concern for Patrick, Nile directed hurtful words toward me, which once again showed me where I ranked.

The sting of Nile's harsh words stuck with me. Regardless of how many times those conversations happened, the hurt I felt after his venomous words never got any easier.

When I cared for my nephew, Doug's compassionate nature and understanding of our cramped living space came to the forefront. Christopher and I attempted to make my tiny cottage our home. We squeezed ourselves into the limited space. It soon became apparent that the situation was far from ideal.

Christopher and I tried to find our footing, and although we were cramped, my nephew never complained. After about a week, Doug stepped in with a solution. Without hesitation, he extended an invitation, free of rent, for Christopher to stay in his house, in a spare bedroom. It had a separate entrance, so we wouldn't bother him if we came and went. I acknowledged the need for Christopher to have a more spacious environment, and I thanked Doug and accepted his gracious offer.

I spent every evening with Christopher. We shared in the joy of him learning to read. At seven, he had yet to unlock the magical worlds hidden within the pages of books. Together, we embarked on a journey through the fascinating realm of *Harry Potter*. We immersed ourselves in the captivating tales that unfolded before us. Despite the challenges we faced, the bond between us grew stronger as we delved into the pages.

In Doug's actions, I saw the embodiment of compassion and understanding. He went the extra mile to ensure Christopher felt both accepted and loved, which fostered a nurturing environment for his development.

During this tumultuous period, there was one decision I knew I had to make. I understood the importance of being a positive influence in Christopher's life. After the breakup with Vanessa, I indulged several times a day in my pot smoking habit. Once Christopher was in my possession, I made the deliberate choice to quit, once again. I was fueled by a deep love and concern for my nephew. I felt strongly that he was entitled to nothing less than the absolute best version of myself.

To let go of my daily crutch was not easy. Pot was a familiar coping mechanism for many years during many challenging times. I wanted to be a positive role model for Christopher, to teach him that resilience, determination and healthy choices were the keys to overcoming adversity—something he, too, experienced.

Life unfolded in Bonny Doon, and Christopher attended the local elementary school, marking a new chapter in his young life. However, amidst the challenges we faced, fate conspired against us. The County of Santa Cruz, unfortunately, failed to process my paperwork for financial help in a timely manner, which left me without the means to continue my caregiver duties. I lived paycheck to paycheck and had recently gone through bankruptcy. The burden of these circumstances, along with the responsibility of providing for and clothing a growing seven-year-old boy, was a huge burden to bear.

Unfortunately, about a year after caring for Christopher, the day came when I found myself unable to provide enough food for him. I knew Doug would have offered for him to stay free of charge, but he already extended so much that I refused to ask him for anything more.

It was a gut-wrenching moment that made me realize I couldn't meet Christopher's needs any longer. Fortunately, my brother's health improved to where he could take on his parental role, once again. It was a bittersweet turning point that required me to make a painful decision; I gave Christopher back to his father.

I held onto the memories we'd shared during our time together. The evenings spent reading Harry Potter, the lessons learned, and the unbreakable bonds we formed will remain forever with us.

NOT MY CIRCUS

During a criminal trial process, the timing varies significantly due to many factors. For my mother's trial, it took about a year and a half for the attorneys to gather the evidence required and to pick the jury. As per the district attorney, this was the most brutal crime in Placer County's history.

Mom was proud of her Irish heritage and always expressed the desire for a wake when she passed away. Rather than people acting sad and morose, she wanted everyone to come together for a celebration, filled with dancing, singing and laughter. She preferred people to commemorate the time they knew her and rejoice in the memories.

However, amidst the lingering uncertainty of the trial, I was in a difficult position. My stepfather, Ron, insisted we should postpone my mother's memorial until after her killer's sentencing. Even though I had mixed emotions, I valued the seventeen-year bond between Mom and Ron and begrudgingly accepted his request.

Not only did Ron deny me the right to plan a wake for my mother, he also asserted that both houses she owned were now his without question. My mom was the main breadwinner between the two of them; Ron was always unemployed. Just a few months before her tragic demise, Mom informed me about the change in her life insurance policy. Her intention was to split it equally between Ron and me.

After Mom passed, I discovered that at the beginning of 2001 the laws changed. Now, it was required that the spouse sign a form that stated they acknowledged this, which he failed to do. Therefore, he was granted the entire life insurance policy, fully aware it did not align with her wishes.

Ron offered me a verbal deal. He agreed to give me ten thousand dollars annually. He made me believe that this was the most advantageous method because of the tax liability I would have faced with a lump sum.

This was not what my mom wanted. She would have wanted me to buy a house with the money and secure my future. However, my pleas were ignored. Ron made one payment before he decided that was sufficient.

While I looked after Ron following my mother's passing, he often made remarks like, "your mother always told me that after she died, I'd be a very rich man." I watched as Ron, an alcoholic gambler, depleted my mother's hard-earned savings as well as her entire life insurance policy. This was heartbreaking, especially since both vices were strictly forbidden by my mother before her death.

Ron's insensitive remarks, his possessive stance on claiming everything my mom worked so hard for against her wishes, and his explosive behavior fueled my suspicions. His actions of miraculously removing the killer from the house just after my mom was gone made him even more suspect. Additionally, the timing of my mother changing her life insurance policy in January 2001 didn't help the troublesome thoughts that plagued me.

Despite these negative thoughts, I tried my best to push them aside and carry on with my responsibilities. To fulfill the role of a strong and emotionally supportive stepdaughter. This is what my mother would have wanted, and I was someone who always tried to make others happy.

It was with deep introspection I realized I needed to create more boundaries in the future in order for me to carve out my healing journey. Eventually, I learned to prioritize myself without feeling selfish.

We impatiently awaited the trial for almost two long and arduous years. Work kept my mind occupied at least during the day, but the time I'd spent waiting to hear when the trial would be scheduled was tumultuous.

Given Ron's vehement insistence on postponing the wake until after sentencing, I felt grateful when Lincoln High School, where my mother taught, organized a balloon ceremony in her honor. This gesture provided a meaningful way for those whose lives Mom touched to come together and pay their respects. It brought me a small bit of closure after her fateful tragedy.

Mom's area of expertise was teaching people to read. Her unique method left a remarkable impact on those who struggled to learn through traditional approaches. The event served as a tribute to her exceptional dedication and the countless lives she transformed with her special approach to education.

During the balloon ceremony, one of my mother's students, who could not read just six months prior, stood in front of the school and read this:

"Hi, my name is Peter. First, I want to give my regrets to Mrs. Niami's family, my prayers are with you all. Mrs. Niami was a kindhearted teacher, who wanted her class to learn as much as they could. She helped me most with my reading. She also helped us in our craft class. The students in her classes will miss her. Mrs. Niami was a great teacher. She had a way of cheering me up. I will never forget the prom last year. It was Mrs. Niami's idea for Andrea and me to go to the prom. She drove us to and from the prom, she was dressed up too. She looked great. We had a fun time. We all knew how much she loved her puppies.

We will miss her so much. She was loved by so many of us here at Lincoln High School. Thank you."

This ceremony was a tribute to my mom and brought a smidgeon of comfort to those who loved her. However, while it appeased me momentarily, I wanted to organize the wake she desired. I longed for the day when I could gather our friends and family and fill the air with music and laughter, like she always wanted.

In preparation for the trial, I begged Nile several times to come up, and he adamantly refused. There were only a few instances I can recall when I explicitly asked something of my brother. I pleaded with Nile to support me through this crazy and challenging time in our lives. I encouraged him to know that we could lean on each other as siblings, but he wouldn't.

On October 16, 2002, the trial finally began. Patrick and I were still rebuilding trust after his attempt to violate me in 1995. During the trial, Patrick showed unwavering support. Thankfully, by this time, his health was much better due to his miraculous recovery from cancer.

Patrick took time off work, stayed in a nearby hotel room, and stood by my side every day of the trial. He'd transformed into the big brother I'd always longed for—caring, supportive, and filled with love. In addition, he now gave the impression that he was astutely aware of his boundaries, which, for me, were non-negotiable. Not to mention, he hadn't taken a trip to Thailand since our conversation years earlier. He'd also become a good dad to Christopher, taking responsibility and full custody of him.

In addition to Patrick, LR, came up to support me during this chaotic time in my life. It meant the world to have my sister from another mister there with me. She held my hand while we sat together, day after day of the trial. We watched as the heinous details unfolded before our eyes. Photos were displayed on a large projection screen of my mother's battered and bruised face. The imprint of Johnson's shoe left a vivid purple bruise on my mother's face, a haunting image I had to confront while eerily projected onto the courtroom wall. Patrick and LR sat right beside me and provided me comfort with gentle squeezes of my hand.

Marc wanted to be with me during the trial but was in rehab at the time. Although I was sad he wasn't by my side, I was grateful he was getting the help he needed.

Despite the turmoil Patrick and I experienced in our relationship, I knew he loved me. Also, I knew that no one had ever shown him sisterly love the way I had. He was appreciative, and his actions spoke volumes about the gratitude he felt.

Nile was too engrossed in his lavish lifestyle to want anything to do with the trial. I couldn't decipher if his refusal to acknowledge the profound hurt caused by our mother's passing was due to excessive pride or pure selfishness. Regardless, his estranged relationship with our mother only added to the difficulty of the circumstances.

Prior to her death, almost two years had passed without Nile and our mother exchanging a single word. I remembered the last time we were in Los Angeles together. Nile and Mom exploded in a screaming match inside Shiraz, a Middle Eastern restaurant on Ventura Boulevard.

On Easter, just mere hours before our mom was killed, she made an effort to connect with Nile and wish him a happy Easter. When Nile's wife answered the phone and heard our mother's voice, she called out for him, "Nile, it's your mom."

Nile uttered, "I don't want to deal with her right now."

His wife and our mother ended the call, and, tragically, the next morning at 5 a.m., she was gone.

The court case that would forever alter the course of my career path began to unfold. From the tender age of five, people would ask me the familiar question, "What do you want to be when you grow up?" My answer, always spoken with immense pride, was, "a judge." My response would surprise some and they would remind me, "you know you have to be an attorney first." I'd heard this remark countless times, and replied, "I know," before I'd run off to play.

I worked diligently at UC Santa Cruz to prove to the advisor that I was worthy of admission to the coveted major of legal studies, which accepted a mere twenty students per year. Concurrently, I majored in sociology. Since I wanted to go into criminal law, it seemed like the perfect double major. I was applying to the bureaucratic world of law school during the time of my mother's demise.

The decision between becoming a criminal prosecutor or a defense attorney lingered in my mind. Regardless, I was steadfast in my decision to become a lawyer, and these were the only areas of law that captivated my attention.

Throughout the trial, my nerves were a wreck, and the sweat on my palms proved it. Patrick, LR, and I sat together in the courtroom. We listened attentively to the testimony. As details emerged, several questions flooded my mind. The foremost among them was why they hadn't questioned Ron to determine if he had any involvement in the incident. The absence of such an inquiry left a nagging doubt, which prompted me to wonder if there was more to the story than what was presented.

I'd invested most of my life thus far into becoming an attorney. Now, the trial that surrounded my mother's death caused me to make a giant shift in my career path. The courtroom resembled a chaotic circus, and amidst the confusion, no one knew which way was up or down, let alone right from wrong. I sat on the hard wooden bench amongst the crowd of spectators, and listened to the gruesome details of the crime.

I pondered my existence. *Why was I here? What was I put on this earth to do? Was it this? Did I really want to be an attorney?* The weight of introspection and soul-searching intensified as my mother's killer, against his attorney's advice, took the stand. The courtroom fell silent, and a whirlwind of emotions consumed me.

I was about to hear from the perpetrator himself, which held me transfixed. With undivided attention, I focused on his testimony. I loathed him and I was determined to convey the depths of the hatred I felt. All the disgust was summoned to the surface. I gave him the most revolting and malevolent look possible, and hoped that he'd see the abhorrence I felt for him deep within my soul. The rest of the courtroom faded away, leaving only him and me locked in a silent battle of emotions.

Johnson's version of events constantly shifted. This included how he arrived at the house, the actions inside, and the details of his brutality against my mother. The stories he told changed by the second. Furthermore, he astonishingly admitted to being the person responsible for taking my mother's life, as well as attempting to kill my stepfather. He even admitted that he caused the dark purple bruise with his shoe by stomping on her face.

I listened to the contradictory accounts and observed his unfeeling and casual admission of this vile act. It was excruciating to watch. The courtroom atmosphere suffocated me as the truth settled in. The sheer ruthlessness left me in disbelief.

Amidst the crowd of spectators, and Johnson's lavish stories, the chaos in the courtroom felt like a wild spectacle. While the testimony echoed in the background, my mind drifted, once again, to thoughts of my career aspirations. In a moment of deep reflection, it hit me: This was no longer the path I wanted to take in my life. The noise and commotion in the courtroom intensified, and my chest pounded harder with each passing second.

I was thirty-one and I reminisced about my entire educational journey. At that moment, I realized it led me down a road that wasn't aligned with my genuine passions.

Johnson continued to weave ludicrous tales in an attempt to avoid prison, clearly hoping for a stay in a psychiatric hospital instead. The audacity of it infuriated me and broke my heart. The entire trial seemed like a sick joke, with my mother's death at the center of it, yet everyone around me appeared so flippant.

A lifetime of dreams were shattered in an instant; everything I'd worked for throughout my education was suddenly gone. The decision not to attend law school and abandon the pursuit of becoming an attorney or a judge consumed me like an exploding avalanche. It felt like an iceberg cracked and dissolved beneath my feet, leaving me adrift in uncertainty. *What was I going to do with my life now?* It felt as if I was outside of my body, watching in despair as my cherished ambition evaporated; like a fleeting speck of dust blown away by the wind.

The prospect of starting anew was both daunting and liberating. I knew it wouldn't be easy. But I also recognized if I stayed on the wrong path that it would lead to a life filled with regrets. I had to summon the courage to embrace change and take charge of my destiny, no matter how uncertain or challenging the journey might be. At that pivotal moment, amidst the chaos, I vowed to listen to my body and alter my course. I was committed to find something that held the promise of fulfillment and aligned with my true self. Even if I wasn't sure what that was at the moment.

Despite the wasted time and resources, I knew deep down that this was an opportunity for growth and self-discovery. I was resolute in embracing this new chapter and exploring the multitude of possibilities ahead.

Once the closing arguments concluded, I felt stifled in the courtroom and wasn't able to take it much longer. I approached the district attorney, who headed up the case.

"Would it be okay if I visited Ron at Kaiser? How long do you think it will take the jury to come to a verdict?"

My stepfather was, once again, in the hospital with complications from the brutal attack.

"They might be out for days. We just never know."

"So it would be okay, you think, if I went and came back?"

"For a few hours, absolutely. I don't expect them to decide today anyway."

"Great, I'll be back as soon as possible. Please call me if anything changes. Can you promise me the jury won't come back into the courtroom until I am back?"

"If it happens—which it never does; they always stay out longer than a few hours. I promise you I will have the judge hold the jury until you can make it back."

"Thank you! Okay, I'm so nervous, I will be back ASAP!"

"Drive safely, take your time. Don't worry; I will call you if anything changes."

I raced to the hospital and prayed that he'd be convicted. Kaiser Permanente in Roseville was about a twenty-five-minute drive from the Auburn Municipal Court. Upon arrival, I made my way to Ron's room and sat by his side for about two minutes when my phone rang. It was the district attorney. Panic consumed me when he declared, "the jury is back."

I knew I was about a half hour away from the courthouse. The urgency led me to speed down the freeway unlike ever before.

During this frantic moment, I gained a newfound understanding and empathy for those who rushed past me at high speeds. Perhaps, like me, they were facing an emergency and not just driving recklessly. The attorney assured me the jury would wait for my arrival, but I couldn't be certain.

I screeched into the parking lot and found the closest spot. I sprinted up the stairs and through the metal detectors toward the courtroom. As soon as I arrived, they called the jury in from the deliberation room. On October 31, 2002, fifteen days into the trial and on my favorite holiday, the verdict was delivered. How fitting it was to convict a monster for such a heinous crime on Halloween?

As the jury got ready to read the verdict, my palms dampened with sweat.

"We the jury, in the case of the People versus Jay Conrad Johnson, find the defendant guilty of first-degree murder of Laurie Niami. We the jury, find the defendant guilty of attempted murder of Ronald Booker. We the jury, find the defendant not guilty on the special circumstance burglary charge."

Unable to hold back the stream of tears that rolled down my cheeks. Patrick, LR, and I hugged each other. Extreme relief filled the courtroom. I experienced lightness, and I could breathe again. My mother's killer was going to prison.

Although it held a hint of justice, a bitter disappointment still lingered in my soul. They did not implement the special circumstance burglary charge, which dashed my hopes of him facing life without the possibility of parole.

It was a bittersweet moment. I was also painfully aware it would never erase the loss of my mother or the newfound fear I'd felt. It signified the end of a long and painful chapter. This enabled me to take a step forward into an uncertain future. The trial left me exhausted, but it was a necessary part of the process to seek justice for my mother's death.

I left the courtroom, and I knew there was still so much healing and growth ahead of me. The path toward closure and forging a new path would be challenging. I navigated this head-on, as I'd done so many times before.

The day of sentencing arrived, nineteen months after his savage crimes. It was scheduled for 8:30 a.m. on December 19, 2002, in Placer County Superior Court Department One. Johnson would now face the consequences of his heinous actions.

The immense weight of the trial and the pain of losing my mother were still fresh, but today marked a crucial moment in obtaining justice for her.

During the sentencing, I had the opportunity to speak to my mother's killer through the form of a statement. Patrick read his first, then my aunt read hers. I was the last of the family members to read my avowal, and when my turn came, I wanted to lock eyes with him.

"May I approach so I can face the defendant, and look him in the eyes when I read this?" I asked the judge.

"I'm sorry, young lady, but you will have to stay there and read the letter."

Johnson doodled during almost the entire trial, except during the few minutes he took the stand himself.

"Okay. Mr. Johnson, please stop doodling and afford me a few minutes of your time to actually listen to what I have to say."

At that moment, he lay his pencil atop his paper, folded his hands, sat back in his chair, and waited.

I read my letter addressed to Jay Johnson, hopeful he would never forget the impact of my words or the pain he had caused.

Dear Santa,

All I want for Christmas is my mom.

One last time for her to stay up until I'm asleep and fill my stocking; one last Santa present wrapped in red tissue paper with my initial on it in gold glitter; one last Easter where I would wake up and find a trail of little chocolate eggs leading me to clues to find my Easter basket; one last Valentine's Day, where I know the only box of chocolates waiting for me in my mailbox would be from my mom; one last Mother's Day to see the surprised expression on her face when I would drive four hours with a balloon bouquet just because I love her.

I know this Christmas, or any other day, I cannot have my mom anymore, thanks to you, jay conrad johnson.

Nobody deserves to die the way you brutally killed my mom, especially not her. She was such a great person. She sacrificed so much of her life to please others. My mom was a special education teacher who worked for almost the same amount of money as her youngest child. She was not the type of person who worked for the money; she worked for the simple pleasure of watching a child learn to read.

I hope my mom was able to watch from up above when one of her students paid homage to her in front of the school. He was a senior and wasn't able to read until my mother taught him at seventeen. He read a tribute to my mom. In it, he stated what a great person she was and how thankful he was that she helped him learn to read. My mom was an incredibly beautiful person. Even though you felt like it was okay to take out all of your aggression on her.

To kill her, and brutalize her face, no matter how hard you try, you can never take away her beauty.

When I saw the pictures of your shoe print on her face and her head swollen like a blowfish, I was devastated. However, these images are not the images that will stick in my mind. Regardless of how hard you tried to steal her beauty, you could not! She radiated from within. It breaks my heart you robbed me, my brothers, my stepdad, my nephews, my aunts and the world of such a wonderful, kindhearted, amazing person.

If your goal was to kill two people when you went into that house, you may have killed a lot more than just that. When you killed my mom, you killed my spirit as well. She was my confidant, my best friend. She was the one person in this world I knew loved me unconditionally, and you took that away from me. You not only robbed me of my mom, but she was so important to so many people. She was a mother of three to Patrick, Nile, and me. A wife, as you know because you tried to kill Ron; a sister; an aunt; and last but not least, a grandmother to Bryce, Nile's firstborn son, who she will never have an opportunity to meet; as well as a grandmother to my seven-year-old nephew Christopher, who will never be able to learn from her the wonderful things she had to teach him.

The death penalty is too easy for your punishment. The brutal way in which you killed my mom deserves a much more just punishment. Getting a needle stuck in your arm and going to sleep does not seem like justice.

Given the brutality of this murder and the fact that Mr. johnson appeared to have no remorse for his crime, it is my request jay conrad johnson be remanded to Pelican Bay penitentiary. I believe this is the most suitable place for a person of his stature. Furthermore, I would request that Mr. johnson be sentenced to a term of life without the possibility of parole.

I hope you will take this request into consideration when placing jay johnson in prison.

Delicia Niami, only daughter and youngest child of Laurie Niami.

I learned in school that Pelican Bay was the most dangerous place for criminals in California. In this prison, perpetrators experienced the weight of their actions in isolation—locked down for twenty-three hours a day. Prior to sentencing, I'd discovered how much Mr. Johnson loved his time outdoors, and I thought this was the most fitting location for his punishment to be carried out.

When the judge handed down the sentence, it brought a bit of closure, yet also a heavy sadness. Whatever time he spent in prison would never be able to replace the void caused by my mother's absence.

Judge Couzens took the bench.

"This is the sentencing in the case of People vs. Jay Conrad Johnson."

Johnson was dressed in an orange jumpsuit and shackled to a chair. He sat emotionless next to Placer County's assistant public defender.

Couzens began, "In the case of The People Vs. Jay Conrad Johnson, with regard to the April 16, 2001, murder of Laurie Niami and the attempted murder of her husband, Ronald David Booker…"

"Excuse me, your honor. May I speak?" Johnson interjected.

"Yes, Mr. Johnson." Judge Couzens replied.

"Listen, I ain't gonna sit here and plead for myself, but I was looking for help! I have a lot of remorse and I really am sorry that I wasn't the one who died, okay?"

"Is that all Mr. Johnson?"

"Yes, sir."

"Mr. Johnson, the crime you have been found guilty of by a jury of your peers is by far the most heinous crime in the history of Placer County. You brutally beat an innocent woman to death in her own home. The worst part is that after she was rendered unconscious, you continued to beat her. You even went as far as to smash her face with your shoe. It is clear that you have no regard for human life. Your testimony did not show any remorse, only justification and excuses for why it was not your fault. You are not even claiming culpability for this brutal murder."

The judge continued, "Mr. Johnson, you are a dredge on society. The jury has unanimously found you guilty. Therefore, I hereby sentence you to twenty-five years to life for the murder of Laurie Niami. In addition, I sentence you to seventeen years for the attempted murder of Ronald Booker."

"Let me be very clear Mr. Johnson that the sentences I have imposed here today are intended for you to spend the rest of your God given life behind bars. That is why I am issuing these sentences to be served consecutively rather than concurrently. I hope you never have the privilege of walking the streets again." Judge Couzens concluded.

"Let it be recorded that the prisoner be remanded to Pelican Bay State Penitentiary for his sentencing term."

I was beside myself, I wanted to clap but controlled my instinct. The judge listened to me. Pelican Bay was the prison where the worst offenders go after they have killed someone in other prisons. I was shocked, yet grateful, that he was sending Johnson there, even though this was technically his first serious offense. I hoped he would stay there forever.

Although the judge granted my wish, and gave Johnson the most severe punishment the law allowed, it brought a mix of emotions. This seemed like an insignificant amount of time in exchange for the pain and loss. I realized that regardless of his sentence, the wounds left behind would never mend.

For myself, the journey toward healing was far from over, but this was another significant step to find closure and move forward.

I attempted to close this chapter of my life, but the questions loomed like shadows. They never left my mind. I continually pondered the mysteries surrounding Ron and Jay's roles in my mother's tragic fate. *Was there a confrontation, a twisted act of revenge that unfolded behind closed doors? Did Ron, driven by greed or fear of her changing her life insurance, have a hand in orchestrating the unthinkable?* The truth remains veiled in uncertainty, and perhaps it always will.

In the wake of my mother's sudden death, I confronted a glaring truth: Life is fleeting, and every moment is precious. The loss of someone so dear has taught me the invaluable lesson that material possessions hold little significance compared to the human spirit. A simple hug or a warm smile—these things are irreplaceable and can never be bought.

I realized that the people we love, the moments we share, and the memories we create together are what give meaning to our lives. In the end, it is the love, the laughter, and the connections we form that become our most cherished treasures.

I now live each day with a newfound gratitude. I strive to embrace the present moment and recognize it as our only true possession. I journey through life, and carry my mother's spirit with me. It's a guiding light that reminds me to embrace each day with an open heart and to cherish the people who fill my life with love and joy.

Chapter Picture References

What Was I Thinking?—Jason and me in our apartment the first time we bought live lobsters and boiled them ourselves. We never knew lobsters could scream...this was just before it broke our hearts.

Unjustified–Mom and me at Frontier Land in San Jose, CA circa 1977.

Stepping-Stones–From left to right: me, Jason, LR, Danny in our Toluca Lake apartment.

Freedom—The two flags that mean the most to me flying together: American Flag and Pride Flag.

My Adventures in Europe—Oli and me in 2018 when I returned for a visit to Bern, Switzerland.

Shattered Illusions—From left to right: Patrick, me and Mom.

Switzerland—My Forever Home?—Snowcapped alps with Swiss Flag.

Finding My Hippie Roots—University of Santa Cruz entrance sign.

Trustworthy Monster #2—Patrick with wine in hand.

Why Does My Body Hate Me?—Me in the hospital, again...

Friend or Foe?—Me smoking a joint at the Reitschule circa 1993.

Uncharted Heartache—From left to right: LR, Tommy, me, Marc at a candlelight AIDS/LifeCycle ride vigil in Ventura for Jason on June 7, 2019.

April 16, 2001—From left to right: Ron, Mom, Nile, me, Patrick first meeting Mother's Day, 1986.

Introspection—Circle above cliffs at Esalen, courtesy of @qsternphotography.

Everlasting Love?—My true everlasting love, Six—July 3, 2002 - May 4, 2024

Unbreakable Bonds—My nephew Christopher and me.

Not My Circus—Photo created by myself depicting the courtroom circus chaos.

Discover the next chapter of Delicia's remarkable journey in "The Queen of Silver Linings," the final book of the ResilientAF series. Delve into the world of alternative medicine alongside Delicia as she explores therapies like plant medicine and transformative breathwork. Despite facing new challenges, Delicia's unwavering resilience, once again, shines through. Delicia's story will inspire readers to find their own strength despite adversity. Join Delicia as she proves that no matter what life throws our way, we are all ResilientAF!

Author Bio
Delicia Niami is an acclaimed memoirist and LGBTQ+ advocate, whose raw and edgy storytelling has touched the hearts of readers worldwide. Residing in Santa Cruz and an alumna of UCSC, Delicia draws inspiration from her own journey of resilience and empowerment. Through her memoirs, she fearlessly addresses topics such as sexual abuse, trauma recovery, and the importance of self-compassion. Delicia's work not only sheds light on difficult experiences but also empowers others to find their voices and embrace their own resilience. Her passion for advocacy shines through in her writing, making her a powerful voice for change and healing in today's world.

https://www.delicianiami.com

www.ingramcontent.com/pod-product-compliance
Lightning Source LLC
Chambersburg PA
CBHW011549070526
44585CB00023B/2519